Love, Money
& Parenting

Love, Money & Parenting

HOW ECONOMICS EXPLAINS
THE WAY WE RAISE OUR KIDS

Matthias Doepke & Fabrizio Zilibotti

PRINCETON UNIVERSITY PRESS
Princeton and Oxford

2516

KH

Published by Princeton University Press
41 William Street, Princeton, New Jersey 08540
6 Oxford Street, Woodstock, Oxfordshire OX20 1TR

press.princeton.edu

Library of Congress Control Number: 2018959969
ISBN: 978-0-691-17151-7

British Library Cataloging-in-Publication Data is available

Editorial: Sarah Caro and Hannah Paul
Production Editorial: Karen Carter
Text Design: C. Alvarez-Gaffin
Jacket/Cover Design: Karl Spurzem
Production: Erin Suydam
Publicity: James Schneider
Copyeditor: Kelly Clody

This book has been composed in Charis SIL

Printed on acid-free paper. ∞

Printed in the United States of America

1 3 5 7 9 10 8 6 4 2

11/16/20

From Fabrizio to María and Nora, and to the memory of
his late parents Francesca and Valter

From Matthias to Marisa, Lukas, Nico, and Oskar, and
to his parents Annemarie and Dietmar

Contents

PART THREE
How Policy Affects the
Way We Raise Our Kids

Preface

The seed of this book is an article that we wrote and published in an academic journal with the title "Parenting with Style: Altruism and Paternalism in Intergenerational Preference Transmission."[1] As we were thinking about parenting from an economic perspective, we realized how many disciplines (anthropology, education, history, psychology, sociology, and, of course, economics) discuss child-rearing practices, often without speaking much to each other. To foster a broader discussion, we published a column on the portal voxeu.org with the title "Tiger Moms and Helicopter Parents: The Economics of Parenting Style." The response we received encouraged us to write a book that would communicate our ideas to a broader audience, one that included parents and general readers who are interested in learning more about parenting. This is how it all started.

Parents and children have been a focal point in our research for many years. Before our research on parenting style, we worked on human capital accumulation and the role of preference and cultural transmission within families. We wrote a number of scientific articles on those topics, and, in the process, we learned more than we could summarize in academic articles. While writing this book, we went back to the work we had done over the years and tried to connect it through a coherent thread. We also went beyond the scientific literature and made contact with a broader range of media (newspapers, blogs, popular parenting books, etc.) to learn more about how people think about raising children.

The book starts from our own experiences as parents and children. We went through the memories of our childhoods and compared them with the lives of our own families today. We realized that we have been very different parents from our own parents, and yet we certainly do not presume to have been better parents than they were. We believe that at the same time, and under the same circumstances, we would have acted much as our parents did. If we raise our children in a different way today, it is not because we have superior knowledge or insights. Rather, we raise our children in a different world from the one in which we grew up. In this spirit, the aim of this book is to explain how the environment in which parents raise their children affects the parenting choices they make. Instead of giving advice on what parents should do, we try to understand the motivations underlying what they actually do.

We also draw on the experiences of Fabrizio's wife María and Matthias's wife Marisa. We realized that their childhood memories were quite different from ours. Once again, none of us claims to have had the "best parents." Rather, we grew up in four different countries: Germany, Italy, Spain, and the United States. Child-rearing practices were different across those countries when we were children. When one digs deeper, one realizes that parenting practices still vary greatly across countries today. Here we could rely on additional personal experiences, as we have both lived in different countries throughout our adult lives. We connected these experiences with our academic knowledge to try to understand why there are large differences in parenting around the world.

Part 1 of the book is about parenting in our time. We document that in the United States and other rich countries, parenting has gotten more intense in recent decades. What explains the sudden emergence of "helicopter parents" and "tiger moms" after many of today's parents had much more relaxed childhoods in the 1970s and 1980s? Our answer is that economic incentives have changed, largely as the result of a rise in economic inequality that took place during the same period. Next, we take a tour around the world and try to understand why parenting practices vary so much across countries. Our answer is that economic incentives differ across countries, too. Third, we observe that in advanced economies a "parenting gap" has opened up between the choices of parents on different rungs of the social ladder. What can account for the gap? We show how economic incentives differ across parents who face different constraints, depending on their income and education.

Part 2 of the book looks back through history. Why was strict parenting so popular for centuries, while today most parents refrain from disciplining their children harshly when they do wrong? We argue, once again, that economic incentives have changed. Using the same lens, we also study the transformation of gender roles in parenting, the transition from large to small families in the course of economic development, the changing attitude of parents toward child labor, and even the formation and transmission of different preferences and values across social classes.

Part 3 of the book looks ahead into the future. There, we study the effect of policies and institutions, focusing first on schools and educational institutions. Then, we consider policy interventions. We argue that the parenting gap between rich and poor families amplifies inequality of opportunity for children from different backgrounds, and we ask what could be done to close the gap. We also look further ahead and ask what parenting will be like for the next generation if the current movement toward higher economic inequality continues.

Writing this book would not have been possible without the help of a great many people. Fabrizio's wife, María, and Matthias's wife, Marisa, encouraged us from the start to take up this project. They were also our partners in our actual parenting experience, which formed much of our thinking about the issues discussed in the book. Throughout, they provided us with constant support and constructive criticism about the development of the book. We also thank our children for the inspiration they provided, for enduring our prolonged preoccupation with the theory rather than the practice of parenting, and for allowing us to draw on our shared experiences in writing this book.

We thank our editor Sarah Caro for her encouragement to pursue this project and for her wonderful editorial guidance from this first proposal to the final draft. We are grateful for the support of our home institutions, Northwestern University and Yale University. The research discussed in this book has benefited from the financial support of the National Science Foundation (grant SES-0820409, Doepke) and of the

Swiss National Science Foundation (100018_165616, Zilibotti). We were fortunate to be able to rely on outstanding research assistants at the University of Zurich, Northwestern University, and Yale University, including Titan Alon, Stefan Binder, Severin Lenhard, Elisa Macchi, Nina Mühlebach, Sebastian Ottinger, Mathias Schief, Veronika Selezneva, Ashley Wong, Rachel Wu, and Laura Zwyssig. Without their help, this book would not exist today. Others who provided us with useful feedback and comments include Helena Appelberg, Gabriele Catania, Kushal Dev, Pamela Druckerman, Luca Fasani, Vanessa Han, Lixing Liang, Liu Liu, Masao Ogaki, Alice Ollino, Jody Ono, Chiara Pronzato, Julian Schärer, Xiang Wei, and Tong Zhang. Our friends and collaborators Fabian Kindermann, Joel Mokyr, and Michèle Tertilt gave us very valuable feedback on the entire manuscript.

Last, but by no means least important, we thank Giuseppe Sorrenti, who has been so much more than an assistant on this project. Without his enthusiasm, ideas, knowledge, and competent input, this project would have never been realized.

Love, Money
& Parenting

INTRODUCTION

When it comes to parenting, people do not usually think of economics. Yet, economics is a social science that aims to understand how people make decisions, and the decisions we make as parents are among the most important ones we face. In this book, we argue that economics can help us understand how many children people have, how much they invest in their upbringing, and what parenting style they choose.

In contrast to many other books on parenting, ours is not a parenting guide. We believe that our task as social scientists is not to tell parents what to do, but to understand the motives and forces behind what they actually do. To this aim, we take the perspective that parents, by and large, know about the pros and cons of different parenting choices. Given this knowledge, they do what they consider to be in the best interest of themselves and their children, whom they care about.

We show that the economic perspective is a powerful tool that can account for many observations on parenting, ranging from recent changes such as the rise of intensive *helicopter parenting* (i.e., supervising children's every move and "hovering" over them) to earlier historical transformations such as the sharp decline in the average number of children per woman that led to the rise of the modern nuclear family.

DRAWING ON PERSONAL EXPERIENCE

In writing this book, we draw not only on empirical data and our economic training but also on our own experience as parents and, earlier in life, as children. For this reason, in this introduction we start out with a description of our own backgrounds. We are two European academics living in the United States who grew up in very different environments (in terms of geography, culture, and economic conditions) from those in which we rear our own children. Our profession has led us to travel extensively and to be exposed to different cultures and child-rearing practices. The great diversity we have observed in the way parents bring up their children—both across countries and over time—motivates us to apply lessons from economics and social science to the study of parenting.

Matthias grew up in a village in Lower Saxony, West Germany, a typical middle-class community close to Hannover, the state capital. His father was a civil servant in state government and also ran a farm. Matthias's mother was a teacher but stopped working in that profession when Matthias was little, as working on the farm and raising four children kept her plenty busy. Later on, she was engaged in local politics and served as mayor of the village for many years. After his studies at Humboldt University in Berlin, Matthias moved at the age of twenty-four to the United States, first to Minneapolis and then to Chicago, where he earned his PhD in economics at the University of Chicago. After taking his first job in California, he married Marisa, an American, who works as a casting director for television shows and movies. Marisa and Matthias had their first two boys, Oskar and Lukas, in Los Angeles and then moved back to the Chicago area in 2010. They currently live in the affluent suburb of Evanston, where their third boy, Nico, was born in 2013. Today, Oskar, Lukas, and Nico are aged ten, seven, and four, respectively. All are fluent in German and English and attend the German International School Chicago.

Fabrizio was born in Emilia Romagna, a highly civic-minded region of Italy, according to Robert Putnam's *Making Democracy Work*.[1] His father was a white-collar worker (more precisely, a technician) working for RAI, Italy's national public broadcasting company, while his mother was a couturier working in the local fashion business. After studying in Bologna, Fabrizio moved to London, where he earned a PhD in economics. There, he met María, a Spaniard, whom he married. María and Fabrizio have moved extensively around Europe: they lived first in Barcelona, then in Stockholm, London, and Zurich before eventually moving to the United States in 2017. Today, they live in New Haven, Connecticut, while their daughter, Nora, is a student at the Swiss Federal Institute of Technology in Zurich.

When she was a small child, Nora attended nursery schools in Stockholm and London, and then kindergarten and primary school in Stockholm. When she moved to German-speaking Zurich with her family in 2006, neither of her parents spoke a word of German: as academics, their working and social language has always been English. Nora, therefore, had to come to grips with different school systems and languages with which her parents were not familiar. Today, she is fluent in English, Spanish, Italian, and German. She is also proficient in French and still remembers some of her early Swedish. Her case is discussed in the book *The Bilingual Edge* by the professors of second language Kendall King and Alison Mackey, who write: "As proud as her parents are of her, little Nora is not an exceptional genius. Rather, she happened to be born into the ideal circumstances to promote *quadra*lingualism."[2]

Apart from having lived in different countries, we also spend a lot of time today visiting other places around the world. Fabrizio spends significant portions of his time in China and Norway, while Matthias is often in Germany and Belgium. What strikes us most is how much diversity in child-rearing practices we observe even across culturally similar countries. It is perhaps not surprising that Chinese and American parents behave differently because, even in a globalized world, these two countries are far apart, have very different economic and political institutions, and their cultures have been different for millennia. However, it is less easy to explain why child-rearing principles differ so much between, say, Sweden and Switzerland, two wealthy European countries that tourists from other continents sometimes confuse with one another.

INTERNATIONAL DIFFERENCES IN PARENTING STYLES

Sweden is the stereotypical example of a culture that encourages an indulgent and permissive parenting style. Loving Swedish parents consider requiring a preschooler to sit quietly at a restaurant table as a breach of fundamental human rights. Most of them disapprove of any form of discipline, including verbal scolding, not to mention corporal punishment—illegal since 1979. What parents in most countries would regard as inappropriate child behavior (e.g., disturbing adult strangers) is understood and forgiven as being inherent to children's nature. María and Fabrizio were once visiting Swedish friends, when the hosts' six-year-old boy screamed at them "Håll tyst! Jag tittar på teve" ("Shut up! I am watching TV"). The parents' response was a complacent smile followed by the gentle suggestion that we, the adults, move to another room so as not to disrupt the child's viewing.

Swedish schools conform to the same liberal philosophy. The vast majority of Swedish toddlers and preschoolers attend nursery schools, free of charge. These are idyllic places, managed by competent and motivated professionals acting under the guiding principle that any formal teaching is taboo. Constraints on children are set to the absolute minimum. Misbehavior is controlled but very rarely sanctioned. Formal education in Sweden does not start before the age of seven, and pupils do not receive grades before turning thirteen. Stress and anxiety are considered the prime evil from which children should be sheltered. Some teachers explicitly discourage ambitious pupils from "overdoing it" and reprimand "irresponsible," pushy parents for stressing their kids out. The competitive spirit of Swedish children is confined to sports activities (an area where Swedes find competition acceptable). Proactive parents face social disapproval. When Nora's parents inquired whether she might start primary school early (at the age of six rather than seven), the answer was, "Of course, she can cope, but I would never do that to my own child."

By international standards, Switzerland also has a liberal parenting culture. However, parenting and schooling practices are definitely stricter than in Sweden. Educators assert their authority from the early grades. Children of all ages are supposed to shake hands with teachers as they enter the classroom, address them by the polite and formal *Sie* (third person), never call teachers by their first name, and listen quietly when teachers speak.[3] Children receive grades and report cards starting in second grade, when their peers in Sweden only just enter school. In sixth grade, Swiss children face an admission test that selects about 20 percent of them for the more academic track (*Gymnasium*) of the high school system (there is no middle school in Switzerland; children move directly from primary to high school). This test, informally called *Gymiprüfung*, is a crucible for twelve-year-old children. Many parents commit them to extra private tutoring in preparation, cutting their children's free time drastically, and some parents even take leave from their jobs to help out. This is not simply paranoid behavior. The Gymnasium is the gateway to university education. Although there are opportunities for children to switch to the academic track at a later stage, the Gymnasium gives access to a more advanced course of study and a selected peer group; thus, the outcome of the exam is undoubtedly important.

While the organization of the school system (e.g., by the existence of a Gymiprüfung) affects parents' behavior, it should not be regarded as the ultimate driving force of Swiss parenting. Rather, the organization of schools is only one manifestation of a different overall approach to education. Competition is more accepted in Switzerland than in Sweden, as is the notion that the more gifted children should be separated and offered a more challenging education than the rest. Parents are proud to have their children stand out academically at school and are willing to invest money and effort to support their individual achievements.

Despite these differences, parenting in Switzerland is not the polar opposite of Sweden. In terms of being demanding and focused on academic success, Swiss parents are far from extreme. As we will document, Swiss parents are less authoritarian and pushy than their French and North American counterparts. Within the United States, even the standard white American helicopter parents are not as demanding as many Asian American parents. Indeed, many white Americans view the strict parenting styles in the Asian American community with a mixture of horror and admiration, colored by the fear that Asian Americans will overtake them in the pursuit of excellence and success. And yet, Chinese parents living in China can be even tougher than Chinese Americans.

What drives these large differences across countries and ethnicities? A common answer is that they reflect cultural differences. However, cultural attitudes are not set in stone. They evolve over time, sometimes rapidly, and very often as a result of socioeconomic transformations. For instance, equality and egalitarianism were among the most important values in Maoist China, and there was very little inequality before the 1980s. After Mao's death, the process of economic liberalization that started under Deng Xiaoping has redesigned the Chinese society and its values, paving the way for a race toward individual economic success. Through recognition of their differences and encouragement of an entrepreneurial spirit, ordinary people were able to climb up the social ladder and millions were raised out of poverty, while economic inequality has grown dramatically. Culture has changed in parallel with this economic transformation. Today, China is a very individualistic society, where parents believe that success can be achieved through hard work and effort.

In contrast, for many years Sweden has been a society with low inequality dominated by egalitarian values. This has not always been the case. Before the twentieth century, Sweden's society was highly unequal. It was also very traditional, classist, and hierarchical. The main factor that produced these changes was a combination of the rise in industrialization and the decline of agriculture, which made ownership of land (the main source of inequality) less important over time, changing the balance of power between the landed aristocracy, the industrial bourgeoisie, and the labor movement. The examples of both China and Sweden show that culture (including child-rearing practices) is not immutable, but rather evolves alongside economic transformations.

ECONOMIC FACTORS MATTER

Our thesis is that economic conditions, and the way they change over time, have an important effect on parenting practices and on what people regard as good parenting. To be clear, this book is not built on the assumption (which some readers might expect from two economists) that parents are selfish beings driven by monetary motivations.

To the contrary, we believe that parent-child relationships are largely motivated by love and altruism. We hold the view that this is true equally across societies: by and large, the Chinese love their children as much as the Scandinavians do. We also do not subscribe to the view that parents in richer countries do a better job because they are more aware of good pedagogy. Like most European parents, we, the authors, dislike the habit of disciplining children by spanking them. Yet, we do not think that all parents who discipline their children are either ignorant or lack parental empathy.

We believe that, broadly speaking, parents try their best to prepare their children for the society in which they will live. Differences in child-rearing practices are rooted in the socioeconomic environment in which parents themselves grew up, in which they interact with their children, and in which they expect their children to live as adults. In other words, parents try to shape their children's values and behavior to prepare them for the challenges that lie ahead. In doing this, parents face a variety of constraints: they may be rich or poor, more or less able to assist their children in doing their homework, more or less busy with their own work, or more or less well informed. In this book, we show that the interaction of economic incentives and constraints (such as financial resources, ability, or time) can explain a great deal of what parents do.[4]

Some readers may be skeptical that economic factors are important to understanding how parents deal with their children. Many of the examples previously discussed compare industrialized nations enjoying similar levels of economic development, and among these countries, there is no clear pattern linking parenting choices with the average living standards. However, average income is not the only relevant economic dimension. Actually, when it comes to parenting styles, we find that income inequality is more important than the overall level of economic development. More precisely, the crucial factors are, on the one hand, the extent to which a child's future economic prosperity hinges on success in education, and, on the other hand, inequality in educational opportunity. In societies where income inequality is high but entirely determined by birth status, it would be futile for parents to push their children to stand out as exceptional students. However, they have every reason to do so when inequality is high because highly educated workers (and those coming from the better schools) earn much more than others.

Throughout our research, we discovered that in countries with low inequality and low returns to education, parents tend to be more permissive, while in countries with high inequality and a high return to education, parents are both more authoritarian and more prone to instill in their children a drive to achieve ambitious goals. The inequality explanation works well for the countries we discussed previously: inequality is very low in permissive Sweden, higher in achievement-oriented Switzerland, and higher yet in the United States, where anxiety-ridden helicopter parents hold sway.

CHANGES OVER TIME: FROM PERMISSIVE PARENTS TO HELICOPTER PARENTS

Child-rearing practices differ not only across countries. Cultural changes over time are equally interesting. When we were young, our parents often told us how much stricter their own upbringing had been relative to ours. This is typical for our generation: we were children during the 1970s, at the climax of the antiauthoritarian wave that had started a decade earlier.

Although our middle-class parents would not claim to have been antiauthoritarian, they still absorbed many of the values of this cultural movement. In many cases, adopting the new permissive values was not an independent choice, but rather reflected changing values throughout society. From primary school onward, teachers would emphasize the importance of freedom, independence, and emancipation from traditional values. In Italy during Fabrizio's childhood, the word *fascism* was (often too) quickly associated with any form of deference to the principle of authority. Parents were urged not to get involved in their children's homework. Traditionalism was under attack on several fronts. While our parents (like our own children sixty years later!) had to memorize multiplication tables, we were exposed to new fashions in the math pedagogy of the time; we learned set theory, binary codes, and Euler diagrams well before seeing any arithmetic. If parents expressed disconcertment at their children's slow progress in summing and multiplying, their perplexity would be met by teachers with complacent smiles. Grading was also deemed to be old-fashioned and blamed for the humiliation of weaker students; thus, it was gradually replaced by verbal assessments (which were not too different in the end, but words were regarded as less offensive than numbers). Children and teenagers were also actively encouraged to sort out conflicts and problems within their peer groups rather than referring to their parents or teachers. Turning to a person in a position of authority would make a youngster extremely unpopular. By contrast, independence and self-reliance were held in high regard. All of these trends apply both to Italy during Fabrizio's childhood and to Germany during Matthias's childhood.

If we think today of the differences between our own upbringing and that of our children, the most striking one is that we are far more involved and intrusive in our children's everyday lives than our parents could have imagined. That came as a surprise to us. Before having kids, we thought we would be relaxed parents because that is how we grew up. But similar to what our own parents experienced in the 1970s, our approach to parenting turned out to be much more informed by conditions in the economy and society that we live in now, rather than by the parenting culture to which we were exposed as children. Indeed, one reason why we started to work on the economics of parenting was the desire to understand why our own behavior as parents turned out to be so different from what we expected.

Our increased involvement as parents manifests itself in ways that middle-class parents today take for granted as the "standard" way to raise children, even though it would have been far from standard a few decades ago. We sign our kids up for music classes and sports, we make sure (discretely) they do their homework, we arrange playdates, and we read books with them. In addition, we generally supervise them closely, with an eye not so much to reduce opportunities for misbehavior, but rather to offer our help and support to induce them to do the right thing by their own "free will." In contrast, our parents did none of these things, or at least not to a comparable extent. When we were children, we often roamed freely until sunset, we went to friends' houses at our own choosing, no one would check our homework, and there were no organized activities until a much older age.

Relationships between parents and teachers are also different today. In the 1970s, many young teachers looked down on the old-fashioned bourgeois lifestyle that, in their view, some families were trying to preserve. But now, the balance of power between teachers and parents has shifted. Teachers are under immense pressure from demanding and opinionated parents, especially in affluent neighborhoods. Some parents complain about the lack of ambition of the school curriculum. Others blame teachers for not recognizing their little darling's genius.

The differences between our own parenting choices and those of our parents are manifestations of a general trend toward a more *intensive* parenting style that we document throughout the book. In our view, this trend can be understood as a response to economic changes that took place during the same period. This is not to say that economic factors are the sole determinants of parenting. However, thinking back to forty years ago, it does strike us that many of the common concerns among today's parents were essentially nonexistent when we were children. In both Germany and Italy, attendance at schools and universities was free, and there was little variation in quality across them (no Ivy League in either country). As long as one made it through high school with the minimum grades to pass, nothing one did in school before age eighteen had long-term consequences. We did not have to take college admission tests, and there were no admission committees evaluating our extracurricular activities. Even for kids that did not go to university, the outlook was bright. In Germany, graduates from the lower-level schools would generally go into apprenticeship programs, and the salaries they would ultimately earn (say, in the Volkswagen factory nearby) would not be much different from those of teachers or even doctors. Unemployment was low, and the social status of working-class values was high. Given this scenario, parents had little to gain from pushing their children hard, so it is not surprising that our parents took a relaxed attitude and let us enjoy a carefree childhood.

Since then, circumstances have changed. Starting in the 1980s, economic inequality has increased sharply, accompanied by the emergence of a "winner-takes-all" culture. In this changing world, parents have become increasingly worried that their children might be left behind. Hence, they push them from a tender age to achieve and succeed. As higher education turned into an essential precondition for economic and social success, increasing numbers of upper- and middle-class parents work hard to help their children succeed in school. High inequality, high returns to education, and high stakes in school achievement are a large part of why we act differently from our own parents and adopt a more intensive parenting style.

BUILDING BETTER INSTITUTIONS

As we stated from the outset, our aim in this book is to explain *why* parents make particular choices, but not to provide another "how to" book that tells parents how they *should* raise their children. This does not mean, however, that no lessons can be drawn from our findings. Our main argument is that parents respond, as best as they can, to the environments in which they raise their children and in which they expect their children's lives to unfold later on. What these environments look like is in part the result of policy choices that vary across societies.

Most directly, we can see this in the design of the education system: features such as variation in the quality of schools, tracking in the school system, the use of high-stakes exams to sort students into different tracks, and the system that admits students into colleges and universities form a large part of the environment to which parents respond. All of these institutional features come down to policy decisions. Other policy choices that are also relevant for parenting include financial support for parents and parental leave policies, the extent to which progressive taxes and transfers redistribute income, and pension policies that partly determine whether aging parents need to rely on their children for financial support.

We can, and should, ask what the consequences of different policy choices are for parenting and whether it is possible to build policies and institutions in a way that leads to better outcomes. We highlight two reasons why policy interventions may be desirable. The first concerns equality of opportunity for all children. We will discuss evidence that the recent increase in inequality in industrialized countries has not only led to more intensive parenting overall but also to larger gaps in the parenting investments between families from different backgrounds. If children from low-income families no longer have the same opportunities as others, there is the risk of a vicious cycle of low social mobility and a further increase in inequality across generations. We will discuss the role public policy can play in addressing this threat.

A second scenario that may call for policy intervention and improved institutions is when parenting turns into a zero-sum competition that leaves all families worse off. Consider a hypothetical country in which success in life depends on a single exam taken at age sixteen (say, the one hundred best test takers receive a prestigious civil service position). Further, assume that the knowledge tested in this exam does not have any real-life relevance; the only function of the exam is to get ahead in life. In such a country, parents have every incentive to push their children hard into studying for this test, to hire tutors, or to pay for "cramming schools" that prepare students for the test. Yet the society as a whole will be worse off because all the studying and cramming as such does not have any true benefits. Of course, studying hard could get a particular child the coveted position, but this comes at the expense of another child that is now left behind: with a fixed number of positions, competition for slots is a zero-sum game. Such a society could benefit from switching to a different system that allows more room for parents and children to enjoy their time together.

Admittedly, there is no country that fits literally the zero-sum scenario we have outlined. While in many countries high-stakes exams play an important role in children's success, generally these exams test some knowledge that has real-life relevance (so, there is value in children acquiring it), and they contribute to selecting the most gifted individuals. In an ideal world where people have equal opportunities, an accurate selection would be valuable for everybody: societies benefit from the ablest individuals occupying positions of responsibility in firms and governments.

Still, we can ask whether a given set of institutions strikes the right balance. In the United States, for example, admission to top universities now depends in equal measure on near-perfect grades in school, near-perfect scores in standardized college admission exams, and on an impressive résumé of extracurricular activities in areas such as music, sports, or volunteering. Families respond to these incentives by putting greater and greater pressure on their children. The result is teenagers having busier schedules than some top business executives. Also, certain ways of testing and selecting children end up benefiting disproportionally children from a wealthy or highly educated family background. Examples include private schools and locally financed public schools that are only attended by children of affluent families and that become stepping stones for admission to elite universities. Another example is expensive extracurricular activities. The ensuing selection may then hinge more on family background than on the child's individual ability. We can use economic analysis to ask whether there is a better way.

Even while considering the role of policies and institutions, we are not suggesting that there is a single best design that fits every society. We certainly think that different parenting practices yield different societies, but it is not always obvious which ones are more desirable. The United States is an individualistic, innovative, and work-oriented (some might say workaholic) society. Scandinavians compensate for their more relaxed work habits with a greater ability to cooperate and work in teams. People often grow attached to their own way of living: many Americans find Europe too relaxed and not meritocratic enough; conversely, many Europeans find the United States too competitive, stressful, and unequal.

We discuss in the book how different patterns of inequality and parenting styles sustain and reinforce each other, even influence the adoption of different institutions. Low inequality in Sweden leads to a way of raising children that, in turn, contributes to keeping inequality low. Children raised in the egalitarian Swedish tradition are more likely to support high taxation and income redistribution as adults. In contrast, children raised in less equal and more competitive societies such as the United States are less prone to support redistribution. We argue that such societies can learn from each other's experiences, and there is also something to be said for trying different approaches.

OUTLINE

The overall thesis of our book is that economic conditions affect the choices parents make and how they interact with their children. In the following chapters, we lay out the economic way of thinking about parenting in more detail, and we apply it in order to understand facts about parenting across countries and historical periods.

Chapter 1 introduces the main elements of the economics of parenting. We highlight how we economists, among the different social sciences, can offer a useful guide to understanding the behavior of parents and children. In doing so, we relate our work to the area of developmental psychology, which is also concerned with the implications of child-rearing choices. From developmental psychology, we adopt the concept of parenting styles. While psychologists have primarily been concerned with the impact that different parenting styles have on child development, we argue that economics can help explain why parents end up choosing a particular style.

Chapter 2 deals with the transformation in parenting that has taken place in rich countries over the last few decades, along the lines of the contrast between our own parenting choices and those of our parents. We argue that changing fashions and parental practices, like the permissive wave of the 1960s and 1970s and the spread of helicopter parenting in more recent times, can be explained by the increase in economic inequality. We present empirical evidence of a rising intensity in parenting and relate these changes to economic trends. We also discuss the implications of different parenting styles for children's success in terms of academic achievement, and how this feeds back into child-rearing choices.

Chapter 3 moves to differences in parenting across countries, such as the contrast between parenting in Sweden and Switzerland that María and Fabrizio encountered when raising their daughter Nora. We discuss how economic differences across countries can help explain why parents in some countries are liberal while elsewhere parents are strict. To this aim, we both use cross-country statistical analysis and zoom in on specific countries. We document that the extent of income inequality plays a crucial role. We also show that over time parents have become increasingly pushy in countries where inequality has increased, while parents remain more liberal in countries where income inequality has decreased.

Chapter 4 places the spotlight on socioeconomic inequality in parenting within countries. We examine how parenting choices vary across groups distinguished by income, education, and racial or ethnic background, and how these differences respond to changes in the economic environment. We discuss the possibility that an increasing "parenting gap" between different socioeconomic groups may contribute to further increases in economic inequality in the next generation and to lower social mobility across different groups in the population. We also use this discussion to open up the policy dimension and ask which policies may be helpful in reducing parenting gaps and thereby contribute to providing equal opportunities to children from all backgrounds.

Starting with chapter 5, we expand our analysis to a historical perspective. We argue that the economics of parenting is equally applicable to parents who lived hundreds of years ago and to those who struggle with how to raise their children today. We begin by mapping out how parenting styles have evolved throughout history, starting in Biblical times. Over a longer historical period, one of the main facts to be accounted for is the decline of strict authoritarian parenting, including the regular use of corporal punishment. We also explore how different economic and cultural factors (e.g., religion and religiosity) explain differences in parental practices.

In chapter 6, we consider the gender dimension and discuss how parents raise girls and boys differently. The historical angle is again salient here: whereas today many parents strive to treat their children in a gender-neutral way, until very recently, girls and boys experienced very different childhoods. We link these differences to the equally divided gender roles that were prevalent in industrialized countries until a few decades ago and that are still relevant in many developing countries today.

Chapter 7 moves beyond parenting style to turn to the more fundamental decisions that parents make, such as how many children to have in the first place. We present evidence of how the number of children has changed in the course of economic development, from the preindustrial era characterized by large families, widespread child labor, and high mortality, to the current era of one- or two-child families in industrialized countries. We examine how decisions on family size interact with parenting style, especially decisions on child labor versus schooling, and we explore specific historical episodes such as the baby boom after World War II.

In chapter 8, we explore parenting choices in a society with deep class divisions. We focus specifically on British society during and before the Industrial Revolution, when the aristocracy, the working class, and a middle class of craftsmen and merchants led sharply distinct economic lives. We argue that economic incentives can explain why these classes also adopted equally distinct parenting values. For example, while middle-class families emphasized patience and a work ethic (similar to many parents today), the aristocratic upper class cultivated a disdain for labor and a heightened appreciation of leisurely pursuits. We also discuss whether the ramifications of sharp class divisions in earlier societies hold lessons for our current era of growing inequality.

In chapter 9, we turn to the role of institutions and discuss the influence of the organization of the school system on parenting strategies. After a historical overview, we describe in detail how the education system is set up in countries such as China, Japan, Finland, Sweden, and France, and how this feeds back into parents' choices.

Throughout the book, we return to the idea that parents actions are shaped by the hopes and aspirations for their children's future. That is certainly true for our own parenting: we often ponder about the world that Lukas, Nico, Nora, and Oskar are going to live in. In the concluding chapter 10, we propose some reflections about what this future might look like in terms of the issues covered in the book. We consider how parenting styles will evolve if current economic trends continue and what role public policy can play in shaping what parenting will be like for the next generation.

PART ONE

Raising Kids in the
Age of Inequality

CHAPTER ONE

The Economics of Parenting Style

What does it actually mean to use economics to understand what parents do? It is a fair question to ask: until a few decades ago, it did not occur to anyone that economists may have useful things to say about parenting. Much of traditional economics deals with money and profit, and, more generally, activity taking place in firms and in the marketplace. In contrast, raising children takes place in the home, and while money is involved, parenting is above all about love and affection.

That an "economics of parenting" is possible today is in large part due to the pioneering work of the Nobel laureate Gary Becker, who was one of Matthias's thesis advisors at the University of Chicago. According to Becker, economics is a general tool used to analyze human behavior that need not be limited to a narrow range of traditional subjects. In his work, Becker extended the realm of economics to cover social phenomena such as crime, politics, religion, and the family.[1] By the time we were in graduate school, Becker's ideas had entered the mainstream, and his work had a profound impact on us. In much of our own research, we have followed Becker's example by using economics to understand issues that were traditionally covered by other fields such as sociology or political science.

The essence of the economic approach to human behavior is that it conceives of people as doing the best they can to achieve their objectives, subject to the constraints that the environment imposes on them. For instance, when we think of the decisions of firms, we envision managers whose objective is to maximize firm profit through actions such as hiring workers, investing in machines, or developing new products, subject to constraints that derive from the firm's production technology, the skills of the employees, the prices of inputs, and the demand for the firm's products.

In this book, we want to examine the decisions people make as parents along the same lines. To do this, just as in the example of a firm above, we need to start with parents' objectives and constraints. What is it that parents are trying to accomplish, and what are the constraints that place limits on what they can do?

PARENTS' OBJECTIVES AND CONSTRAINTS

Let's start with parents' objectives. In everyday speech, the adjective "economic" is often used to mean "monetary" or "financial," and in certain situations, it makes sense to think of parents as pursuing monetary goals using children as their economic resources. In some societies, young children are a source of income for families. Child labor is a widespread phenomenon in many developing countries today and was equally common in today's industrialized countries in the past (we discuss the specific issue of child labor in chapter 7). Likewise, in some societies parents may decide to have children in the expectation that they will support them in old age. Either as workers or as caregivers, one can regard children, in part, as economic assets in which parents can invest.[2]

Yet envisioning parents as having children mainly for financial reasons is a caricature that misses the main picture. Financial matters may play some role, but for most parents, child-rearing is first of all about compassion, empathy, and love. Parents' concern for their children includes both the present (parents would like their children to be happy) and the future (parents would like them to do well in life).

If parents' objectives are for children to be happy and to do well in life, what are the constraints that they need to take into account? When we speak of constraints, we mean all limitations or restrictions that people are subject to when making choices. In traditional economics, the most familiar constraint is the budget constraint: people would love to buy many things (a bigger house, a nice car, an expensive vacation) but are restricted by what they can afford.

In terms of parenting, limited funds may restrict parents' ability, for example, to pay for the best private schools or to satisfy their children's demands for the latest gaming console. Yet constraints, like objectives, need not be exclusively of a financial nature. For many parents, the most significant constraints are time and capabilities. Some parents need to work long hours, cutting down the time they can spend with their children. In some instances, time constraints can be extreme: some parents are locked in jail, and others migrate without their families in pursuit of work, enduring separation from their children for years. Limits to parents' knowledge and abilities are equally important. Some parents may have the time and resources to care for their children, but fail to provide them with an appropriate diet because they are unaware of the nutritional properties of different types of food. Others underestimate the importance of education as a means of getting on in society and do not put effort into motivating their children to do well in school. In emphasizing the different constraints and opportunities that people (especially, the rich and the poor) face, our thinking is heavily influenced by the work of the British economist Tony Atkinson, who was one of Fabrizio's mentors at the London School of Economics. His lifelong research on inequality and poverty would have made him a likely Nobel laureate had he lived longer.

That parents face certain constraints is an undeniable fact of life, and even saying that they have objectives should not be controversial. The point where we economists depart from other social sciences is that we take the perspective that, by and large, people act deliberately to achieve their objectives. Commenting on Becker's work on fertility choice, the American economist James Duesenberry wrote, "Economics is all about how people make choices; sociology is all about how people don't have any choices to make."[3]

In the end, whether or not our choice-based method is fruitful hinges on its ability to explain social phenomena. In the specific case of parenting, how far can the economic approach go in explaining how parenting practices evolve over time and across space, and how they differ among individuals? In other words, the task is to link changes in parenting to changes in the incentives and constraints that parents face, given their objectives. In this book, we argue that the economic method is remarkably successful in explaining what parents do.

DIANA BAUMRIND'S PARENTING STYLES

One central choice that we would like to understand is that of *parenting style*. This concept was coined in the field of developmental psychology. Therefore, we start by laying out how psychologists think about parenting styles and how their approach differs from ours. In developmental psychology, parenting style refers to the broad strategies that parents employ in raising their children. A number of empirical studies in this field (some of them reviewed in later pages) document that parenting styles matter for child development—in other words, children exposed to different parenting practices grow up with different preferences, attitudes, and skills.

The seminal contribution of developmental psychology to our understanding of parenting styles was made by Diana Baumrind of the University of California, Berkeley. Baumrind identified three main parenting styles: *authoritarian, permissive,* and *authoritative*.[4] We now briefly introduce these three basic types of parenting.

AUTHORITARIAN PARENTING STYLE

As the name suggests, the authoritarian style is one where parents demand obedience from their children and exercise strict control. In Baumrind's words:

> The authoritarian parent attempts to shape, control, and evaluate the
> behavior and attitudes of the child in accordance with a set standard
> of conduct, usually an absolute standard, theologically motivated and
> formulated by a higher authority. She [the parent] values obedience

as a virtue and favors punitive, forceful measures to curb self-will at points where the child's actions or beliefs conflict with what she thinks is right conduct. She believes in keeping the child in his place, in restricting his autonomy, and in assigning household responsibilities in order to inculcate respect for work. She regards the preservation of order and traditional structure as a highly valued end in itself. She does not encourage verbal give and take, believing that the child should accept her word for what is right.[5]

A fictional authoritarian parent is the Lutheran bishop Edvard Vergérus in the Swedish director Ingmar Bergman's movie *Fanny and Alexander*.[6] Austere, strict, and humorless, Vergérus is prepared to inflict merciless punishment on his stepson Alexander for even minor disobedience and disrespect. This includes beating, whipping, and humiliating the wretched child. Alexander's misery is made worse by the lively memories of his life prior to the death of his natural father, when he grew up in the liberal and joyful atmosphere of a family of artists (among them, his mother, Emily). Yet Vergérus is no sadist: he believes that he acts in the long-term interest of Alexander and in deference to God.

Authoritarian parenting can often involve corporal punishment. However, we need to draw a line between authoritarian parenting and outright child abuse. In reality, physical abuse is often a symptom of dysfunctional families where parents suffer drug or alcohol addiction or other forms of psychological disorders. We do not address such social pathologies in this book, and it is not what we have in mind when we speak of authoritarian parents. Instead, we focus on generally well-meaning parents who think that children should obey their parents because this will eventually turn out to be in their own interest.

Mike Agassi, the father of the famous tennis player Andre Agassi, is another example of an authoritarian parent. A former boxer and later tennis coach of his son, Mike made clear to Andre from a tender age that he had to become the best tennis player in the world. Neither Andre's personal taste for playing tennis, nor his passion for other activities, nor any concern for his current well-being were supposed to matter or interfere with this goal. In his autobiography, Andre recalls what happened when one day he expressed a desire to play soccer instead of tennis. His father shouted at him: "You're a tennis player! You're going to be number one in the world! You're going to make lots of money. *That's the plan, and that's the end of it.*"[7] Mike was a strong-willed father and, like Vergérus, was no sadist. Rather, both Mike Agassi and Vergérus believed they alone knew what was best for their sons.

While the methods used by Vergérus and Andre Agassi's father are heavy-handed and borderline abusive, authoritarian parents need not be harsh. Some parents may be strict and demand obedience, while at the same time being loving and affectionate. A benign incarnation of an authoritarian parenting style is Teresa, María's mother (i.e., Fabrizio's mother-in-law). María grew up in a Catholic family of six during the Francoist dictatorship in Spain. Teresa is an example of a loving mother who believed her mission was to enforce "a set standard of conduct . . . formulated by a higher authority." Rules were neither to be explained, nor to be agreed upon, nor to be internalized. They were just to be obeyed. In Baumrind's words, Teresa believed that children should accept their parents' word for what is right. Different from Vergérus and Mike Agassi, Teresa did not make her children's life miserable. On the contrary, María's parents were generous and prepared to make large economic sacrifices for their children's future: all children received support for higher education and material needs, though always on their parents' terms.

After the two elder daughters adopted the rebellious mood of the 1970s—allegedly because of an excess of freedom and "bad" peer influence—María was sent by her parents to a boarding house run by the Catholic conservative organization Opus Dei. She lived there while she attended college at the University of Valencia. Her parents took on the full economic burden of the boarding house, including food, lodging, and the strict invigilation services of its pious wardens. The rules of the house included a rigid curfew and an appropriate amount of religious ceremony. While María recalls her college years as the saddest time in her whole life, her mother maintains that this was the best gift she could have given to her daughter, and the seed of her future adult-life academic achievements. In spite of holding different views about this and other matters, María loves her mother and regards herself as a lucky daughter.

The story is similar with Matthias's paternal grandfather, Otto. Matthias and his siblings remember Otto as a grumpy old man who had little tolerance for loud children in the house and who would scold them even for minor perceived infractions. For Matthias's father, Dietmar, Otto's authoritarian ways had more severe implications. Otto's view was that for the first twenty-four years of each of his five children's lives, he alone got to decide on what they should study and which career they should pursue. As the first-born child, Dietmar had to bear the brunt of this attitude. For Otto, there was no question that Dietmar's place in life was to ultimately take over the farm. Decisions on Dietmar's career followed from this long-view plan; his own preferences did not matter. Accordingly, after finishing school, Dietmar served as an apprentice for another farmer. He had no role in deciding on this or even in picking the farm where he was supposed to learn the trade: Otto took care of all of that and simply dropped him off at the chosen establishment. After finishing the apprenticeship, Dietmar was enrolled to study to be a teacher because Otto (a teacher himself, like his own father) felt that teaching was an occupation that went along well with farming. Once again, Dietmar's own preferences (he would have rather studied physics or law) did not play any part in the decision-making process. Later on, Otto's aggressive interventions in Dietmar's life led to a temporary falling-out. Yet overall, Otto achieved what he had intended: Dietmar finished his studies, took over the farm, and also had a career in civil service similar to Otto's own. Dietmar's younger siblings were able to gain more independence, but even they were far from free in choosing their own path in life.

PERMISSIVE PARENTING STYLE

The second of Diana Baumrind's parenting styles, permissive parenting, is the polar opposite of authoritarian parenting. Permissive parents follow a laissez-faire approach and let children make their own choices, encouraging their independence. Baumrind writes:

The permissive parent attempts to behave in a non-punitive, accep-
tant, and affirmative manner towards the child's impulses, desires,
and actions. She [the parent] consults with him [the child] about
policy decisions and gives explanations for family rules. She makes
few demands for household responsibility and orderly behavior. She
presents herself to the child as a resource for him to use as he wishes,
not as an ideal for him to emulate, nor as an active agent responsible
for shaping or altering his ongoing or future behavior. She allows the
child to regulate his own activities as much as possible, avoids the
exercise of control, and does not encourage him to obey externally
defined standards.[8]

In the same way that we do not view authoritarian parents as bad parents, we also do not attach any negative connotation to the term permissive.[9] To be sure, there are some parents who neglect or completely
abandon children to themselves. We will refer to such parents as *neglectful* or *uninvolved*, borrowing the terminology from the psychologists
Eleanor Maccoby and John Martin.[10] In contrast, permissive parents
care about their children and want them to do well, but believe that
granting a lot of freedom is a good way to accomplish that. In our terminology, the notion of permissive parents could as well be replaced
(as we will occasionally do) by that of liberal parents.

The artist and designer Bruce Zeines is an example of someone who
has adopted a self-consciously permissive parenting style. A proponent
of a radical form of independent learning, Zeines is a founder of the
Brooklyn Free School (BFS), a "democratic free school" in New York.
The only strict requirement for pupils at the BFS is that they attend the
democratic all-school meetings designed to empower students to speak
freely. According to Zeines, the school maintains that students can pursue anything as long as it does not interfere with anyone else's pursuits.
If it does interfere, then the person involved can call a meeting.

In his article "The Opposite of Tiger Mom," Zeines argues that his
views developed in reaction to his own experience in public education.[11] "I spent a lot of time drawing and I wasn't interested in what the

teacher was doing. . . . I began a path of learning that was forged on my own. I learned more outside of school than inside." This experience turned him into a permissive parent: "As a parent my perspective is pretty much just to leave them alone. Let them find their way. You could call us laid back parents." He would never force his son to do anything he dislikes; rather, he lets him learn through his own enthusiasm. "In public school, kids read because you make them, but forcing kids to do anything makes them not like it. Public school is about obedience, respecting authority. Do we want obedient children? Or do we want free-thinkers, people who can help us out of messes?" He claims that his radical approach has made his child fearless and ready to question adults when he thinks they are wrong or superficial.

Two fictional permissive moms are Mrs. George, Regina's mother in the teen comedy film "Mean Girls," and Lorelai Gilmore, one of the two protagonists of the television series "Gilmore Girls." Mrs. George calls herself a "cool mom" and behaves pretty much like a teenager. She speaks to her daughter using teenage jargon, something that makes her look silly but that also allows her to make contact with her daughter's feelings. She is liberal and unconventional to the point that she allows minors to drink in the house, does not object to her teenage daughter indulging in sexual promiscuity, and even offers Regina condoms when she brings Shane Oman to her house. In short, Mrs. George is a permissive mother insofar as she seconds her young daughter's inclinations without imposing any traditional adult values.

Lorelai Gilmore is less radically permissive than Mrs. George. The unhappy daughter of an authoritarian mother and a workaholic father, Lorelai has herself been a rebellious, independent girl. After becoming pregnant, she leaves home, gives birth, and rears Rory as a single mom. As a mother, she tries to be all that her own mother had not been for her. She is never judgmental and is instead open, caring, sympathetic, and supportive of her daughter. Lorelai always takes Rory's opinions seriously and, in fact, often consults her daughter about her own business and emotional life. While Rory is allowed to make the final decision for everything that concerns her own life, Lorelai is ultimately a very engaged mother. She cares about Rory's everyday welfare but also about her educational success. One might say that her parenting style is 90 percent permissive and 10 percent authoritative, the parenting style to which we turn next.

AUTHORITATIVE PARENTING STYLE

The authoritative parenting style occupies a middle ground. Like authoritarian parents, authoritative parents aim to influence their children's choices. However, rather than doing so through command and discipline, they achieve their goal by reasoning and attempting to shape their children's values. In Baumrind's words:

> The authoritative parent attempts to direct the child's activities but in a rational, issue-oriented manner. She encourages verbal give and take, shares with the child the reasoning behind her policy, and solicits his objections when he refuses to conform. Both autonomous self-will and disciplined conformity are valued. Therefore, she exerts firm control at points of parent-child divergence, but does not hem the child in with restrictions. She enforces her own perspective as an adult, but recognizes the child's individual interests and special ways. The authoritative parent affirms the child's present qualities, but also sets standards for future conduct. She uses reason, power, and shaping by regime and reinforcement to achieve her objectives, and does not base her decisions on group consensus or the individual child's desires.[12]

Baumrind's quote reads like a recommendation of the type that dozens of recent books, webpages, and blogs offer to parents seeking advice. It rhymes well with what many of today's middle-class parents in the industrialized world aspire to. We must confess that Baumrind captures well what the two of us try to do in our own life as fathers. If this book were another guide to modern parenting, the rest of it would contain recipes for how to be a truly authoritative parent. However, our goal is a different one: we want to understand *why* parents adopt a particular parenting style, and how their choice depends on the socioeconomic conditions of the society in which they live. Before we can do that, we need to explore what the various parenting styles actually accomplish.

THE IMPACT OF PARENTING STYLE ON CHILD DEVELOPMENT

In developmental psychology, there is a great deal of research that aims to understand how specific parenting styles affect child development. A main finding in a number of empirical studies is that, on average, the children of authoritative parents perform better in school than children exposed to other parenting styles. A frequently cited article by Sanford Dornbusch of Stanford University and a number of coauthors considers a sample of 7,836 high school students in the San Francisco Bay Area and finds that children who experience authoritative parenting obtain higher grades.[13] Several other studies using data from other areas of the United States confirm their findings.[14] Sociologists Tak Wing Chan and Anita Koo study the effect of parenting styles beyond school performance.[15] Using the Youth Panel of the British Household Panel Survey, they document that children exposed to an authoritative parenting style not only obtain stronger academic results but also report higher levels of subjective well-being and self-esteem. In addition, these children enjoy better health and are less likely to indulge in risky behavior such as smoking cigarettes, consuming drugs, or engaging in fights.

What is it about children of authoritative parents that makes them do well in school? According to a study of Swedish adolescents led by psychologist Kaisa Aunola, an important determinant of adolescents' academic success is their *achievement strategy*, in particular, how they respond to challenges.[16] The study documents that when facing difficulties, adolescents exposed to an authoritative parenting style are less likely to be passive and helpless, less afraid to fail, and less prone to attribute failure to their own lack of ability. In addition, they are less susceptible to depression and better at concentrating and staying focused on a task. Interestingly, her study also finds that the performance of Swedish children subject to a permissive parenting style is very similar to that of children subject to an authoritative parenting style. In contrast, children exposed to either authoritarian or neglectful parenting do worse. In chapter 3, we will show that permissive parenting is popular in Sweden and very common among the educated middle class. So, there may be other good reasons why this parenting style is associated with good school performance in Sweden. We return to this point in the following pages.

Another reason why children of authoritative parents do well may simply be that these parents put a lot of effort into getting involved in their children's school activities. A study of nine high schools in Wisconsin and northern California led by psychologist Laurence Steinberg documents that authoritative parents are significantly more likely to help their children with homework, to attend school programs, to watch their children in sports or extracurricular activities, and to help students select courses.[17] Moreover, these parents are more aware of what their own children do and how they perform in school. Finally, authoritative parents praise academic excellence and the importance of working hard more than other parents do.

If authoritative parenting leads to strong school performance, how does the stereotypical Chinese American tiger mom fit into the picture? Psychologist Ruth Chao notes that Chinese American children typically perform well in school, although most Chinese parents are more authoritarian than authoritative.[18] Are these children different? According to Chao, the issue is that the usual classification into three basic parenting style hides some important nuances. Chinese parents may set many rules and prohibitions, but also emphasize training and are prepared to invest a lot of time in motivating and supporting their children's learning activities. Such a parenting style combines features of an authoritative and authoritarian parenting style and is fundamentally different from the traditional authoritarian approaches of María's mother and Dietmar's father, discussed previously (although one might argue that it has some commonality with the approach of Mike Agassi).[19] In the rest of the book, we sometimes refer to a notion of *intensive parenting* that combines elements of an authoritarian and an authoritative parenting style—that is, it captures heavily involved parents who strongly interfere with their children's lives.

We should note that, taken by itself, the empirical association between the exposure to an authoritative parenting style and strong school performance does not prove that this parenting style is the ultimate cause of kids doing well in school. To establish that children perform better *because* they are subject to an authoritative parenting style, one would ideally run an experiment in which parenting styles were randomly assigned to different parents. In such a hypothetical study, the researchers in charge of the experiment would tell parents which of the styles to adopt in raising their children, and the parents would abide by their instructions, irrespective of their own convictions and inclinations. Clearly, such an experiment is not actually possible in a free society. Even if the researchers could get the approval of an ethics committee, they would not be able to find many parents who would be willing to take part in such an experiment. Most readers would object to dispensing corporal punishment to their children for the sake of generating scientific knowledge!

Given that such a randomized experiment is unachievable, survey studies like those previously reviewed provide the best available evidence on the effects of parenting styles. These suggest that an authoritative parenting style is associated with desirable outcomes, especially in schools. However, it is possible that this correlation is, at least in part, due to other factors that lead to a better school performance and happen be more prevalent among parents who choose to adopt an authoritative parenting style. For instance, we may suspect that richer or better-educated parents are both likely to have children who do well in school and to be authoritative parents. We can address such concerns, at least in part, by comparing the effects of different parenting styles across parents of the same income or with similar educational achievements. In the following chapters, we provide additional evidence of the effects of parenting styles on education outcomes, test scores, and social mobility in different countries, while accounting for the effects of additional factors such as parents' income and education. We will show that the main findings from developmental psychology (such as children with authoritative parents doing well in education) hold up well.

THE ECONOMISTS' PERSPECTIVE ON PARENTING STYLES

Having reviewed evidence on the effects of parenting styles from developmental psychology, let us move back to economics. As we have seen, the focus of the research in psychology is on how the use of a particular parenting style affects child development. This is usually done by comparing a set of otherwise similar children (say, who all attend the same school) who are exposed to different parenting styles. Our approach is different in three ways. First, we put the spotlight on the parents and ask *why* they make particular choices, rather than taking these choices as given and only looking for their effects. Second, we are interested in broader comparisons and ask why parenting differs so much across countries and generations, rather than looking at a particular time and place. Third, in answering these questions we use the economic approach—that is, we envision parents as making deliberate choices to achieve specific objectives, subject to constraints.[20]

By following the economic approach, we refrain from classifying parents as good or bad. For centuries, the vast majority of parents were authoritarian. Why? Were our grandparents too ignorant to understand what good parents should do, or was the permissive trend in the 1970s the result of a collective delusion? Have today's parents finally been rescued by a few enlightened experts who showed them the right way to raise kids? Such a view of the world would be as superficial as it would be arrogant; so, our book takes a different tack.

We maintain that parents' decisions are driven by objectives that center on concern for their children and by their views on the pros and cons of different parenting strategies in helping them achieve these objectives. This does not mean that we assume that parents are perfectly informed about the effects of every parenting style: predicting the future is hard for parents, just as it is for economists or other social scientists. In fact, limits to their knowledge or their capability to implement a particular parenting style are part of the constraints that parents face. Nevertheless, we work from the assumption that parents broadly know what they are doing and that their choices make sense given the environment they face.

We should also note that our economic approach allows for the possibility that parents make decisions more or less consciously. It probably would be hard to find parents who, after having their first child, entered into an explicit debate involving spreadsheets with a detailed comparison of the various pros and cons to choose their parenting style. Most of the time, we parents make particular decisions because they just seem right to us, without going into deep thought as to exactly why this is so. Yet we argue that the outcome of this process can be understood *as if* the parents carefully weighed all their options before coming to a decision. Parents do often try to envisage the society their children will live in as adults, and the core of the economic approach is to assume that decisions on parenting style are informed by these deliberations. If the parents expect that the society will become more unequal and competition will be stiffer, they respond by adopting a parenting style that prepares children to survive, and hopefully thrive, in a more competitive environment. Our argument applies beyond income or other financial factors. For instance, in countries with strong civil liberties, we would expect parents to encourage children to be outspoken, whereas in a repressive state parents would be more likely to advocate restraint.

Using the economic approach, we would like to figure out the incentives that drive how parents actually parent—and how parenting styles can change in response to changes in economic incentives. Our ultimate goal is to understand the broad pattern of variation across countries, time, and socioeconomic groups in the adoption of parenting styles. As already stated, it is our view that the primary objective that drives parents' decisions is love and affection for their children. This does not mean, however, that parenting is always designed to maximize children's immediate happiness, as the examples of authoritarian parents make clear. To understand why love and affection can still drive such parenting decisions, we need to explore more deeply the specific forms that parents' concern for their children can take.

HOW WE CARE FOR CHILDREN: ALTRUISM AND PATERNALISM

Parents are typically concerned for both the current and future well-being of their children. The way parents behave—including the parenting style they adopt—may reflect how relatively important they regard each of these two objectives. Some parents think that childhood should be the happiest stage of human life and that children should primarily be helped to enjoy it without worrying too much about their future. Conversely, others believe that childhood is the time to sow, while adulthood is the time to reap. Children should be guided, or even pushed, to make the necessary investments for a successful adult life.

In our own recent research, we argue that in order to understand the behavior of parents it is useful to think of their love for their children as comprising two different forces, which we label *altruism* and *paternalism*.[21] We do not argue that some parents always act altruistically and some always act paternalistically. Rather, we believe both forces to be present in each parent, although some parents are more altruistic while others are more paternalistic.

Following Gary Becker, we define parents as altruistic toward their children if they are prepared to take actions that are costly to them (either in monetary terms or because they are intrinsically unpleasant) but that increase the children's overall well-being.[22] By overall well-being, we mean not only the pleasure of the moment but also the enjoyment of future happiness or success.

What costly actions are we thinking about? For instance, altruistic parents might decide to sacrifice a plan for a hiking trip in the mountains (of which the parents themselves would be fond) in order to go for the children's preferred option of a trip to Disneyland. Or they may be willing to give up going to the cinema or opera in order to stay at home and play with the kids. As parents we, the authors, have often played board games with our small children, not necessarily for our own enjoyment (some can be pretty tedious), but to see our children happy. Being altruistic does not mean giving up everything for the child: the parent still weighs costs and benefits. An otherwise affectionate mother, María has always found board games too boring and painful relative to the reward of seeing her beloved daughter's smile.

The key feature of parental altruism is full empathy with the children. In other words, altruistic parents accept their children's own opinion of what is good for them—they look at their children through the children's eyes, rather than imposing their own views on what is best. Since altruistic parents (in our definition of altruism) agree with their children's preferences, a parent who is driven solely by the altruistic motive would always let the children rule and thus adopt the permissive parenting style.[23] Like Mr. Zeines, altruistic parents would never force their children to do anything they dislike, even under circumstances in which they would themselves make a different choice.[24] For instance, if a child were told that eating sweets for breakfast may cause tooth decay and future painful visits to the dentist, and yet the child decided that the passion for sweets is so strong that it is worth taking the risk, a purely altruistic parent would support the child's choice. Similarly, if an older child decided to drop out of high school early to travel the world, a fully altruistic parent should raise no objection.

Most parents have some altruistic tendencies toward their children, but few would go as far as agreeing with all their children's decisions as a matter of principle. They would try hard to dissuade their children from overeating sweets or leaving school. Why? Because of the second motive of parents' behavior: paternalism. Like altruistic parents, paternalistic parents care about their children, but they also believe that sometimes the children's autonomy should be restricted for their own good. This is because paternalistic parents have their own views on what is good for the child, and these views may disagree with what the child is thinking. As a result, paternalistic parents may object to what their children would like to do and try to influence their behavior. Paternalistic parents are not concerned solely with what makes children happy. Rather, they weigh the pros and cons of their children's behavior from their own adult perspective.[25]

We believe that all parents have paternalistic motives to some extent. After all, the word paternalism stems from the Latin word *paternus* for "fatherly." It is almost inevitable to be paternalistic at least toward young children, who truly do not know yet what is good and bad for them. Even concerning older children, being altruistic or paternalistic is not an either-or question, but a matter of degree. To draw a drastic example, imagine that an adolescent joined a street gang and got involved with drugs. Very few parents would be impressed if the child argued: "I know what I am doing and am aware of the consequences, but this is too much fun to give up." Even very liberal parents would try to stop this from happening. Wealthier parents might consider moving to a different neighborhood; others might impose a strict home curfew; some parents might try to get help from a psychologist.[26] At the same time, there may be other choices (say, of an extracurricular activity or of a romantic partner) where the same parents feel that it is best to let the adolescent decide on his or her own.

Perhaps the most common source of disagreement between parents and children is the trade-off between the enjoyment of the present and the long-term consequences of current actions. Parents are often more concerned with their children's future than are the children themselves. Therefore, paternalistic parents are prepared to take costly actions that may reduce children's current happiness, but that they judge to be in the long-term interest of the children.[27]

The paternalistic motive can explain why many parents adopt an authoritative or authoritarian parenting style, both of which aim to influence children's choices, rather than the permissive style, which an entirely altruistic parent would choose.[28]

HOW THE ENVIRONMENT AFFECTS HOW WE CARE FOR CHILDREN

Having laid out the basic motives that underlie parenting decisions, what determines the parenting style a particular parent will adopt and the popularity of different styles across countries and over time? One possibility is that parents may simply be different from each other.

Just like some people like soccer and others like opera, some are relatively more liberal and altruistic and others more paternalistic. Some of these differences are related to socioeconomic factors: artists like Bruce Zeines tend to be more liberal than farmers or clerks, whereas religious people are more prone to paternalism (see chapter 5). Yet, not all individual variation can be ascribed to social factors: we know many academics in a socioeconomic position similar to our own who are more relaxed than we are about parenting, and we know just as many who are far stricter.

A second, more interesting possibility is that equally paternalistic parents may decide to adopt different parenting styles depending on the environment in which they live. Take two liberal parents, one of whom lives in Beirut and the other in Tehran. If each parent had a daughter who would like to wear a miniskirt, the parent in Beirut (where the dress code is liberal) would probably be supportive or indifferent, whereas the otherwise identical parent in Tehran (where "inappropriate" dress for women used to lead to trouble with the morality police) might act in an authoritarian way and prohibit this choice. Similarly, Marisa and Matthias do not let their sons explore their hometown on their own, in large part because in the United States police sometimes pick up unaccompanied children and accuse their parents of child neglect. When visiting family in Germany, where children move around independently from a young age, Marisa and Matthias adapt to the environment and grant more freedom of movement. More generally, the socioeconomic environment in which parents expect their children to live should be an important driving force of parenting decisions.

We would like to apply these ideas to understand how parents choose between the parenting styles illustrated in figure 1.1. The figure envisions the parenting styles as arising from two dimensions of parent-child interactions, namely, how responsive parents are to their children and whether they interfere with their children's choices. In this scheme (which forms the basis of many empirical studies of parenting styles, including our own in the following chapters), a parent who is neither responsive to the child nor tries to influence the child is considered neglectful. While neglectful parenting might arise if parents simply do

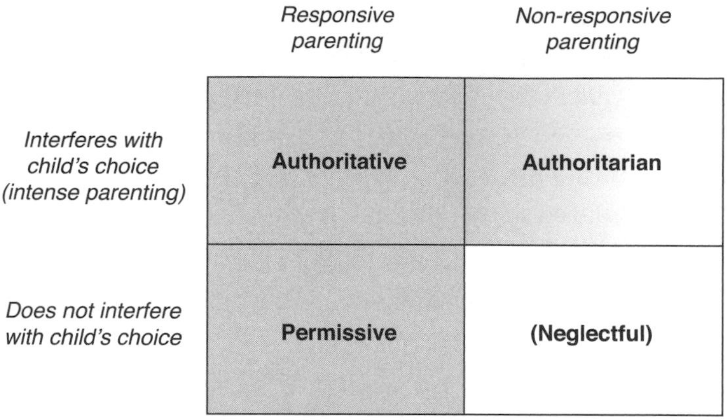

	Responsive parenting	Non-responsive parenting
Interferes with child's choice (intense parenting)	Authoritative	Authoritarian
Does not interfere with child's choice	Permissive	(Neglectful)

FIGURE 1.1. The chart shows how Baumrind's parenting styles can be broken down in terms of parents' responsiveness and interference with the child's choice.

not care much about their children (that is, they are neither altruistic nor paternalistic), our primary interest here is in the choice between the principal parenting styles: permissive, authoritarian, and authoritative. How do the objectives and constraints of parenting lead parents to choose? When do parents determine that it is better not to put pressure on their children and choose to follow a permissive parenting style, and when do they prefer, instead, to be pushy? When should we expect parents to emphasize rules and when freedom?

THE STAKES IN PARENTING AND
PERMISSIVE VERSUS INTENSIVE STYLES

Consider, first, the choice between permissive parenting on the one hand and the intensive parenting styles (authoritarian and authoritative) on the other hand. The key distinction is that intensive parents interfere with their children's choices, while permissive parents do not. As outlined earlier, we view altruism toward children as the force that leads to permissive parenting, and paternalism as the force that pushes toward intensive parenting. Hence, we would expect a parent who was entirely altruistic to be permissive, whereas an entirely paternalistic parent should adopt an intensive parenting style. However, most parents have a combination of altruistic and paternalistic motives. For such parents, the choice between permissive and intensive parenting hinges on their socioeconomic environment.

All parents who are at least somewhat paternalistic have views on the choices children should ideally make, which often differ from what the children would choose to do. The key question that determines whether the parents decide to interfere is how important they deem the consequences of the child's choice to be. This, in turn, hinges on how much is at stake, and that is where the environment matters. When the stakes are low, meaning when taking the "wrong" action does not have any major repercussions for the future of the child, the parent might decide to let the child have his or her way. When, from the parent's perspective, doing the right thing is crucial for the child's future success, the drive to interfere will be much stronger.

Exactly what the stakes are differs depending on the question at hand; for example, parents might worry about the child's health, career prospects, or future relationships. It is possible, even likely, that parents will adopt a more or less paternalistic attitude depending on the specific action at hand. Thus, some parents might be very protective (and paternalistic) when it comes to risk of injury, but more permissive in terms of career choice.

THE ROLE OF ECONOMIC INEQUALITY AND RISKY BEHAVIOR

Parents and children disagree on many things, but if there is one question that stands out, it is how to weigh having fun in the present versus investing for the future. We do not know of any parents who wish that their children would spend less time on homework and more on video games. Most of the time, parents worry about the child's future prospects, while the child is more interested in instant gratification.

When parents decide whether to impose their will on their children and push them to study more, what matters is whether the stakes are high enough to make the effort worthwhile. This is where economic inequality becomes a key determinant of parenting style. Consider a child who finds school boring and would like to drop out to take a low-skill job. In a society where wage inequality is low and blue-collar workers enjoy a high social status, parents may worry less about schooling outcomes than they would in a more competitive and unequal society. In other words, in a society where school dropouts earn only slightly less than doctors and engineers, parents can afford a more relaxed attitude toward education, and thus, permissive parenting should be more prevalent. In fact, an intensive parenting style (be it authoritarian, authoritative, or a combination of the two) in such a society may unnecessarily constrain the child's sense of independence, preventing her from discovering her true talent (e.g., choosing a profession that best suits her). In contrast, in a society where education and effort are highly rewarded and where people with little education struggle, parents will be highly motivated to push their children hard, even at the cost of repressing their personal development. Thus, we would expect economic inequality to be associated with intensive parenting styles. In the rest of this book, we will see that this prediction is strongly supported by the data, both in terms of changes in parenting over time and variation in parenting across countries.

Parents might also be less concerned about education if they live in a society where good jobs are assigned by birth status or social connections rather than according to merits and skills. Fabrizio's uncle Gianni, who is now a retired engineer and was a successful business owner, was the first member of his family to attend university. His progress in education was kept under close scrutiny by his lower-middle-class family, for whom a nonworking grown-up child meant a significant economic sacrifice. In contrast, many of his wealthier fellow students were far more relaxed, alternating a little study with a lot of partying. Taking ten years to graduate was not an issue in a society where university was a privilege for the rich. These wealthy young people knew that they would have no difficulty finding a good job, not so much because of the academic degree they would eventually earn, but rather for the family names they bore.

The importance of working toward future success versus having fun in the present is not the only source of tension between parents and children. Another one, especially important for adolescents, is the propensity to indulge in forms of risky behavior that parents may disapprove of, ranging from riding motorcycles to premarital sex. Parents often tend to be more risk averse than children. Indeed, we observe a trend in many societies toward increasingly protective parents. The downside of this attitude is that it can make children fearful and unable to take initiative. Once again, the environment can shape incentives. In deprived neighborhoods populated by gangs and drug dealers, exposure to juvenile crime can lead children to make choices that could ruin their lives. There is far less risk in middle-class neighborhoods. In such safer environments, parents may be more prone to allow their children to experiment and take initiatives without fearing that they suffer severe consequences in case of failure. Such an upbringing may lead to a more positive attitude toward choices that involve different types of risks, such as innovation and entrepreneurship, later in life.

HOW TO BE AN INTENSIVE PARENT: FORBID OR PERSUADE?

Let us say that the economic environment is such that parents feel it important to guide their children and hence choose an intensive parenting style. Such parents would like to influence the children's choices so they align with their own adult preferences. Parents can follow two strategies to achieve this objective. First, they can use coercion—that is, forbid certain behaviors or impose specific choices on their children—which is characteristic of an authoritarian parenting style. Direct monitoring and the enforcement of strict rules through punishment are also associated with this parenting style. Authoritarian parents do not bother to convince children that what they want them to do is right or in their own interest; they just tell them to do it.[29]

The alternative approach is persuasion—that is, parents attempt to shape their children's values and preferences in such a way that the children will make the choices desired by the parent, but of their own accord. For example, parents may instill in their children a strong work ethic or an aversion to (or fear of) recreational drugs. Or, closer to our experience, they can try to convince them that academic success should be a major priority in life. This approach amounts to authoritative parenting. It also echoes the concept of *soft power*, coined by political scientist Joseph Nye of Harvard University in the context of international relations. Nye distinguishes soft power from coercion and bribery, defining it as the ability to shape the preferences of others through appeal, attraction, and subtle communication.[30] Soft power, according to Nye, is an effective way to induce others to behave the way one wants. This is what authoritative parents try to achieve with their children.

How to choose between these two approaches? In our view, neither one is obviously more correct than the other. To be sure, the coercion that is part of the authoritarian parenting style has negative connotations, and if coercion relies on corporal punishment, that comes with now well-known repercussions. However, we also acknowledge that, contrary to permissive parents, authoritative parents do not accept children as they are, but rather attempt to guide (some might say manipulate) them into thinking and behaving like adults. For instance, if children have an innate tendency toward fun and games in the company of their peers, authoritative parents might attempt to devalue their enjoyment relative to doing homework. Authoritative parenting could be considered the most intrusive among all parenting styles, since it aims to reshape children's values. In contrast, even authoritarian parents accept children's nature for what it is; they simply regulate their behavior.

When neither of the two styles is clearly better, the choice comes down to the relative costs and benefits. From the perspective of parents, all parenting styles entail some costs. Authoritarian parents spend time and effort monitoring their children. Similarly, authoritative parents work hard to indoctrinate their children into believing, say, that delaying gratification is a great idea, or that they should evaluate their choices from the perspective of long-run success. Some may also spend time pushing their children to participate in activities that they hope will shape the children's preferences in the direction parents like. Classical music or athletics, for instance, may foster children's ability to concentrate, work hard, and work toward achievements. However, such activities are typically expensive and time-consuming for parents.

Apart from these direct costs, there may be a psychological burden: since all parents have an altruistic self, they may dislike the pressure that an invasive parenting style imposes on their children. From this perspective, permissive parenting is less costly than the intensive parenting styles, as permissive parenting exempts parents from either monitoring or indoctrinating their children. However, even permissive parenting has some costs, such as putting parents at the mercy of their children or having to deal with unhappy neighbors or friends. Fabrizio has a Scandinavian friend who is a fervent believer in a permissive parenting style. When their children, who were of the same age, were young, the two families would sometimes organize picnics together. However, on several occasions, the friend's four-year-old child would have a temper tantrum and demand to do something else. The father would then announce: "Sorry, my son is getting stressed"—and the picnic was over. Plates and tablecloths were quickly gathered, and the whole plan was called off amid apologies. Telling the child, "No, we are eating now," was never an option.

Parenting styles also come with different benefits. Many of the benefits from the authoritative parenting style pay off when children grow up. For instance, a solid work ethic may induce resilience and perseverance, which are important character traits in most careers. Yet, the permissive parenting style can also bring some advantages. The stereotypical Scandinavian child is not a nerd, but instead might grow up to be more independent and self-reliant, and might be in a better position to discover her or his own inclinations. Brainwashing children into liking "useful" subjects such as math or finance may sound sensible to many parents, but can also stifle hidden talents. Some children raised in an intensive parenting style may be prevented from becoming world-class soccer players or inspired artists. The children of permissive parents may learn to be assertive about what they like and follow their natural inclinations, while the children of authoritative parents may internalize all of their parents' fears. Even an authoritarian parenting style may be less intrusive than an authoritative one when it comes to occupational choice. María's brother (who, recall, had a benignly authoritarian mother) is a successful professional painter. In contrast, María and Fabrizio's daughter would have never embarked on an artistic career; her authoritative parents would have made every effort to dissuade her from choosing a career with such an uncertain economic future.[31]

A big downside of the authoritarian style is that it relies on constant parental monitoring. If a child has to make important decisions at a time or place when such monitoring is impossible, the child of the authoritarian parent will not be able to do the right thing on his or her own. In contrast, authoritative parenting works by making children internalize the values and attitudes of the adult. If done successfully, the child will then make "adult-style" decisions even when on his or her own. In other words, a key benefit of the authoritative, relative to the authoritarian, style is that it can work even in situations where direct monitoring is not feasible. We believe that this benefit is crucial to explaining the choice made between the two intensive styles in the data. We will show throughout the book that authoritarian parenting is more common in situations where parents are able to closely monitor their children, say, because children continue living with their parents on the family farm. In contrast, authoritative parenting dominates when children need to make important choices independently, such as in societies where success depends on attending schools or universities far from home.

NATURE VERSUS NURTURE

We have argued that authoritative parents aim to shape their children's values and preferences. However, can parents really attain such a goal? There is a long-running debate about the extent to which child-rearing actually matters, with one side taking the view that children's personalities are mainly hard-wired, that is, determined by genetics as opposed to child-rearing.[32] Some might think, for example, that children from an upper-middle-class background are generally successful not because of their exposure to a nurturing family environment, but because of a superior gene pool. A somewhat inconclusive debate between anthropologists and population geneticists has raged for years about the relative importance of nature versus nurture.[33] However, there can be little doubt at this time that nurture matters—big time. For example, studies of adoptive children suggest that family upbringing is very important.[34]

Genetic factors do matter a lot for basic personality traits, such as extroversion versus introversion. In contrast, child-rearing is central to the development of skills over time. Most of the child characteristics that authoritative parents try to influence are so-called noncognitive skills, including patience, risk aversion, and work ethic.[35] Patience, for example, may depend in part on personal traits such as impulsivity, but also is partially acquired. When parents try to help their children become more patient, they teach the ability to think carefully about the consequences of their actions and to envision long-term repercussions that may affect them years or decades later. Children do not come endowed with a natural ability to make such considerations, but it is a skill they can be taught.

The evidence that family upbringing and the social environment have a strong effect on noncognitive skills is by now uncontroversial. For instance, the Nobel laureate James Heckman documents that financial programs targeting disadvantaged families can have a strong positive effect on children's noncognitive skills.[36] These children become more motivated to learn, less likely to engage in crime, and altogether more prone to think about the future consequences of their choices than are children who grow up in poor families that did not receive support. As support can affect the families' child-rearing practices, but cannot change their genes, this evidence shows that noncognitive skills are not just genetically determined. These soft skills are important for individual success in life. In his research with a number of collaborators, Heckman documents that they are a driving factor for success in the labor market and social behavior.[37] A number of empirical studies focus specifically on the transmission of risk tolerance and patience, traits that have a central role in our discussion. Research using the German Socioeconomic Panel documents that parents who invest more effort in child-rearing can shape their children's trust and attitude toward risk.[38] In sum, the evidence strongly supports the notion that parenting choices can have a substantial impact on the values, attitudes, and, ultimately, the decisions of their children.

OTHER CONSTRAINTS: ARGUMENTATIVE SKILLS AND PARENTS' AWARENESS

So far, we have explored how the socioeconomic environment shapes the objectives that parents pursue in their parenting, and how the parenting styles differ in terms of the constraints they impose. When we consider why parenting choices differ among parents who live in the same society, additional factors that vary from family to family are also important. For instance, parents may differ in their abilities or opportunities to influence their children's values and behavior through the use of soft power. Parents working long hours far from home find it more difficult to enforce strict rules than parents who spend most of their time close to home and who can more easily monitor their children. Well-educated parents may have acquired argumentative or debating skills that enable them to persuade their children more effectively by making a better defense of their "adult" case. Richer parents likely have an easier time paying for music classes or athletic activities that build concentration and academic focus. All of these factors might help explain which parenting style different parents choose.

Another possible constraint is knowledge: some disadvantaged families may suffer from insufficient information about the effects of parenting. The economist Orazio Attanasio documents that in some developing countries parents fail to invest in their children's human capital because they underestimate the economic value of education. For instance, parents are not always aware of the benefits of simple forms of interaction such as speaking to small children.[39] Such lack of information may be particularly important in the rural developing world, where illiteracy is still a severe problem and information spreads slowly. Yet, these knowledge gaps are certainly less severe and widespread in industrialized countries where information is easily accessible.

In one of the earliest studies of child-rearing practices made by economists, Bruce Weinberg argues that poor parents lack the resources to be able to affect their children's behavior through monetary rewards and must therefore resort to corporal punishment to control their behavior.[40] For instance, rich parents can promise their teenage child a motorcycle or enrollment in an expensive tennis club in exchange for a certain behavior. Poor parents simply cannot afford to reward compliant behavior in this way. This explains, in Weinberg's opinion, why in the United States corporal punishment is more widespread in low-income families.

We believe education to be even more important than income. Some parents may find it difficult to persuade their children to follow their advice and ultimately resort to more authoritarian practices. Educated middle-class parents can also more easily complement their introduction of the "right" values with active support. For instance, they may help their children with homework in differential calculus and Latin, which would not be possible for parents who were not exposed to these subjects. In Switzerland, many sixth graders must pass an exam to access the academic track (the "Gymiprüfung" mentioned in the introduction). Mathematical ability is tested through sophisticated problem sets that would be relatively easy for children who possess more advanced knowledge of math tools (e.g., how to solve systems of equations). Children must prove their ability to use basic logic to get through these hurdles without using sophisticated techniques. The local school authorities attempt to assign exams that elicit the pure cognitive ability of children and that cannot be prepared for through rote learning. Nevertheless, practice is useful. Life is easier for math-literate parents; they can turn into instructors and credibly tell their children: "You can make it!" This creates a disadvantage for less-educated families.

UNDERSTANDING SOCIAL CHANGES: FROM PERMISSIVE TO HELICOPTER PARENTS

We now have all the pieces in place to understand how parenting choices vary across countries and over time, using the economics of parenting. To do this, we need to map out how the stakes in parenting have changed, and how the costs and benefits of the different parenting styles differ across families.

We start by turning our attention to what we find a fascinating question for social scientists. Why have so many children who grew up in the antiauthoritarian 1970s, raised to question authority and to hold materialism in disdain, turned into intensive helicopter parents as adults? In chapter 2, we lay out how the rise of helicopter parents in the United States and other countries can be traced to a major economic transformation that took place during this same period of time.

CHAPTER TWO

The Rise of Helicopter Parents

"Mother hovers over me like a helicopter. . . . I'm entitled to sneeze without explanation," wails despairing teenager Lenard in the classic parenting guide "Between Parent and Teenager" by child psychologist Haim Ginott, which was a best seller when it was published in 1969.[1] Despite Lenard's complaints, parents at that time were generally far less obsessed than they are now with controlling their children's lives. Today, the expression *helicopter parenting* is widely used to refer to the heavily involved, time-intensive, controlling child-rearing approach that has become widespread over the last three decades. The trend toward more intensive parenting is not just about supervising and protecting children but also about getting immersed in how children perform in school, which activities they pick up, and even who their friends and romantic interests are.

TIGER MOM AND OVERPARENTING

This intensive parenting style is in sharp contrast with the more permissive parenting approach that prevailed in the 1970s, when many of today's helicopter parents grew up. What has turned the independent youngsters of the 1970s into a generation of parents obsessed with their children's individual success? People who lived that experience have different memories. Wendy Wisner, a popular writer for the website Scary Mommy, recalls her happy childhood as the daughter of a hippie family, "running around half-naked and barefoot on Martha's Vineyard, and then spen[ding] the rest of it moving all around the country," with her parents "always on a mission to find themselves, change the world, explore."[2] While feeling lucky to have enjoyed such a childhood, she confesses that since becoming a parent, she "embraced a more traditional family lifestyle in some ways, while still maintaining a bit of a counterculture, natural-minded edge." The well-known US television news anchor Tom Brokaw sums up the change as follows: "These people would ingest anything you handed them. Now they hover over their kids, have them in soccer camp, college prep courses, fret over getting them into the top colleges and shop at Whole Foods. The change is amazing."[3]

Parents' invasion in their children's lives can take different forms. An extreme version of the pushy and demanding parent is Amy Chua, a Chinese American professor at Yale Law School. Her best-selling book, *The Battle Hymn of the Tiger Mother*, makes a brilliant (and humorous) defense of the stereotypically tough, East-Asian approach designed to produce self-confident, hard-working children devoted to success. Amy Chua believes in pushing rather than pampering children: "Western parents worry a lot about their children's self-esteem. But as a parent, one of the worst things you can do for your child's self-esteem is to let them give up. On the flip side, there's nothing better for building confidence than learning you can do something you thought you couldn't."[4] Rather than "providing positive reinforcements and a nurturing environment . . . the best way to protect their children is by preparing them for the future, letting them see what they're capable of, and arming them with skills, work habits, and inner confidence."[5]

Is Amy Chua the role model of an authoritarian or of an authoritative parenting style? Her creed involves elements of both. On the one hand, Chua believes that building up the children's inner confidence requires forcing them to do things they do not like, which is an authoritarian element. She says: "What Chinese parents understand is that nothing is fun until you're good at it. To get good at anything you have to work, and children on their own never want to work, which is why it is crucial to override their preferences. This often requires fortitude on the part of the parents because the child will resist; things are always hardest at the beginning, which is where Western parents tend to give up."[6] On the other hand, Chua also believes that children must ultimately be self-motivated in their pursuit of success, as do authoritative parents.

While Amy Chua's style is often associated with Chinese culture, intensive parenting has become increasingly popular across a number of industrialized countries, albeit with varying characteristics.[7] Some parents suffocate their children with attention and advice, but are more protective than forceful. Fabrizio knew of an Italian mother who rented an apartment in the village where her twenty-five-year-old son was doing his military service so that she could prepare warm dinners for him to recover from the fatigue of hard training. If all Italian mothers were this protective, the government might have to arrange special camps for accompanying mothers along the front line. The psychologist Hara Estroff Marano has labeled this child-rearing approach *overparenting*. In her book with the contentious title *A Nation of Wimps: The High Cost of Invasive Parenting*, she blames overparenting for the supposed loss of independence of young American adults.[8] Indeed, she asserts that parental intervention has extended its scope progressively into adulthood and that parents increasingly get involved in their children's education well beyond high school and college. For instance, a growing number of parents meddle in their children's admission process to graduate schools, visiting campuses and calling up and asking to meet with graduate admissions officers. Marano relates with horror that this parental invasion has now reached business and law schools, institutions that traditionally value applicants' motivation and self-reliance.[9]

Marano is only one of the many critics of the overparenting frenzy. British journalist Tanith Carey, the author of a best-selling book about "taming" the tiger parents, blames overparenting for choking off creativity and individualism, and for potentially producing a generation of cookie-cutter people lacking personality or imagination, all aiming to go to the same universities and to get the same jobs.[10] A passionate advocate of a permissive rather than authoritative parenting style, Carey suggests that parents should broaden their notion of success. In her view, parents should help their children to become happy, thriving human beings rather than forcing them to work harder and harder. In a recent book, Julie Lythcott-Haims, Stanford University's former dean of undergraduate advising, echoes Marano's and Carey's critiques.[11] She blames parents who do their children's homework for them, then pay for expensive private tutors, and eventually get involved even in their children's application for jobs or for graduate school for raising passive, dependent, and unimaginative children. She urges them to break free from the "overparenting trap."[12]

EMPIRICAL EVIDENCE ON INTENSIVE PARENTING: PARENTS SPEND MORE TIME WITH THEIR CHILDREN

Parents who call up graduate admissions officers or prepare warm meals for their children in military service make for telling anecdotes, but as economists, we look for systematic evidence to corroborate the view that this is symptomatic of a more general pattern. This is true of our approach throughout the book: when we consider a change in parenting and a potential explanation, we look at the data from many parents and children to see if there is real evidence that the explanation is credible.

To measure whether parenting really has gotten more intense in recent decades, the natural first step is to look at survey diaries that record how people spend their time.[13] In a growing number of countries, statistical offices collect information on how people spend the twenty-four hours that they have at their disposal each day. For instance, in the United States the Bureau of Labor Statistics collects data on how Americans spend their time in a project called the American Time Use Survey (ATUS).[14] Similar projects are run in other countries.[15] The data confirm that over recent decades, parents have devoted an increasing share of their time to child-rearing.

Figure 2.1 shows the weekly hours spent by mothers (upper panel) and fathers (lower panel) on child-rearing in Canada, Italy, the Netherlands, Spain, the United Kingdom, and the United States. The plots for the Netherlands and the United States are especially revealing because the data go back all the way to the 1970s. In 2005, Dutch mothers spent about four more hours a week on childcare than in 1975, while Dutch fathers spent three extra hours. This means that, on average, children

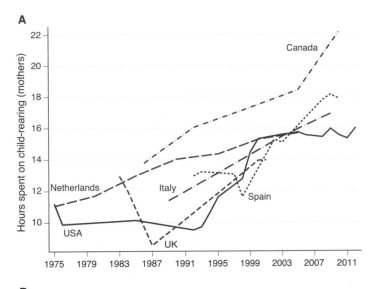

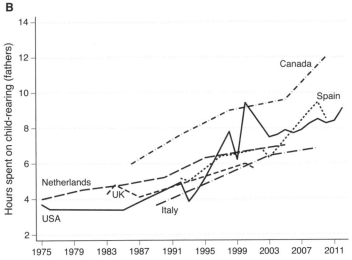

FIGURE 2.1. Hours per week spent on child-rearing by mothers (upper panel) and fathers (lower panel) in six OECD countries

in 2005 got a full extra hour per day of interaction with their parents compared to children in 1975. In the United States, the increase in time spent on parenting is even larger: between the late 1970s and 2005, the time mothers and fathers spent per week with their children went up by approximately six hours each, which translates into an additional hour and forty-five minutes of parent-child interaction per day. For Canada, Italy, Spain, and the United Kingdom, data are only available for shorter time spans, but in all cases, there is clear evidence of an increasing trend in time spent on parenting.

The effect of this increase on the attention received by each child is further amplified if one takes into account the decline in fertility that took place during the same time. In the Netherlands, the average number of children per family (as measured by the total fertility rate) fell from 3.1 in 1960 to 1.7 in 2014, and in the United States it fell from 3.7 to 1.9 during the same period. If one takes into account that today there are fewer children to care for, our estimate that parent-child interactions went up by one to two extra hours a day is actually an understatement of the additional attention received by each child.

Another element to take into account is the "quality" of the time that adults spend with their children—watching TV together is different from truly engaging with a child in a joint activity. This dimension is harder to quantify, but certainly parents are, on average, better educated today than a few decades ago, which is likely to be related to the quality of parent-child interactions. Parents also have access to cheaper and more effective educational tools. In fact, an entire industry has sprung up that develops educational toys, web sites, apps, and electronic devices designed to "stimulate" children and assist in their development. However, the net effect of these changes is hard to assess, as surely technology is also prone to misuse. A BBC News Education Report from Judith Burns argues that overuse of smartphones by parents disrupts family life. She quotes the results of a survey in which more than a third of adolescents stated to have asked their parents to stop checking their devices all the time.[16] This calls into question whether the quality of child-adult interaction is actually higher than in the past.

Another interesting observation is that in both the United States and the Netherlands, the time spent on childcare activities has increased more for college-educated parents than for less-educated parents. In the Netherlands, in 1975 college-educated mothers spent one hour a week more on child-rearing activities than did non-college-educated mothers.

For fathers, the educational gap in childcare time was half an hour. In the first decade of the current century, the gap went up to about two and a half hours for both mothers and fathers. During the same period, the change was even larger in the United States. In the 1970s, less- and more-educated parents spent about the same time on childcare. Today, there is a gap of more than three hours between these groups. We return to this observation in chapter 4.

The diaries also tell us what activities parents do with their children. Back in 1976, the average couple in the United States spent two hours a week (76 minutes for mothers and 43 minutes for fathers) on playing, reading, and talking to their children, and seventeen minutes a week (10 and 7 minutes, respectively) on helping them with homework. In 2012, the average couple spent six and a half hours a week (204 and 184 minutes) on playing, reading, and talking to their children, and more than an hour and a half (65 and 31 minutes) on helping them with homework. Overall, the time American parents spend on these activities went up by a factor of 3.5, from less than two and a half hours to more than eight hours per week.

The results are similar in Italy. In 1989 (which is the earliest available data), the average Italian couple spent less than two hours (53 minutes for mothers and 71 minutes for fathers) on playing, reading, and talking to their children, and more than an hour (41 and 13 minutes) on helping them with homework. In 2009, twenty years later, the average couple spent seven hours (257 and 165 minutes) on playing, reading, and talking to their children, and about one hour and a half (77 and 25 minutes) on helping them with homework.[17] Overall, the time Italian parents spend on these activities went up by a factor of 2.9, from three hours to eight and a half per week.

The rise of homeschooling in the United States may be another symptom of the growing desire of some parents to have full control and to be able to shape their children as they see fit. The US Department of Education reports that the estimated percentage of the school-age population that is homeschooled has doubled from 1999 to 2012, to about 3.4 percent. Is this a sign of helicopter parenting? The fact that over 90 percent of homeschooling parents said that "a concern about the environment of other schools" was an important factor in their decision would suggest so.[18]

The impact of intensive parenting is reflected in children's experiences. In the United States, the percentage of kids walking or biking to school fell from 41 percent in 1969 to 13 percent in 2001.[19] Among six-to-eight-year-old Americans, free playtime decreased by 25 percent between 1981 and 1997, whereas time spent on homework more than doubled. This is interesting, as one might have suspected that parents have simply learned to enjoy fun and games with their children. They may do that too (especially with games that have a high educational content that parents enjoy more than children do), but the lion's share of the new intensive parenting consists of pushing children to become early achievers.

To sum up, the evidence shows unequivocally that parents spend much more time with their children today than a few decades ago. The question is: Why? Are today's parents wiser, more aware, perhaps even more loving than their own parents were? Is this increase in parent-child interaction time bringing up a great generation of super-educated and highly motivated adults? Or rather, as suggested by critical authors such as Marano, Carey, and Lythcott-Haims, is this just the sign of an irrational frenzy that will grow a generation of "mama's boys" and "daddy's girls" lacking independence and imagination?

Our goal in this book is to understand what circumstances have brought about the shift in parenting style. Our theory is that parents are responding to changes in incentives, especially concerning the economic environment in which their children will live as adults. What happened that makes parents increasingly obsessed with what their children are up to? To answer this question, we go back to our personal experiences as children in the 1960s and 1970s.

BACK TO OUR CHILDHOOD

In our own childhood, we were expected to show up for family meals, but otherwise we were largely unsupervised for the rest of the day. As this was true for most of us at that time, the streets were full of kids roaming around. Moreover, because it cost nothing to play in the street, there was a lot of interaction between children of different classes and backgrounds, made all the easier by the low levels of residential segregation in Europe in the late 1960s and 1970s.

Fabrizio moved from the countryside to the city of Bologna when he was five. Bologna is known as "the Red One," a pun playing on the color of its tiled roofs and its left-wing political tradition (Bologna elected a mayor from the Communist Party without interruption from the country's liberation in 1945 to the party's dissolution in 1991). Fabrizio's family settled in a suburban neighborhood that had a mixture of middle- and working-class housing. Neither children nor parents attached much importance to social distinction. If anything, the prevailing social norms encouraged white-collar workers to hide their own class background and express a sense of shared class identity with blue-collar workers. Any expression of pride in economic success or educational achievements was frowned upon.

The school system, which was almost entirely publicly funded, forcefully promoted values of justice and equality. Primary school children would be asked to write essays about the Vietnam War or attend lectures about the defense of world peace. Fabrizio's parents were nonpracticing Catholics who voted in national elections for moderate center parties that were part of the national government coalition, but voted for parties on the centre-left in local elections. Overall, they were a fairly typical middle-class family, leaning toward the conservative relative to the surrounding environment. In spite of that, family values were imbued with the egalitarian culture of the time. Once elected to the local school council, Fabrizio's father, a no-nonsense, white-collar worker, supported measures aimed at preventing wealthy families from segregating their children by sending them to the elite schools in the city center.

At school, regular classes took place mostly in the morning, although parents could put their children's names down for after-school activities in the afternoon. These activities were a free social service offered to disadvantaged families where both parents worked (a rarity at the time, as female labor participation was low). Yet, there was strong peer pressure for the children of more affluent parents to also attend the after-school activities in the interest of social integration. The few parents who did not conform were criticized and challenged by both teachers and school principals. Fabrizio's family felt compelled to abide by the social norm.

Apart from the activities organized by the school (mostly, relaxed supervision of children roaming around), extracurricular activities were rare. Some children got involved in organized sports (mostly soccer for boys, dance or volleyball for girls), but this was the exception rather than the rule. The school itself was not very challenging. Until eighth grade, grade repetition was rare and usually decided on in agreement with the parents. At some point, numerical grades were banned and replaced by verbal evaluations intended to play down differences in academic performance, such differences being viewed as a sign of failure by the school to compensate for unequal backgrounds in income and opportunities. The notion that children might differ in innate abilities was taboo.

The street culture was unfriendly to studious kids: success in school did not make one popular among peers. Fabrizio remembers being shy and reticent about his school achievements. When teachers publicly praised him, he felt more embarrassed and worried about his peers' reaction than proud. His parents were naturally pleased with good grades, but saw no reason to push an already well-performing child further. This was not a sign of neglect. As he was doing well academically, his parents thought it more important to encourage him to go out, socialize with his peers, and learn to interact with other people in a socially diverse environment. While parents would be vigilant when it came to access to drugs or other hazardous activities, there was not much concern about who their children chose to be friends with.

Parents and teachers perceived school as a vehicle for fostering an independent personality rather than for promoting future economic success. When Fabrizio's parents moved to Bologna, checking out the quality of the local schools was not an issue. Most parents would send their children to the nearest school, and the idea that there are good and bad schools was alien to them. Fabrizio's parents regarded living in a mixed neighborhood as a blessing. The odd fight would strengthen the child and give him the experience to cope with future difficulties and conflicts. When problems with other children arose, they would discourage him from involving teachers or other adults unless things turned really sour. The rule was to "never be aggressive or unfair, but when attacked, stand firm and fight back!"

The economic environment in which Fabrizio's family lived was fundamental to this laid-back approach. Until the end of the 1970s, unemployment was not a major issue in Europe (especially in a prosperous Northern Italian city like Bologna). Inequality, which was already low to begin with, fell sharply in the 1970s following the high-inflation episode associated with oil price shocks. Italy had a special labor market institution, known as the "escalator," that indexed wages to inflation by granting regular adjustments to living costs. The law ensured that salaries would adjust periodically to compensate workers for the loss of purchasing power. Crucially, the absolute inflation allowance was the same for all workers, instead of being proportional to the wage. In times of high inflation, the "escalator" had a dramatic equalizing effect.[20] Wage differences between white- and blue-collar workers were drastically curtailed, falling to a historic minimum.

The political situation in the 1970s did not suggest any likely reversal of this trend. The Italian Communist Party (PCI) reached a historic peak in popularity. In the national elections of 1976, it scored a vote share of over 34 percent, almost matching that of the Christian Democrats, the traditional front runners. There was a wide expectation that Italian politics would move further to the left in the years to come.

Matthias's personal history is similar. Matthias spent his childhood in a village just north of Hannover, a city with a population of about 500,000. It is a transportation hub and also a manufacturing center, including car and tire production, and the headquarters of Volkswagen in Wolfsburg is close by. Matthias's family owned a small farm, and its roots in the village can be traced back to the early seventeenth century. However, by the time Matthias was born, farming had already become a secondary source of income for the family for two generations, with both Matthias's father, Dietmar, and grandfather, Otto, making their main living as civil servants in the state government. Indeed, while there were still a few old farming families present, the village with a population of five thousand had become more like a suburb, with most of the main breadwinners commuting to Hannover for work.

In Germany in the 1970s, the male breadwinner model was the norm, with most mothers staying at home to care for their children. Day-care services for young children did not exist. Four-year-old children had the option to attend kindergarten, but Matthias got out of that by crying continuously for the first few days. Elementary school started at age six and took only a few hours per day, with the children expected to walk home for lunch after class. Overall, the education system was built on the expectation that a mother would always be available to take care of her children when required. It is no surprise then that Matthias's mother stopped working as a teacher soon after having her first two children (including Matthias, the second). Childcare and the work on the farm kept her busy enough.

Among Matthias's friends in school, a few had mothers who worked outside the home part-time. Having a mom who worked full-time was both rare and, more likely than not, a sign of trouble, such as a father in prison or parents who had separated. However, such cases were rare. The village was solidly middle class with hardly any truly rich families (the top of the income distribution was mostly made up of local dentists and pharmacists), hardly any poverty, and most families living in similar conditions in modest single-family homes.

Like Fabrizio, Matthias remembers a much more relaxed and laid-back childhood compared to that of his own children. School took only a few hours per day, and after lunch on most days, Matthias and his three siblings were left free to roam. As long as everyone returned for dinner, it would not have occurred to Matthias's parents to worry about the children's whereabouts. Many days were spent playing at friends' houses, building forts in the haystacks, and playing soccer with other kids from the village. The few demands that Matthias's parents placed on their children primarily had to do with farm work, such as helping feed the calves, make hay, and gather the harvest.

The liberal approach of Matthias's parents extended to matters of school and education. How much to study for school, or whether to study at all, was mainly left to the children to decide. Matthias's parents might express some concern or hire a tutor if one of the children accumulated failing grades and started to be at risk for repeating a grade. But as long as a child kept up in class, she or he was left alone.

Matthias found out early on that there was little point in doing homework under these conditions. Given that he was able to get passing grades by paying attention in class, his parents did not bother to push him to study. At school, many teachers were not systematic in checking homework, either, and instead kept calling on one of the few hardworking students to read out the answers. In the case of the occasional teacher who did expect students to show their work, it was sufficient to scribble some rudimentary answers while on the bus to school to avoid serious repercussions. With so many more fun things to do in the afternoon, Matthias stopped doing homework entirely for years, and did not start again in earnest until twelfth grade, when grades start to count for the *Abitur* (the high school degree that allows access to university studies).

Some of the choices Matthias's parents made have personal roots. Matthias's father experienced a strictly authoritarian upbringing, with his own father leaving him little leeway to chart his own course in life. School proved to be a burden as well, where teachers used corporal punishment on an everyday basis. Given these often painful experiences, Dietmar was determined to grant as much freedom as possible to his own children and let them make most decisions on their own. Matthias's mother, Annemarie, was under less pressure as a child, partly because, as a girl, she was not the one who was expected to continue her family's farm. Nevertheless, she also grew up in an environment where most children had little choice in what to do with their lives, and she perceived the freedom that she was able to attain as a privilege she wanted her own children to share.

At the same time, personal history is only one part of the story. After all, while Matthias's parents may have been more liberal than most, the majority of kids that he grew up with had a broadly similar childhood. What was equally important was the economic environment, which at the time was characterized by historically low levels of inequality and low levels of unemployment, especially in suburban villages such as the one where Matthias grew up. There was also little crime, and issues such as drug addiction were mostly confined to the bigger cities. Parents had little reason to worry that their kids would get into serious trouble, and even if they did not excel in school, children could still expect to make a good living later on. In this environment, it made no sense for parents to push their children very hard.

The comparatively tranquil times of the 1970s and 1980s, when Matthias grew up, stand in marked contrast to the conditions when Matthias's parents were children in the 1940s and 1950s. Annemarie and Dietmar were both born during World War II. Their parents lived through two world wars, the worldwide economic recession of the 1930s, two hyperinflations in the 1920s and at the end of World War II, and periods of widespread hunger and poverty. Their families escaped from all of this relatively unscathed, in large part because of the relative stability that owning and farming land provided. Given their experiences, it should perhaps not be surprising that Dietmar's and Annemarie's parents felt that holding on to the land and continuing the family farm was essential for their families' survival. This background helps explain, at least in part, why Otto forcefully pushed Dietmar into following in his footsteps. Similarly, the very different conditions in the 1970s, when small-scale agriculture in Germany was in a steep decline, presumably contributed to Dietmar's approach to parenting.

In addition to economic conditions, the organization of the school system also matters in the choice of parenting style. The German school system at the time when Matthias grew up (and to a lesser extent today) was characterized by early tracking. After grade four, children entered one of three different types of schools, only the most academic of which prepared them for university (the *Gymnasium*), whereas the other two were supposed to prepare children for vocational training (*Realschule* and *Hauptschule*). As a result, one might expect that parents experienced some anxiety about which type of school their child would be recommended for, and perhaps engage in intensive parenting to increase their child's chances of making it into a more challenging school.

Indeed, this has been increasingly true in recent decades. For example, it has become common for parents to engage their children's teachers directly, going as far as begging for the "right" (i.e., Gymnasium) recommendation. In the 1970s, however, parents were more relaxed even at that juncture. There are at least two reasons for this. First, the stakes were not that high. Even the lower tracks could provide good prospects for children, as these schools were usually followed by apprenticeship programs that used to place most children into secure employment. In addition, there was an element of social convention to deciding the "appropriate" school for children from different backgrounds. Children from a working-class background would be expected (including by their own parents) to go to Hauptschule, and parents from more privileged backgrounds (say, the children of doctors, lawyers, or pharmacists) would be expected to go to Gymnasium, even if they did not excel academically.

Once in the Gymnasium, academic excellence was not particularly important. In Matthias's group of friends, the parents were primarily concerned with the possibility that their children might repeat a grade (*Sitzenbleiben*), but even this was common and not a source of shame. Indeed, often the (slightly older) children who had repeated a grade were the "cool" kids in school. Certainly, there was little of the anxiety over grade point averages that is familiar to American parents today.

If we look at what happened after Gymnasium, it is easy to understand why. Graduating from Gymnasium with any passing grade gave students access to a university education. In the 1970s and 1980s, this meant the ability to enroll at nearly any university in nearly any subject, no questions asked. As a result, higher grades did not determine children's future lives. It is then understandable why neither children nor parents were overly stressed about school performance, beyond the minimum required to make the next grade.

At the time, the main exception to the rule that children did not care much about grades were those who planned to study medicine at university. Here, demand for slots exceeded supply, and university slots were allocated based both on grades and on a special *Medizinertest*, broadly similar to the college entrance exams used in many other countries. Among Matthias's classmates, it was striking that kids who had set their minds on a medical career (often the children of doctors) were noticeably more grade-oriented and stressed about school than those focusing on other fields.

The experience of Italy and Germany in the 1960s and 1970s is representative of a broader trend during that period of time. Recent research by French economists Thomas Piketty and Emmanuel Saez documents that in industrialized nations a period of declining inequality that started after World War II reached a historical trough in the 1970s.[21] This low-inequality period coincided with the growing popularity of permissive parenting and the demise of authoritarianism.

Clearly, economic factors were not the whole story. The reaction to fascism after World War II was especially important in Europe. The growing popularity of psychoanalysis and the Freudian school, including key figures such as Wilhelm Reich, Carl Jung, and Erich Fromm; Bertrand Russell's social criticism; Jean-Paul Sartre and Simone de Beauvoir's marriage of existentialism, feminism, and Marxism; and the philosophy of the Frankfurt School were among the many intellectual forces that pushed the Western culture of the time in radically anticonformist directions. The underground artistic and literary rebellion of the Beat Generation in the 1950s evolved into an explosion of social and political activism in the 1960s. Antiauthoritarianism reached its first apex with the hippie movement and continued with the more abrasive and antagonistic antiestablishment, punk subculture of the 1970s. Common themes of these movements included free love and sexual liberation, feminist emancipation, a strong egalitarian drive, and a permissive attitude toward drugs. This intellectual atmosphere also contributed to the popularity of increasingly permissive parenting practices.

THE TURNING POINT OF THE 1980S: RISING INEQUALITY AND HIPPIES VERSUS YUPPIES

The 1980s were a turning point for Western countries in political, economic, and cultural terms. A conservative counterrevolution started to unfold in the late 1970s. In 1978, the Polish cardinal Karol Wojtyla became pope as John Paul II, marking a sharply conservative turn in the Catholic Church. His energetic and charismatic (if controversial) leadership aimed at restoring the Catholic Church's prestige, popularity, and power, while directing public attention at the oppressive nature of institutions in communist countries like Poland.

In 1979, Margaret Thatcher became the British prime minister. Her political manifesto celebrated individualism and rejected the egalitarian values that had been thriving for a few decades. For instance, in an interview in 1987 she stated that there "is no such thing as society." Instead, there are "individual men and women and there are families[,] and no government can do anything except through people and people look to themselves first."[22]

On the other side of the Atlantic Ocean, Ronald Reagan became the president of the United States in 1981. Reagan and Thatcher promoted many shared values, such as the virtue of free markets and individualism, and a profound disdain for both socialist and communist ideals. Their leaderships reshaped the world, revamping conservative liberalism and contributing to the collapse of the Soviet Union.

There were also sharp changes in economic inequality. Figure 2.2 displays the ratio between the income share accrued by the richest and poorest 10 percent (also known as the S90–S10 ratio) of the working population for four countries in the Organization for Economic Co-operation and Development (OECD).[23] The figure shows a trend of increasing inequality since the 1980s. The increase in inequality is especially strong in the United States and the United Kingdom. In the United States, the ratio more than doubled between 1974 and 2014 (from 9.1 to 18.9). In the United Kingdom, it increased from 6.6 to 11.2 during the same period. In Italy, it went up from 7.7 in 1984 (first available

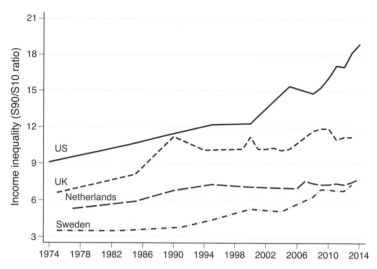

FIGURE 2.2. Income inequality (ratio of income shares accruing to the richest versus poorest 10 percent of the working age population) over time in the Netherlands, Sweden, the United Kingdom, and the United States

data) to 12.6. Even countries that were traditionally highly egalitarian witnessed an increase in inequality: the S90–S10 ratio increased from 3.5 to 7.3 in Sweden, and from 5.3 to 7.8 in the Netherlands. Although the level of inequality remains far below that of Anglo-Saxon countries (neither the Netherlands nor Sweden have reached today the level of income disparity that prevailed in the United States in the 1970s), it is still a substantial increase.

A significant portion of the surge in income inequality during the 1980s was driven by increasing returns to education. In the United States, the ratio between the average wages of college-educated workers and those of high school graduates increased from 1.5 to 2. In addition, there was a sharp increase in the return to postgraduate education.[24] The British economists Joanne Lindley and Steve Machin show that in both the United Kingdom and the United States the wage premium for workers with postgraduate education has increased relative to workers with only a college degree.[25] In the early 1970s, the average wages of the two groups were about the same, whereas in 2009 a worker with a postgraduate qualification earned, on average, a third more than a college graduate (and as much as 136 percent more than a high school graduate). These figures are likely to underestimate the value of a post-graduate degree, since many of those earning these degrees end up in academic or teaching jobs that are not very highly paid (except for a few elite schools) but are associated with significant nonmonetary benefits (such as prestige, research freedom, and job security). Today, the return to postgraduate education is very high, and the increasing appeal of advanced education is apparent in that the share of workers holding a postgraduate degree has boomed over the years.

Another contributing factor to the rise in overall inequality is an increase in wage inequality among people with the same education level. This shift is explained both by higher pay differences across subjects (such as the significant increase in wages for graduates with finance and engineering degrees relative to humanities and social sciences) and by pay differences across graduates who obtained their degrees from different universities.[26] All these changes to inequality have a common consequence: they increase stakes in education.

Why did inequality go up? One common culprit is the political swing to the right during the same period that led to less redistributive economic policies. However, most economists believe that political change was not the primary cause. The most widely accepted explanation for the trend to higher inequality is technological change.[27] The onset of the information technology revolution dramatically changed labor market conditions, reducing demand for less-educated and increasing demand for more-educated workers. The political and institutional transformations during the same period played an amplifying role by reducing the ability of governments to mitigate the impact of technological change through income redistribution and social policies. Some studies even argue that technological change might have been the cause of political and institutional change. For instance, the economists Daron Acemoglu, Philippe Aghion, and Gianluca Violante assert that the rise in the education premium induced high-skill workers to break out of unions, leading to the progressive decline of unionization.[28] Another team of economists, including Fabrizio and his coauthors John Hassler, José Rodríguez Mora, and Kjetil Storesletten, constructed and tested a politico-economic theory where the increase in wage inequality is the cause rather than the effect of the political changes that occurred in the 1980s.[29] In the world of low inequality and a low return to education in the 1960s, most people (including highly paid workers) found welfare state programs attractive. These programs provided security and safety nets, and in times of low unemployment, they were not expensive to finance. During the 1980s, the richer part of the population broke this social contract and decided to look out for themselves: they invested more in their education and individual success, while deeming social protection less important. When it was time to vote, they supported right-wing governments promising to lower taxes and scrap social transfers. Those left behind were not sufficiently empowered to fight policies that would harm their interests.

Culture and the role models people aspired to emulate came to reflect these changes. The egalitarian spirit of the 1970s suffered a backlash in popularity, becoming eclipsed by the ascent of individualism in the 1980s. Two well-known acronyms sum up these shifts in attitude: hippie and yuppie. The hippies were a radical antiauthoritarian, youth-oriented political movement from the 1960s, which originated in the United States but whose popularity spread quickly across the globe. A yuppie, a term first coined in the early 1980s that was short for "young urban professional," was a young, well-educated, highly paid professional stereotypically obsessed with her or his career and the material trappings of success.

Two founders of the hippie movement were the activists Abbie Hoffman and Jerry Rubin. While Hoffman remained loyal to his radical ideas until his death in 1989, Rubin's parable personifies the cultural shift that occurred in the early 1980s.[30] A dropout from the University of California at Berkeley, Rubin became famous in the 1960s for his battles against racial discrimination and for leading antiwar protests, culminating in the organization of rallies to obstruct the transportation of troops and weapons destined for Vietnam. But in the late 1970s, Rubin lost faith in political activism. He turned into a successful entrepreneur and eventually became a millionaire. In 1986, he engaged in a

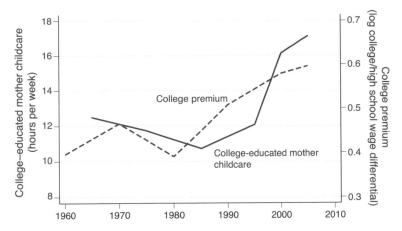

FIGURE 2.3. Time spent on childcare by college-educated mothers and the financial returns to education (ratio of average wage of college-educated versus high school–educated workers) in the United States

series of debates with Hoffman titled "Yippie vs. Yuppie," where Rubin defended his conversion, blaming the hippie culture for destructive abuses of drugs, sex, and private property. He now put his hopes in a new generation of innovating entrepreneurs who would take the future into their hands and produce a major social, economic, and political transformation of society.

We believe that the increase in economic inequality, in addition to prompting a shift in cultural values, also changed the behavior of parents. In particular, parents became increasingly convinced that their children's success would hinge on educational achievements. In a world of high stakes, the appeal of permissive parenting faded. Middle-class parents started pushing their children to adopt adult-style, success-oriented behavior. It is in this context that "helicopter parenting" has gained wide currency.

Consistent with our view, figure 2.3 shows how the time college-educated mothers in the United States devote to childcare has evolved vis-à-vis the college premium—that is, the ratio of the earnings of workers with a college degree relative to those without.[31] The two variables exhibit remarkably similar trends. The increase in the college premium in the 1980s is followed by a sharp increase in the number of hours educated mothers spend caring for their children.

We argue that the change in economic conditions is responsible for at least part of the increasing investments parents make in their children. For this argument to be credible, it is crucial that parenting styles really matter in terms of success in school and life. How strong is the evidence that an intensive parenting style or, more broadly, the time parents spend interacting with children improves their school performance? In chapter 1, we have already described a number of studies in developmental psychology that support this view. We now consider evidence from two data sources that allow us to examine this question in more detail, using data from a number of countries.

PARENTING MATTERS: EVIDENCE FROM PISA

We first consider data from the Program for International Student Assessment (PISA) study of the OECD. Officially launched in 1997, with a new test being administered every three years, PISA tests the knowledge of fifteen-year-old school pupils in mathematics, science, and reading. The project involves more than seventy countries, with over 500,000 participating students in recent surveys. Each country randomly selects from schools that participate in the survey, and the sample of students is representative of the population—namely, they come from a broad range of backgrounds and abilities. Children around the world answer the same questions translated into the local language in order to make the results comparable.

Most public attention to the PISA study focuses on comparing the performance of different countries and school systems. Here, we are interested in the dimension of parenting. In some of the recent surveys, students and their parents are asked to answer a questionnaire that includes information about how parents and children interact. The replies to these questions are then linked with the test score of each child. In our analysis, we focus on the questionnaires administered in 2012.

We use the answers to questions about the extent of parental involvement to construct a measure of the intensity of parenting style. More precisely, we classify the parenting style as intensive if all of the following criteria are satisfied: the parents discuss the child's well-being at school at least once a week, the parents have a conversation with the child at least once a week, and they eat a meal with the child at least once a week.[32] Clearly, this is a mild definition of intensive parenting. Looking back at our own child experience, our parents used to talk to us and eat meals with us every day. Yet, they probably would have failed to talk with us about school every week. So, our parents would have been classified as practicing a nonintensive parenting style.

Consider first the results for South Korea, an East Asian country whose children are among the top performers in PISA. Only the pupils from Shanghai (the only city in mainland China that participates in PISA), Singapore, Hong Kong, and Taiwan get higher average scores than the Koreans. For instance, the math score of Korean children is 554, which compares with a score for the Unites States of 481, and with an OECD average of 494 (the OECD is an organization comprising the most industrialized, high-income economies). Among Koreans, the average for children of nonintensive parents is 540, while the average for children of intensive parents is 563, a difference of 23 points (see fig. 2.4).[33] The differences in the reading and science scores are similar at 24 and 22 points, respectively.

A difference of 23 points in the PISA test score is large. It is similar to the difference between the math test scores of Finland (the top European performer, along with Switzerland) and those of average OECD countries like France or Great Britain, whose scores are considered disappointing.

One might worry that the difference in performance among children subject to different parenting styles may in fact be a reflection of parental education: intensive parents are, on average, better educated than less-intensive ones. More-educated parents are better placed to support their children in school, for example, by helping them with homework. For this reason, it is useful to compare parents from an identical educational background. Since PISA provides information about parents' education, we can use standard statistical techniques (multiple regression) to separate its effect from that of parenting style.[34] Somewhat surpris-

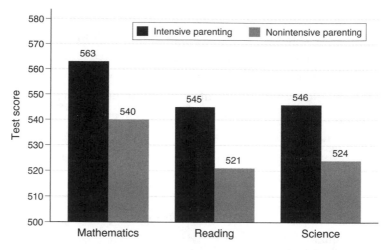

FIGURE 2.4. Intensive vs. nonintensive parenting and test scores in South Korea according to PISA 2012

ingly, for a given choice of parenting style, having better educated parents does not appear to have a large effect. Having two highly educated parents only adds 7 points to the average math test score, while an intensive parenting style adds more than 20 points across parents of equal levels of education. Therefore, the use of an intensive parenting style is associated with a much larger improvement in the child's performance than is the education level of the parents on its own. The results are similar for the reading and science test scores.

Do the findings for Korean children hold up in other countries? PISA 2012 provides information about parenting style for eleven countries: Belgium, Chile, Germany, Hong Kong, Croatia, Hungary, Italy, South Korea, Macau, Mexico, and Portugal. In nearly all of these countries, our measure of intensive parenting is positively correlated with test scores. The effects are the largest for Italian children (34 points for the average of the three test scores). The only exceptions are Belgium and Germany, where the effect of intensive parenting is close to zero.

Since the score of Korean children is likely to differ from that of Mexican children for reasons other than parenting styles (e.g., a large part could be due to differences in the school system), it makes sense to compare Korean children with Korean children and Mexican children with Mexican children, but not children from different countries. It is possible to use statistical techniques that calculate the average effect within the eleven countries (in the jargon used by economists, we run regressions controlling for country fixed effects). When we do that, we find that children subject to an intensive parenting style perform substantially better than those subject to nonintensive parenting within the same country. The difference is between 14 and 17 points across the three test scores. When one compares the children of parents with the same education, the effect is only slightly smaller, ranging between 11 and 14 points. All the effects are statistically significant.

PISA also contains information about the specific activities that parents do with their children. In particular, the 2009 questionnaire asks about the frequency with which parents read books with their children, tell them stories, or discuss various issues such as politics or movies. Using the same statistical techniques as outlined above, we can calculate correlations between these parental activities and test scores, holding constant the education level of parents. Since many parents engage in multiple activities (e.g., both reading books and telling stories), we estimate the effect of each single activity holding the others constant. Reading books with children is associated with an increase in the score of 16 to 18 points across the math, reading, and science tests, while telling stories has an average effect ranging between 2 and 7 points. Interestingly, discussing politics with children is associated with an increase in the test score between 9 and 12 points, which is a large difference.

One should be cautious about giving these findings a causal interpretation. We do not claim (as certain parenting books do) that parents can expect a large improvement in their child's proficiency simply by reading more books with them. Rather, it is likely that parents who spend time on reading books, telling stories, or discussing politics with their children are more closely engaged with their children in multiple dimensions than parents who do not engage in any of these activities. The findings should therefore be interpreted as the effect of broader differences in parenting choices that are all closely related, but only some of which are measured. In line with this interpretation, we find the largest effects for the children of parents practicing all three activities (reading books, telling stories, discussing politics). If done with a sufficiently high frequency, these children score, on average, about 32 points higher across tests than children whose parents do not engage in any of these activities. For PISA 2012, the effect is comparable with that of having an intensive parenting style. Overall, the data of PISA 2009 and 2012 yield a consistent picture: an intensive parenting style is associated with a significant improvement in school performance.

THE EFFECTS OF PARENTING IN THE UNITED STATES: NLSY97

The second data source we use to examine the effects of parenting style on children's educational achievements is the National Longitudinal Survey of Youth 1997 (NLSY97) in the United States. The NLSY97 is a nationally representative survey that follows the lives of nine thousand young Americans who were twelve to sixteen years old as of December 31, 1996. In the initial interviews in 1997, both parents and children were interviewed about a number of topics, which included a set of questions on parenting style. The youths are subsequently interviewed annually as they progress through adult life, which allows us to go beyond test scores and link information on parenting to children's adult outcomes.

We classify parenting styles according to children's responses to two questions. The first question concerns the extent to which the child perceives parents to be supportive. Children are asked, "When you think about how s/he acts toward you, in general, would you say that s/he is very supportive, somewhat supportive, or not very supportive?" We classify parents as "supportive" when the response is "very supportive" and as "not supportive" otherwise. The second question is about how strict parents are: "In general, would you say that s/he is permissive or strict about making sure you did what you were supposed to do?" Here, the admissible responses are "permissive" and "strict." The responses to the two questions are then combined to produce a "parenting style" measure (for each parent) that has four categories:

uninvolved (permissive and not supportive), authoritarian (strict and not supportive), permissive (permissive and supportive), and authoritative (strict and supportive).[35]

This method of measuring parenting styles has limitations. Most importantly, the classification is based on children's subjective perceptions. In families where there is a lot of conflict, children are more likely to report their parents as nonsupportive or overly strict. This may bias some results for authoritarian parents because we may pick up the effect of conflict in addition to the effect of authoritarian parenting. Similarly, the survey may lead us to classify some parents as permissive who are in fact authoritative. Children who generally have a good relationship with their parents may be reluctant to label them as strict, even when they guide them firmly into adhering to certain codes of behavior. It is also possible that when asked about their parents' strictness or supportiveness, children use their peer group as a benchmark. For instance, some white children may regard practices as strict that many Asian American children would not find unusual. However, even with these caveats in mind, this classification (which is widely used in the literature) paints a consistent picture of the effects of parenting styles.

Table 2.1 shows how the educational achievements of a child vary with the mother's and the father's parenting styles. The children of uninvolved mothers are 37 percent more likely to be high school dropouts compared to the average, and they are significantly less likely to earn a college degree. For uninvolved fathers, the likelihood of a child not completing high school is 26 percent higher than for the average father. The poor performance of the children of uninvolved parents should not be surprising, since the classification is likely to pick up truly neglectful parents and families from disadvantaged social backgrounds. The more interesting comparison concerns the three groups of involved parents. Among them, authoritarian parents clearly perform the worst. The proportion of children not attaining a college (bachelor's) degree is 76 percent for authoritarian fathers, which compares with 66 percent for authoritative and 69 percent for permissive fathers (with an average of 71 percent in the total population answering the questions). The pattern

TABLE 2.1. Percentage of children attaining different educational degrees broken down according to the different parenting styles (of the mother and father) to which they have been subject

	Mother's parenting style				
	Uninvolved	Permissive	Authoritative	Authoritarian	Total
Less than high school diploma	32%	22%	22%	25%	23%
Less than BA	51%	51%	50%	54%	51%
BA and MA degree	16%	25%	27%	20%	24%
PhD or professional degree	0.8%	1.3%	1.8%	1.1%	1.4%
	100%	100%	100%	100%	100%
	Father's parenting style				
	Uninvolved	Permissive	Authoritative	Authoritarian	Total
Less than high school diploma	25%	19%	17%	22%	20%
Less than BA	55%	49%	49%	54%	51%
BA and MA degree	19%	30%	31%	23%	28%
PhD or professional degree	1.1%	1.2%	2.3%	1.1%	1.6%
	100%	100%	100%	100%	100%

is similar for mothers, albeit differences across parenting styles are less pronounced. The children of authoritative parents achieve better educational outcomes than those of permissive parents. The largest difference is at the postgraduate level. An authoritative mother is 40 percent more likely to see her child earn a PhD or a professional degree than a permissive mother. While the fraction of children attaining postgraduate degrees is altogether small, this is still an important observation because the economic return to such degrees has increased dramatically (as documented previously).

Once again, we should interpret the results with caution. The different parenting styles could mask important socioeconomic differences. For instance, table 4.1 in chapter 4 shows that both uninvolved and authoritarian parents are, on average, less educated than permissive and authoritative parents. Since the education of the parents can have a direct effect on child performance (for instance, more-educated parents may be better at helping their children with homework), some of the correlation could be driven by educational background rather than parenting style. Other socioeconomic factors may also be important, such as the different family structures across ethnic and racial groups and the age of the parents. How socioeconomic characteristics affect the choice of parenting style will be discussed in more depth in chapter 4.

To isolate the effect of parenting style from confounding factors, we use a statistical method known as multivariate logistic regression analysis. Since we use this method many times in the book, we will now explain the statistical concepts of *odds* and *odds ratio*.

ODDS AND ODD RATIOS (A QUICK DETOUR)

Consider an event whose outcome can be success or failure, like the probability of passing a certain exam in a particular school. The ratio between the probability of success and that of failure is the odds of success. Suppose, for example, that historically one third of female students and one quarter of male students have passed the exam in question. Then, the odds of success for females and males are 1:2 and 1:3, respectively. The relative odds ratio is the ratio between these two numbers. For instance, the odds ratio for female relative to male students is 1.5 (one-half divided by one-third) in the example above. Here an odds ratio larger than one indicates that female students are more likely to succeed than male students.

Logistic regression allows us to estimate the odds ratio of different parenting styles for parents of equal socioeconomic characteristics. In other words, the odds ratio of parenting style X versus parenting style Y yields the relative success of two otherwise identical parents who only differ in their choice of parenting style. Note that while the absolute probability of success of the two parents hinges also on socioeconomic factors, the statistical model assumes that the odds *ratios* are independent of such factors. This ends the detour.

BACK TO NLSY97: RESULTS

Consider, first, the effect of mothers' parenting styles (ignoring fathers for the time being) on completing college. The relative odds ratio of a permissive mother relative to an uninvolved mother is 1.7; that of an authoritarian mother relative to an uninvolved mother is 1.3; finally, that of an authoritative mother relative to an uninvolved mother is 2.1. This means that in order to obtain a college degree, having an authoritative mom is best, followed by a permissive, authoritarian, and then uninvolved mom.

To translate these odds ratios into more standard probabilities of success, consider an example with four hypothetical white girls: Jane, Jessica, Jill, and Judith. In this fictitious example, the four girls' mothers have identical socioeconomic characteristics (i.e., same education, age, etc.), but their moms adopt different parenting styles. Figure 2.5 visualizes the results. Suppose Jane's mother is uninvolved, and Jane has a 20 percent probability of obtaining a college degree. Given this information, we can use the estimated odds ratios to calculate the probability of graduation for the other three girls. This calculation gives us a sense of how important differences in parenting styles are. Jessica (permissive mom) will graduate with a 30 percent probability. Jill (authoritarian mother) will graduate with a 24 percent probability. The most likely to succeed is Judith (authoritative mother), who will graduate with a 34 percent probability.

As anticipated, other factors also matter for success in education, some no less important than our measures of parenting styles. Having a well-educated mother increases the probability that a child earns a college degree, for any given parenting style. Girls are more likely to graduate from college than boys. However, the single most powerful predictor of success is being of an Asian origin. Given all other factors (including parenting style), an Asian or Pacific origin increases the odds of success by a factor of 2.5. Returning to the example above, consider two Asian girls, Jiao and Ju, whose mothers share the same socioeconomic characteristics as the mothers of Jane, Jessica, Jill, and Judith. Suppose Jiao's mother is uninvolved, whereas Ju's mother is authorita-

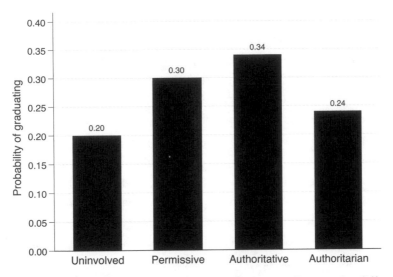

FIGURE 2.5. Estimated probability to graduate from college under different parenting styles for fixed socioeconomic characteristics

tive. Jiao will earn a college degree with 39 percent probability, which is already much higher than Jane's 20 percent; Ju will graduate with a probability above 56 percent.

What explains this large correlation between Asian origin and school success? We believe that cultural and behavioral differences, rather than genetic factors, play the most important role. Our data provide only a coarse measure of the actual parenting style. In the end, the classification relies on whether children find their parents to be strict and/ or supportive. No matter what children report, interactions within many Asian families may be different from those within families of other origins, corresponding to nuances in parenting style that our classification misses. For instance, if our own children were interviewed, our wives, María and Marisa, might well end up in the same bin as the tiger moms portrayed by Amy Chua. Yet, in reality they may well be "softer" than the average Asian-American mother. So, an Asian origin may be important precisely because children with an Asian family background are subject to a more stringent authoritative parenting style than other groups.

What about dads? The picture is similar overall to that for moms. Take as an example a fictitious girl named Jacqueline whose father and mother are both uninvolved. Let us suppose that her probability of finishing college is 20 percent (the same as Jane's above). Consider, next, four additional girls, Jennifer, Jody, Julia, and Jingjing. Jennifer has two authoritarian parents; Jody has two permissive parents; Julia has two authoritative parents; so does Jingjing, who is, however, also Chinese American. Jennifer's probability of graduation is 23 percent, only marginally above Jacqueline's. Here, the interesting new feature is that the correlation of authoritarian dads with school success is as low as that of uninvolved dads, in contrast with the earlier finding that authoritarian mothers have significantly more successful children than uninvolved mothers. Jody and Julia's probabilities of success are 36 percent and 40 percent, respectively. Hence, having two permissive or authoritative parents (rather than just a mom with these styles, as in the examples of Jessica and Judith) further increases the chance of graduating from college. Finally, Jingjing's probability of success is a full 65 percent!

The effect of parenting styles becomes even larger when we consider postgraduate degrees, such as a PhD or a professional degree. The main insight is that an authoritative parenting style is associated with a major increase in children's success rate relative to a permissive parenting style. Let us return to our previous example and suppose that Jacqueline has a 0.5 percent probability of earning a PhD. The probability for Jody (two permissive parents) to earn a PhD barely increases to 0.8 percent. In contrast, Julia (two authoritative parents) has a probability of earning a PhD equal to 1.3 percent. Recall that Jody and Julia have about the same probability of earning a college degree. Being permissive versus authoritative is not associated with a large difference in the probability of one's children finishing college. However, the authoritative parenting style has a significant edge over the permissive style for postgraduate degrees. In this example, there is a large increase in the probability of success as one moves from a permissive toward an authoritative parenting style. Once again, Asian origin is important: Jingjing's probability of earning a PhD is as high as 5.4 percent.

Parenting styles are also correlated with exposure to risky behavior. Using the same dataset, we studied the effect of parenting style on the probability of incarceration, age at first sexual relationship, use of condoms, smoking, alcohol abuse, and use of drugs. The pattern is consistent across all behaviors. Uninvolved and authoritarian parents are associated with riskier behavior in their children than permissive and authoritative parents. Overall, the children of authoritative parents (and especially authoritative mothers) engage in the least amount of risk-taking.

TAKING STOCK: THE ECONOMIC ROOTS OF HELICOPTER PARENTING

The data from the PISA and the NLSY97 surveys confirm that parenting styles have an impact on school performance and risky behavior. The children of involved parents who adopt an authoritative parenting style are more likely to do well in school and to receive higher degrees, and are less likely to engage in potentially harmful risky behaviors. In terms of education outcomes, the children of permissive parents are in the middle, and the children of authoritarian and uninvolved parents do less well. All the results hold true when we hold constant the parents' education background.

There are additional differences that are not captured by our classification of parenting styles. Within the United States, an Asian origin is associated with a significant increase in the odds of success. We discussed why this is also likely to be related to parenting styles: our coarse definition of parenting styles may fail to capture important variations in the nature of parent-child interactions. Since we do not believe that learning abilities differ significantly across racial groups, we conjecture that the large effects that we find are related to differences in the way children interact with their parents and their own peers.

All these pieces of evidence are consistent with our general thesis: there has been a shift in the intensity of parenting, as measured by the time parents devote to interacting with their children. This shift has occurred in a period characterized by increasing inequality, a booming return to education, and more generally higher stakes to bringing up children. As a result, parents have become increasingly worried about their children's school performance and responded by engaging in more intensive parenting, choosing parenting styles that are conducive to children doing well in education. Hence, the rise of helicopter parents can be understood as a rational response of parents to a changed economic environment.

CHAPTER THREE

Parenting Styles around the Contemporary World

The thesis of this book is that economic incentives shape the way parents rear their children. When rising inequality increases the stakes in education, parents respond by choosing intensive parenting styles that are conducive to their children's success. In the previous chapter, we showed that the economics of parenting accounts very well for broad changes in parenting over the last three decades: tiger and helicopter parenting grew increasingly popular just when inequality rose sharply.

Relative to explaining changes over time in the popularity of different parenting styles, explaining why parenting differs so much *across* countries is a much more ambitious task. Countries differ in many dimensions, such as political history, ethnic diversity, and culture, and each of these may play a role in parenting. When it comes to relations between parents and children, it would seem natural to assume that local culture and traditions passed down from generation to generation play a central role. In comparison, how important can economic factors really be?

In this chapter, we will argue that the economics of parenting is, in fact, remarkably successful at predicting how parents behave in different countries around the globe. We find that many parenting choices that at first seem to be part of local culture turn out to be rooted in economic conditions. Once again, the degree of economic inequality takes center stage.

Both the levels of and changes in income inequality vary substantially across countries. In the United States, the increase in inequality has been particularly pronounced, with a widening gap between those in the middle and those at the top of the income distribution. The real income of the median household has hardly changed since 1980. Meanwhile, the income of the richest 1 percent has risen quickly. The share of total income earned by this small group more than doubled, from 10 percent to 21 percent, from 1980 to 2014.[1] Today, a family in the richest 1 percent earns thirty-eight times as much as a family in the poorest 10 percent.

Income inequality is comparatively lower in Europe. In the United States, a worker at the 90th percentile of the income distribution earns 6.5 times as much one at the 10th percentile. The corresponding gap is only a factor of three in Scandinavia. In France and Germany, the gap is slightly larger than in Scandinavia, but still much lower than in the United States. Inequality has gone up in Europe over the past three decades, but not as quickly as in the United States. In most European countries, the income of the median household has increased steadily over time, albeit at a lower rate than the income of the rich.

According to our theory of economic incentives, parents should be more permissive in more equal societies like those found in the Scandinavian countries. Conversely, tiger and helicopter parents should be more common in countries with high inequality. The economics of parenting also makes predictions for changes over time. Parents should *become* more intensive (especially, more authoritative) in societies where inequality grows faster and more permissive in societies where the income distribution becomes more equal. If all societies become more unequal, the popularity of intensive parenting styles should grow faster in societies where inequality grows faster. We will see that the empirical evidence lines up well with these predictions.

PARENTING VALUES ACROSS COUNTRIES: IMAGINATION, INDEPENDENCE, AND HARD WORK

We examine cross-country differences in parenting styles using data from the World Values Survey (WVS), a survey run by a Stockholm-based network of social scientists studying changing cultural values and their impact on social and political life.[2] The WVS includes a series of questions about the values that parents regard as most important to rearing children. In this chapter, we mostly focus on industrialized countries that are members of the OECD (which, recall, comprises the most advanced economies in the world) because socioeconomic differences other than inequality are less likely to play an important role compared to a study including both developed and developing countries.[3] For instance, the countries in our sample have broadly similar income per capita (as measured by gross domestic product [GDP], per capita). We provide a comparison of a broader set of countries further below.

The questionnaire asks people which attitudes or values they regard as most important for children to learn at home. Respondents can choose up to five values from a menu containing independence, hard work, feeling of responsibility, imagination, tolerance and respect for others, thrift and saving money, determination and perseverance, religious faith, unselfishness, and obedience. Obedience is the value most closely associated with authoritarian parenting, which we discuss in chapter 5. In this chapter, we focus on imagination, independence, and hard work, where hard work is associated with intensive (more specifically, authoritative) parenting, and imagination and independence are characteristic of permissive parenting.

By checking how these parenting values vary with the level of inequality in countries, we can test our prediction that intensive parenting should be more popular in countries with higher inequality. Figure 3.1 plots the share of respondents in each country who list, respectively, imagination, independence, and hard work against the Gini coefficient, a standard measure of income inequality. A higher level of the Gini coefficient indicates higher inequality.[4]

The patterns are striking. In high-inequality countries, many parents emphasize that hard work is an important value for children to absorb, whereas in low-inequality countries parents attach a higher value to independence and imagination. We can measure the strength of these relationships with a statistical measure called "correlation coefficient."

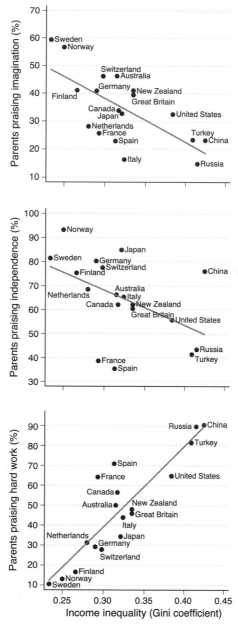

FIGURE 3.1. Income inequality (Gini coefficient) and percentage of parents praising the values of imagination (upper panel), independence (center panel), and hard work (lower panel) in child-rearing across OECD countries (plus China and Russia)

This coefficient can take values between minus and plus 100 percent. A correlation of zero indicates that there is no relationship between two variables. A positive correlation of 100 percent is the closest possible positive relationship between two variables (if one goes up, so does the other), and a correlation of negative 100 percent would be the closest possible relationship in the opposite direction (if one goes up, the other goes down).[5] We find an extremely strong positive correlation between inequality and hard work (+89%), whereas both independence and imagination are strongly negatively correlated (−48% and −68%, respectively) with inequality.

Consider hard work. Sixty-five percent of Americans mention hard work as a key virtue, while the percentage is as low as 11–17 percent in Nordic countries. Similarly, less than 30 percent of German parents praise hard work. This goes against the cultural stereotype of hardworking Germans (which Matthias finds overrated!), but is in line with the observation that inequality in Germany is rather low. In countries with intermediate levels of inequality such as Italy and Australia, parents are less enthusiastic about hard-working children than in the United States, but more than in Germany and the Scandinavian countries. There are a few countries that do not immediately fit into the general pattern. For instance, hard work is a popular value to instill in children in France and Spain, despite the fact that inequality is moderate in both these countries. We return to these exceptions in the pages that follow. However, the dominant pattern is a strong positive association: the more unequal a country, the more parents think that children should learn the virtue of hard work.

The opposite pattern emerges for independence.[6] Nurturing independent children is very important to Nordic parents, especially Norwegians, 93 percent of whom mention it as a top-five value. Central European parents also value independence, whereas only half of the American parents include it among the five most important values. Another country where parents highly value independence is Japan. This appears to be typical for East Asian parents, an observation to which we come back later.

Similar to independence, imagination is held in high regard by a large share of Nordic parents. In contrast, far fewer parents choose imagination in countries with high inequality. For instance, less than a third of American parents single it out. The same is true in Turkey, which is also a country with high inequality. To Fabrizio's dismay, Italy is the OECD country where imagination is appreciated the least, despite Italian history being so rich with great poets, inventors, and artists. Matthias can instead cheer up: more than 40 percent of Germans praise imagination. Once again, economic explanations prevail over cultural stereotypes: Italian sport commentators have a never-ending habit of claiming that the German soccer team is solid and well organized but less imaginative than the Italian one!

China and Russia are two large countries that experienced communist revolutions in the twentieth century and where income inequality has become very high after they returned to market economies. For comparison, we also include them in our plot even though they are not OECD members. In both cases, the attitudes of parents fit our hypothesis: 90 percent of Chinese and Russian respondents praise hard work, while imagination attracts the favor of only 15 percent of Russians (a lower score than for Italy) and 23 percent of the Chinese.

In summary, the WVS data provide a strong indication that economic inequality is indeed a key determinant of the choice between a more permissive versus a more intensive parenting style across countries. In countries with low inequality (such as Germany, the Netherlands, and the Scandinavian countries), parents single out the importance of children being independent and imaginative, values that we associate with permissive parenting. Hard work is popular in unequal countries such as the United States, China, and Russia. These patterns are based on a comparison of the average popularity of different child-rearing values across a country. Later in this chapter, we will delve deeper into the data and consider individual replies to associate each person surveyed in the WVS with a particular parenting style. Before going there, we consider how intensive versus permissive parenting relates to the happiness of children and then take a closer look at how parents behave in a selected group of countries.

THE HAPPIEST CHILDREN IN THE WORLD

One should not confuse a relaxed parenting style with half-hearted parental involvement. Our thesis is not that the Americans or the Chinese are better parents than the Europeans. Nor that they are worse. There are pros and cons to different parenting styles, and their appropriateness varies with the economic context.

Arguably, permissive but caring parents can end up with happier and more independent children, even though they may be less prepared to face the challenges of a competitive world. A study of child well-being across countries by UNICEF ranks Dutch kids as the happiest children in the world.[7] The Netherlands is followed (among the countries included in our WVS sample) by Norway, Finland, Sweden, Germany, Switzerland, and Denmark. These are all low-inequality countries whose parents praise independence and imagination and are less obsessed with instilling a strict work ethic in their children.

The UNICEF ranking considers a broad set of measures in five categories: material well-being, health and safety, education, behavior and risks, housing and environment. The measure that relates most directly to parenting style is the time that parents spend with their children to enhance their well-being, such as eating breakfast together daily or exercising regularly with them. In these, as in other dimensions, Dutch and Nordic children top the ranking. Parents in these countries may be more relaxed about achievements, but they engage with their children, respond to their needs, and care a lot for their health.

One might suspect that the various measures of child happiness simply capture the virtue of being wealthy. However, it turns out that the relationship between GDP per capita and overall child well-being is rather weak. For instance, the Czech Republic ranks ahead of Austria, Slovenia higher than Canada, and Portugal higher than the United States. In each of these comparisons, child happiness is higher in the poorer country. Two large, wealthy nations fare especially poorly: Britain and the United States. While Britain is ranked 16 in child happiness, the United States is only number 26, in spite of having the third highest GDP per capita in the sample, after Norway and Switzerland.

THE NETHERLANDS: JUST BE NORMAL, THAT'S ALREADY CRAZY ENOUGH

In the Netherlands, the parents of the happiest children in the world encourage children to be independent. For instance, children are expected to prepare their own lunch and to learn to ride a bicycle from an early age. In line with the low emphasis on hard work in the WVS, it is unusual to hear of Dutch parents pushing their children to achieve from a young age or expressing excitement about their child prodigies. Far from the tiger mom's ethos, they believe in the value of being down-to-earth, under the credo "doe maar gewoon, dan doe je al gek genoeg," which translates as "just be normal, that's already crazy enough."[8]

Relaxed standards apply to child-adult relationships across the board. Dutch parents do not hover over their children. Playgrounds are often located next to coffee shops or restaurants where parents meet and chat while their small children play together unsupervised. Parents are even tolerant of some risky behavior. Fewer than 30 percent of Dutch children wear a helmet when cycling in the city, which is significantly below the European average.[9] Although cycling is relatively safe in the Netherlands, every year eighteen thousand children below age twelve visit the emergency rooms of hospitals for bicycle-related injuries. Children claim to dislike helmets both because they are cumbersome and inconvenient to wear, and because their peers do not find them "cool." Dutch parents have an indulgent attitude toward such arguments. Rather than providing a role model for safe practices, they often do not wear a helmet themselves in the presence of their children.

School practices reflect this relaxed child-rearing culture. Dutch children below the age of ten have no homework. In early grades, there is very little competition between students, and failing a grade is unusual. This laid-back approach does not appear to stand in the way of high academic achievement. In PISA 2015, Dutch pupils were among the top performers in Europe. In the math test, they ranked second in Europe after Switzerland. The share of low achievers in the math and science tests is consistently smaller than in the United States. The Dutch pupils also report the highest level of life satisfaction among all countries participating in PISA, in marked contrast with Korea, Japan, and China, where children's academic performance is stronger than in the Netherlands, but children report low happiness levels.

SWEDEN: OUTDOOR NAPS AND LET CHILDREN BE CHILDREN

Like the Dutch, the Swedes are committed to the welfare of their children. Swedish parents never walk alone, meaning that they receive strong support from the state. Parents are entitled to a combined sixteen months of paid parental leave (*mamma-* or *pappaledig*), with the condition that neither parent can take more than thirteen months of leave, a measure intended to foster the commitment of *both* parents (especially fathers) to spending time with their children. The right to mamma- or pappaledig extends until the child turns seven. Many parents add unpaid leave to their statutory right. This generous parental leave policy encourages young people to have children. It is no surprise that Sweden has one of the highest fertility rates across the whole of Europe. Parental leave is only one of the many social policies supporting families. Day care and kindergarten are heavily subsidized by the government—being de facto almost free of charge. More than 80 percent of children in the relevant age group attend preschool institutional care.

One might argue that these and other redistributive policies explain the Swedish approach to parenting. Individual economic success may become less urgent if the state takes care of many expenses, and by subsidizing public childcare, parents are incentivized to raise their children in one particular way. Policy-driven incentives are certainly important factors explaining how the Swedes behave. Yet, one should not forget that policies and institutions do not fall from the sky. In-kind transfers to families enjoy widespread popular support and have been kept in place by governments of different political color. Any party proposing to cut the provision of welfare policies for families would face a resounding electoral defeat.

Swedish parents are among the most permissive in the world. Parents believe that children should be granted the maximum freedom, at least as long as this does not jeopardize their safety. Since small Swedish children are like small children everywhere else, conflicts in the playground happen with regularity. A common pattern is for one child to hit another and the victim then runs to mom or dad in tears. As an Italian father, Fabrizio was accustomed to the idea that each parent should ensure that her or his child causes no harm nor disturbance to others. A good Italian parent would feel the urge to deliver a brisk reprimand when her or his child crosses the line. The hotheaded child's parent is also expected to apologize profusely to the victim's parents. There is no such clear-cut rule on Swedish playgrounds. Parents sit leisurely in coffee shops and do not actively monitor what their kids do. Even when problems arise, they are reluctant to step in: according to the Swedes, the children will sort it out their own way. When troubles arise, the Swedish conflict resolution protocol is activated. The aggressor is gently invited to empathize with the victim. A hug between the children would uneventfully end the incident, while parents would nonchalantly comment: "Well, they are only children." After digesting the cultural shock, María and Fabrizio had frequent opportunities to observe how small children learn to exploit this lenience: their "sincere" and "spontaneous" apologies would often be followed by a victorious smile. However, Swedish boys and girls are no more likely to grow into thugs than other children. To their surprise, María and Fabrizio saw that they gradually learned to play and coexist peacefully.

With the notable exception of sports, organized extracurricular activities are rare in Sweden. Authoritative María and Fabrizio gently pushed Nora into piano lessons offered by a demanding (and authoritarian) professional East European teacher. Most kids attending these lessons were foreigners, and the majority were of Asian origin. Nora's achievements made her parents feel moved and proud. Yet, Swedish friends would more often frown upon the overbearing parents than show admiration for their little prodigy child. In Sweden, most parents do not drive their children to music lessons or enroll them in courses for precocious math wizards. In the same vein, nursery schools make a point of offering no formal teaching, be it reading or writing. Mandatory schools do not start until age seven (like in other Nordic countries). Nonetheless, one often hears parents express great concern for their little eight-year-old being forced into the cruelty of formal learning, and some parents demand an even later start. The grounds for these concerns are dubious: even in formal learning, the Swedish classrooms are anything but formal. Children enjoy frequent breaks and can often decide on their own whether they want to sit at the desk or roam around the room. To an Italian, the classroom situation is best described as controlled chaos.

Much of a child's early experience in Sweden involves outdoor activities. This may sound surprising as Swedish weather is not exactly mild. In Southern Europe, babies are rarely taken out in winter because it is considered just too cold. On the other hand, Swedish people believe that there is no such thing as bad weather, only bad (i.e., inadequate) clothing. Back in 1999, when newborn Nora was about to leave Danderyds hospital in Stockholm a couple of days after birth, her parents had received warnings about what to do if the temperature fell below $-10°C$ (14°F). It was a cold winter, with the thermometer showing $-18°C$ (0°F). In response to their inquiry, a nurse said, "You should not be worried as long as the temperature does not fall below $-20°C$, and the baby is well dressed." María and Fabrizio quoted the more cautious advice they had received. The nurse smiled: "People in Stockholm worry so much! I am from Boden (a cold city in Northern Sweden) and can assure you that there is no danger." The two southerners soon learned that well-protected babies love to nap outside in the cold winter and simply adapted. Swedish people know what they are doing; after all, child mortality in Sweden is the lowest in the world.

María and Fabrizio could not bring themselves to adopt all the Swedish customs. For example, some of their friends signed their children up for forest nursery schools, where children play outdoor all year round with only basic shelters for when the weather conditions turn rough. When their enthusiastic friends explained that small children attending such schools would be exposed to fewer bacteria and fall ill less often, María and Fabrizio nodded politely but opted instead for a more conventional indoor school.

Scandinavian people are generally easy going. Yet, when it comes to parenting, they hold firm beliefs. They think that the rest of the world is a little crazy. At some point, María and Fabrizio decided to move to the German-speaking part of Switzerland. During the transition, they considered moving Nora to a German school in Stockholm for one year to ease her transition. Their friends thought this was a terrible idea. Apparently, Scandinavians perceive German parents and the German education system to be brutally authoritarian.

GERMANY AND SWITZERLAND: RELAXED PARENTS (UP TO A POINT)

That is, of course, an exaggeration. German parents may be somewhat stricter than Scandinavians, but perceptions about parenting style are largely a matter of what you are accustomed to. Americans might see German parenting in a very different light. For instance, an article published in *Time* magazine relates the perspective of an American mother moving to Berlin: "All the German parents were huddled together, drinking coffee, not paying attention to their children who were hanging off a wooden dragon twenty feet above a sand pit. Where were the piles of soft padded foam? The liability notices? The personal injury lawyers?"[10] The culture shock did not end there. The American mom noted with surprise that the *Kindergärten* in Germany are not academically focused, nor do parents push their preschool children to learn to read and write. The biggest shock was that school kids of all ages walked unsupervised to school and roamed around the neighborhood. The story ends with the American mom putting on a brave face and letting her daughter go to the bakery on her own . . . while watching her from the balcony the whole time.

Matthias often witnesses this cultural clash at the school his three boys attend, the German International School Chicago. The teachers are from Germany, Austria, or Switzerland, and having arrived in Chicago only recently, they are still used to the more relaxed Germanic attitudes to children's play. In the early days of the school, much consternation was caused by incidents where a child suffered a minor cut or bruise in the playground, without the school providing any explanation of what had happened. In these situations, American parents (used to American preschools) expect, at a minimum, a detailed written "incident report" describing exactly what happened and why, followed by a meeting with a teacher (and ideally the school director) for further discussion and assurances that such events will be prevented at all costs in the future. Instead, the German teachers would just shrug and say, "It happened in the playground, we were not looking," leaving some American parents aghast.

Parenting in Switzerland is also relatively relaxed. Overparenting is not part of the local culture. In May 2015, the *New York Times* published an article with the suggestive title, "In Switzerland, Parents Observe. In the US, Hovering Is Required."[11] A Swiss mother living in the United States sits in a cafeteria and witnesses her daughter having a minor conflict with a smaller boy. Acting like a typical Swiss mother, she sees no reason to get involved in such an insignificant episode and prefers to let children independently find a way to resolve the conflict. Then, she is confronted with the appalled reaction of the boy's hovering mother, who disapproves of her nonchalant attitude and requests a proper apology from both mother and child.

Independence ranks high in the Swiss parenting culture. Children attending primary school and even kindergarten walk to school together with other kids, unsupervised by adults. The Swiss authorities work hard to ensure that nobody gets harmed by this practice and the streets are full of signs warning drivers that they are in an area near a school. Driving styles are expected to adapt to parenting styles (and punishment for reckless driving is draconian)!

However, the claim that Swiss children are relaxed and subject to little pressure needs some qualification, or at least an age limit. While children can enjoy a relaxed childhood until the early grades of primary school, stress levels rise as they progress in their education. As already mentioned, in Switzerland children take the Gymiprüfung, which assigns high school students to either an academically oriented or a vocationally oriented track. This exam is a turning point and a major source of stress in Swiss family life. In the area of Zurich, the examination takes place in grade six, when children are twelve years old. Many parents enroll their children in demanding preparatory courses and spend long hours helping them study. The day of the Gymiprüfung is full of drama: crowds of anguished parents wait in front of the exam sites, trying to read in their children's faces signs of success or failure as they exit. This example shows how, in addition to economic inequality, institutional features such as the design of the school system also help determine parenting choices. This is what economics predicts: high-stakes exams raise the stakes in parenting and hence provide incentives to engage in more intensive parenting. We will return to this point in chapter 9.

Switzerland is also an interesting case because, in spite of being a small country, it features great regional diversity in terms of language, economic characteristics, and even school systems. In a recent thesis at the University of Zurich, the economist Julian Schärer examined the relationship between inequality and parenting style across Swiss regions (cantons) using data from the Swiss Survey on Children and Youth known as COCON (Competence and Context).[12] This is a longitudinal study started in 2006, which covers the German- and French-speaking parts of Switzerland. Schärer classifies parenting styles according to parents' answers to a set of questions about the parent-child relationship. Since authoritarian parenting is uncommon in Switzerland, he focuses on the choice between a permissive and an authoritative parenting style. His analysis shows that the proportion of authoritative parents in each canton increases with the level of income inequality. The share of authoritative parents is high in high-inequality cantons such as Schwyz, Vaud, or Basel. It is substantially lower in low-inequality cantons such as Aargau, Solothurn, Biel, or Bern. This is the same pattern that we found across countries.

THE GROWING POPULARITY OF OVERPARENTING IN THE UNITED KINGDOM

Differences in the dominant parenting style do not simply reflect the cultural divide between Europeans and Americans. Not all Europeans believe that relaxed parenting styles foster independence and imagination. In January 2016, only a few months before his government was brought down by the Brexit referendum, British Prime Minister David Cameron gave a speech to an audience of parents in Islington, North London. There, he urged parents and school educators to adopt the tiger mums' ethos and do all it takes to instill the virtue of hard work into their children. Public schools should transmit Amy Chua's faith in "try hard, believe you can succeed, get up and try again" rather than an "all must have prizes" culture. In his words: "Character—persistence— is core to success. . . . No matter how clever you are, if you do not believe in continued hard work and concentration, and if you do not believe that you can return from failure, you will not fulfil your potential."[13] His passionate speech about moral values did not touch upon the importance of selective admission into elite private schools, such as Heatherdown Preparatory School and Eton College, which Mr. Cameron himself attended.

In spite of not telling the whole story, Mr. Cameron may have been preaching to the choir. The parenting style of Britons, especially among the more-educated classes, is more intensive than that of Germans and Scandinavians. The popularity of helicopter parenting in the United Kingdom has been growing fast since the 1990s. It is increasingly common for parents to take an active role in guiding their children in their choice of university and to visit campuses with them, just as many American parents do.

This recent trend has gone so far that visiting days at universities now target parents of prospective students as much as the students themselves. During such visits, parents are more and more vocal. Confronted with this trend, universities often schedule separate presentations for the parents and the students at the same time, to avoid parents "gatecrashing" the students' session. Anecdotes include mothers showing up (uninvited) at parties intended for master's students, so that they can talk to professors about the progress of their twenty-plus-year-old kids. Interestingly, it appears that a turning point in British parents' change of attitude was the Teaching and Higher Education Bill passed in 1998, which raised tuition fees and abolished students' maintenance grants, replacing them with a new system of means-tested loans.[14] Since then, fees have increased from 1,000 to 9,000 pounds a year, and competition among top schools has stiffened. Before the reform, maintenance grants were typically available to a large share of the students (for instance, a university lecturer's salary would be low enough for her child to qualify). In contrast, under the new regime, many lower-middle-class parents simply cannot afford for their children to abandon their studies or to change course or university after a few years. Nor can they afford for their children to choose a course that is not likely to lead to relatively well-paid and secure employment. In other words, the financial stakes are higher after the reform, and these increased stakes in education go hand-in-hand with the boom in helicopter parenting.[15]

CHINA: WHERE PARENTS KNOW WHAT IS BEST FOR THEIR CHILDREN

If one is looking for a country where intensive parenting is the norm, China is the place to go. In the United States, Amy Chua believes that parents of Chinese origin are more focused on their children's academic success than Westerners are: "Chinese parents spend approximately ten times as long every day drilling academic activities with their children. By contrast, Western kids are more likely to participate in sports teams."[16] The data from the WVS align well with the stereotypes about the strict Chinese parenting culture (see fig. 3.1). The value of hard work is singled out by 90 percent of the Chinese respondents (compared with 65 percent in the United States and only 11 percent in Sweden). According to a survey reported in the *China Daily*, the strict parenting approach promoted by Amy Chua is popular in China. "Among 1,795 people polled . . . 94.9% said they know women who are strict mothers, and 55.1% said they see merit in Chua's parenting." Only "18% said tiger moms deprive their children of childhood fun."[17] According to a professor of education at a Beijing university, as reported in this same article, the merits of this parenting style result in smarter children who are better prepared to face harsh competition in the future.

In China, the tiger mom myth is so popular that it became the subject of a television series starring famous actors Zhao Wei and Tong Dawei. The three main characters are Shengnan (the "tiger mother"), Su (her husband), and Qianqian (their five-year-old daughter). Shengnan (which in Mandarin means "being better than men") is the senior CEO of a successful company. She is strong-willed, strict, and prepared to exert enormous effort to guide her daughter to success. In comparison, Su is a more permissive parent. The story revolves around the humorous disputes between the two parents.

A recurrent theme in the series is the importance of giving Qianqian the best education. One day, Shengnan discovers, to her dismay, that Qianqian is wearing makeup in order to look pretty, which angers her mother. The mother-daughter conflict lingers until Qianqian delights her mom by telling her that she no longer wants to wear makeup and wants instead to study hard like her friend Dudu. Shengnan wants to learn more about this wonderful Dudu. She finds out that Dudu is a pupil at the No.1 Primary School where there are hundreds of kids like her. Shengnan's goal in life becomes to send Qianqian to that school. A condition to earn admission is to live in the school's enrollment zone, which is very expensive. Shengnan decides to sell the two-story apartment in which they live to buy a shabby, old, and cramped "elite school property" (*xue qu fang*) that costs 90,000 RMB (US$14,000) per square meter. When Su and his family try to dissuade her from getting a 2-million RMB mortgage that would turn their life into misery, Shengnan tells her story: her father was poor, yet he spent most of his money on her education. Thanks to that, she could go to the best schools and eventually become successful.

In spite of her family's great sacrifice, Qianqian fails to enter the dream school because of a change in the admission rule by which only families residing in the school zone for at least two years receive priority in enrollment. Shengnan does not give up, and rather than sending her daughter to an ordinary primary school, she defers her admission until the following year. Yet, keeping Qianqian idle during the hiatus is out of the question. Shengnan quits her career job and subjects her daughter to hyperintensive home schooling and strenuous daily physical exercise, paying extra tuition for drawing and music lessons. But Shengnan has no doubt: "Our careers can be sacrificed, but our daughter's future cannot. We live for our daughter."

Shengnan personifies the stereotype of a committed Chinese mother who believes that hard work is the avenue to success—a belief that is reflected in the responses of Chinese parents in the WVS. She can be merciless. One day, Qianqian cannot finish her assignments because her grandmother takes her out for a whole day. When Shengnan comes home at night, she pulls her daughter out of bed and forces her to finish her homework. Is this merely the exaggeration of a fictional story? Not entirely. One day, Fabrizio asked a Chinese friend admiringly about his daughter, who was a piano prodigy. Where did all this talent spring from? The friend answered earnestly that he believed that his daughter was no more musically talented than many of her schoolmates; she was simply willing to crank out more hours of practice than the others. Many Chinese parents agree with the famous quote often often attributed to Einstein: "Genius is 1% talent and 99% hard work."

The example of China supports the economic theory of parenting. Inequality is very high in today's China. It is higher yet than in the United States, and far higher than in any Western European country. In addition, the stakes are exceptionally high in education. Finally, as in Shengnan's own account of her life experience, hard work is a powerful vehicle for social promotion. In school, the door to success is a test called *gaokao*, a high-stakes exam that over nine million students take every year to earn admission to higher education institutions. A strong gaokao performance can grant a student admission to a top university; a bad result will deny any access at all. Contrary to the United States, where admission to elite colleges hinges not only on grades and test scores but also on other factors such as extracurricular activities and socioeconomic background, grades are all that matter in China. We discuss the drama that the gaokao creates in chapter 9.

Do we believe that economic inequality and high stakes in education explain everything about the dominating parenting style in China? While we think that these factors are very important, we grant some aspects of Chinese parenting are rooted in older cultural traditions rather than current economic conditions. For instance, the traditional respect for authority and hierarchy may explain the authoritarian twist that distinguishes intensive Chinese parents from those living in Western countries where inequality is also high. In the words of Amy Chua: "Chinese parents believe that they know what is best for their children and therefore override all of their children's own desires and preferences."[18]

JAPAN: SEND THE BELOVED CHILD ON A JOURNEY

The Japanese parenting culture provides an interesting contrast to China. While China and Japan are very different countries today, they share some long-standing cultural traits. For instance, education and academic achievements are highly regarded in both China and Japan. Respect for parents and the elderly are also important traditional values the two countries share. Thus, if one believed ancestral cultural factors to be the main determinant of parenting style, one should expect similar parenting practices in the two countries. However, the economic situation in Japan is very different from that of China today. To start with, Japan is a much richer country (its GDP per capita is 2.5 times higher than that of China), although China has grown much faster than Japan in the last two decades. More importantly, income inequality is much lower in Japan than in China. The Gini coefficient of Japan is also much lower than that of the United States and in between those of Germany and the United Kingdom. In line with these economic differences, parenting values are also different between Japan and China. In the WVS, Japanese parents emphasize hard work much less than Chinese parents do. Only one-third of Japanese respondents list this value among the most important values for child-rearing, compared to 90 percent in China. Conversely, Japanese parents hold imagination in higher regard than do the Chinese. Thus, China and Japan diverge in a way that conforms well to what our economic theory predicts.

However, the parenting cultures of China and Japan converge when it comes to the importance of bringing up independent kids. Independence is singled out as a very important value by 76 percent of Chinese respondents and by more than 80 percent of Japanese respondents, much higher proportions than the 56 percent of US respondents. The strong emphasis on independence is summarized by the Japanese proverb *"kawaii ko ni wa tabi o saseyo,"* which translates in English as "send the beloved child on a journey," or less literally but perhaps more accurately, "let the beloved child travel alone." This proverb illustrates the importance of fostering self-reliance within children. From a tender age, Japanese children ride public transport and run errands such as grocery shopping without adult supervision.

The importance of raising independent children is so deeply rooted in the Japanese parenting culture that a popular Japanese TV show titled *"hajimete no otsukai"* (my first errand) is dedicated to young children running their first errand (for example, brother and sister going out to buy groceries for the first time). The show has aired on Japanese TV for more than twenty-five years.[19] Why is independence so popular among Japanese parents? Possibly because of the great social trust and sense of community that is present in the Japanese culture. In addition, crime rates in Japan are exceptionally low, and children are taught early on that they can rely on other members of the community for help whenever needed.[20]

Although Japanese parents are less obsessed with the work ethic than the Chinese, intensive parenting is still spreading, especially with regard to supporting children's education. The Japanese have long cared about education. Mothers have been in charge of ensuring that children progress, and the expression *kyoiku mamas* (education mothers) has been used for years to refer to this role. This tradition appears to have evolved in a peculiar way. A team of child development scholars who studied the relationship of Japanese mothers with their children's teachers in preschool and elementary school concludes that the traditional kyoiku mamas of the 1960s, generally shy and supportive toward schools' goals and methods, have evolved into today's "monster parents" who interfere heavily with every aspect of their children's lives.[21] Monster parents frequently come into conflict with school teachers, whom they blame for not delivering education that meets the parents' expectations.[22]

WHERE AUTHORITARIAN PARENTING SURVIVES
IN EUROPE: FRANCE AND SPAIN

In the countries discussed so far, parenting choices line up well with the thrust of our theory. We now turn to two European countries that provide more of a challenge: France and Spain. The WVS data show that while the attitude toward hard work is roughly in line with what our theory would predict, French parents value independence and imagination far less than would be warranted by the intermediate level of inequality in their country. Instead, obedience scores high, with 43 percent of respondents listing this value among the five most important ones. This is a far larger share than in Germany (17%), Sweden (17%), and the United States (30%). Spain is similar to France: 42 percent of parents believe in obedience.

The authoritarian twist of French and Spanish parents is also reflected in their general acceptance of corporal punishment, though in recent years the two countries have had different laws: corporal punishment has been illegal in Spain since 2007, while it has remained legal inside the home in France until as late as 2017. Yet, parents in both countries admit to a generous use of this practice. In a study carried out in five European countries (Sweden, Austria, Germany, France, and Spain), five thousand parents were interviewed about their views, actual use of corporal punishment, and their own experiences with violence.[23] More than half (55%) of the Spanish parents reported slapping their children in the face, 80 percent slapping their bottom, and 7 percent having beaten them with an object. The corresponding numbers for French parents are 72 percent, 87 percent, and 5 percent, respectively.

A possible explanation is that Catholic parents are especially inclined to authoritarian methods. In line with this view, a study by the American sociologist Gerhard Lenski looks at differences in parenting styles between Catholics and Protestants living in Detroit.[24] Detroit Catholics were more traditional than Protestants in their relations to their children and held values that put more emphasis on obedience to authority than on personal autonomy or self-direction. Catholics were also more likely to use corporal punishment. This study is based on the United

States and dates back to half a century ago. The international evidence from the WVS for more recent periods is only partially supportive of this conjecture. The value of obedience is highly praised in most Catholic countries included in the study, for example, Argentina (48%), Chile (58%), Colombia (67%), Mexico (64%), Peru (61%), Brazil (55%), and Poland (55%). However, Italy (29%) is a Catholic country whose parents attach low importance to obedience. Moreover, our analysis of the behavior of parents within countries (see chapter 5) suggests that while religious parents are on average more authoritarian, there is no major difference between Catholics and religious people from other denominations. Other possible explanations center on political history (Spain is a relatively young democracy and experienced civil war in the 1930s) and features of the education system, which is an issue we return to in chapter 9.

USING INDIVIDUAL DATA IN THE WORLD VALUE SURVEY

After our in-depth look at a few selected countries, we return to a more detailed analysis of the data from the WVS. At the beginning of the chapter, we showed how specific parenting values are related to inequality across countries, using data from a single edition of the WVS (choosing the edition with the largest coverage). There is more information that we can extract from these data. First, we can use the information on parenting values to infer the specific parenting style of each respondent. Next, since many countries have participated repeatedly in the WVS, we can test whether changes in the popularity of different parenting styles track changes in income inequality. In other words, we can test whether, as countries become more unequal, the authoritative parenting style gains ground at the expense of the permissive style. Finally, the WVS provides rich information on the socioeconomic characteristics of individual respondents, such as age and level of education. Since these individual characteristics are likely to have an effect on the choice of parenting style, we can use statistical techniques to separate the effect of these additional factors from those of income inequality at the national level.

To assign each respondent in the WVS to a particular parenting style, we use four characteristics: independence, imagination, hard work, and obedience. Given that parents are asked to indicate their five most important values from a large menu, they may pick more than one of the four values we are interested in. With this in mind, we classify all parents that mention obedience as one of the top values as authoritarian, irrespective of what other values they choose. Demanding obedience is a distinctive characteristic of the authoritarian parenting style that is not shared by the others because authoritative parents aim to convince their children to do the right thing on their own accord, and permissive parents do not interfere with their children's choices. Among the remaining (nonauthoritarian) parents, we classify those who list hard work as authoritative because pushing children toward higher performance is characteristic of this parenting style, but not of permissive parenting. Finally, we classify parents who are neither authoritarian nor authoritative as permissive if they pick independence or imagination among the preferred values because both of these values are naturally associated with permissive parenting. This leaves us with parents who pick none of the four values that form the basis of our classification. Given that this category comprises only 9 percent of the total number of respondents, we omit them from our analysis.

THE MORE INEQUALITY GROWS, THE MORE PARENTS TURN AUTHORITATIVE

Figure 3.2 shows how the percentage of parents who adopt each parenting style varies with the level of inequality across countries.[25] Here we measure inequality as the ratio between the earnings of the workers at the 90th and 10th percentile of the income distribution, respectively, among full-time, dependent employees (note that this measure differs from that reported at the beginning of the chapter and also from the S90–S10 ratio discussed in chapter 2). The results would be very similar if we used the Gini coefficients as in figure 3.1, but we have better measures over time for this indicator.[26] The figure reports only one observation for each country, namely, the average over the available editions of the WVS.

Consider, first, the permissive parenting style (top panel of fig. 3.2). Higher inequality is associated with a smaller share of parents adopting the permissive parenting style. Many Swedish parents are permissive, and inequality is low in Sweden, while only few American parents are permissive, and inequality is very high in the United States. Given that we have data from several editions of the WVS, we can also consider changes over time within countries. These data are analyzed more systematically in our earlier published research.[27] There, we document that changes over time in the popularity of different parenting styles track changes in inequality within each country. In most cases, as a country experiences an increase in inequality, the popularity of the permissive parenting style declines. Take Norway, for instance. Norway is a country with very permissive parents, on average. Yet, as inequality increased between 1996 and 2007, Norwegian parents became less permissive. The same is true for Finland, Germany, New Zealand, and the United States, all of which started from very different levels of income inequality. In contrast, as inequality fell in Spain between 2007 and 2011, Spanish parents became more permissive. As is often the case in social science studies, no theory predicts the data perfectly, since theories focus on one aspect (in our case, inequality) while abstracting from other factors that can also be important. For instance, inequality did not change much in Germany between 2006 and 2013, yet parents became more permissive.

The middle panel of figure 3.2 shows that higher inequality is associated with more parents adopting the authoritative parenting style. This style is unpopular in Scandinavia, nor is it commonly adopted in the Netherlands, Switzerland, or Germany. Instead, authoritative parenting is popular in the United States, as well as in Turkey, France, and Spain. Our earlier research also reveals that changes in the popularity of the authoritative parenting style track changes in income inequality within each country. Consider the United States. The sharp increase in in-

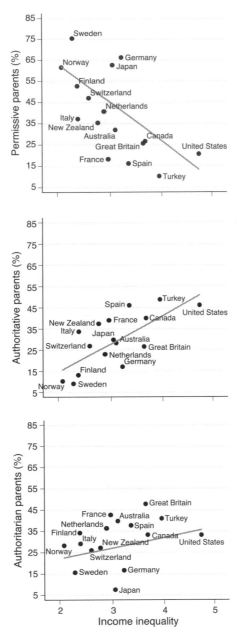

FIGURE 3.2. Income inequality (ratio of 90th to 10th percentile of the earnings distribution) and percentage of parents adopting a permissive (upper panel), authoritative (center panel), and authoritarian (lower panel) parenting style across OECD countries

equality between 1995 and 2011 is associated with an increase in the popularity of the authoritative parenting style from 39 percent to 53 percent.

Finally, the bottom panel of figure 3.2 shows the relationship between inequality and the authoritarian parenting style, which emphasizes obedience. Higher inequality is associated with a larger share of authoritarian parents, although the relationship is less strong than for the other two parenting styles. In line with our discussion of Japan, very few Japanese parents are authoritarian. There are also some surprises: many more Finnish parents are authoritarian than are Swedish parents. We will see in the following chapters that the main determinants of an authoritarian style are the parents' socioeconomic status and the level of economic development rather than inequality at the country level.

HOW LARGE ARE THE EFFECTS OF ECONOMIC INEQUALITY?

The cross-country analysis of the WVS data provides support for the hypothesis that an increase in income inequality is associated with less permissive and more authoritative (and, to a lesser extent, authoritarian) parents. However, these relations deserve some further scrutiny. So far, we have only considered the effect of macroeconomic inequality in isolation. However, at the individual level, parenting styles are likely to depend also on a variety of socioeconomic characteristics of the parents, such as their levels of education. At the country level, differences in parenting may in part be due to cultural heterogeneity (e.g., the heritage of Confucianism in China or that of Puritanism in the United States). Abstracting from these determinants might lead us to overstate the effect of inequality on parenting.

To address these concerns, we return to the statistical methodology already used in chapter 2 (multinomial logistic regression). Rather than aggregating the data at the country level, we perform our analysis on the original individual data, where the unit of observation is the person interviewed for the WVS. This method allows us to separate the effect of increasing inequality from that of parental educational or demographic characteristics.[28] In other words, we estimate the probability that parents with *identical socioeconomic characteristics* adopt each parenting style for different levels of income inequality. To deal with country-specific factors such as cultural influences, we can take advantage of the fact that we have data from multiple surveys (run in different years) from each country. This allows us to examine the effect of inequality on parenting style by comparing parents living in the same country, holding constant country-level factors. This method of analysis is known as "regression with country fixed effects."

Overall, this analysis yields results similar to the less sophisticated analysis outlined previously. Changes in inequality at the country level are associated with changes in the probability that parents adopt each of the parenting styles.[29] More concretely, when a country becomes more unequal, parents of identical socioeconomic characteristics turn significantly less permissive, significantly more authoritative, and somewhat more authoritarian.

To get a sense of the quantitative importance of changes in income inequality for reshaping parenting style, consider the following example. Take a hypothetical Swedish parent with average characteristics (age, education, etc.) in 1996, when the inequality measure is 2.3. The probability for such a hypothetical parent to be permissive, authoritative, and authoritarian are assumed to be, respectively, 75 percent, 6 percent, and 19 percent, close to the national average data in figure 3.2. Next, suppose that we relocate this parent and drop her in a different economic environment with an inequality at the level of the United States in 2011. We can use the estimated effects to infer the probability that this parent would choose to be permissive, authoritative, and authoritarian in the US-like society. This parent would be permissive, authoritative, and authoritarian with probabilities of 21 percent, 26 percent, and 53 percent, respectively (see fig. 3.3).[30] These figures are very different from the original ones! The switch from a permissive to an authoritative parenting style is especially large and highly statistically significant. The drop in the fraction of permissive parents is almost

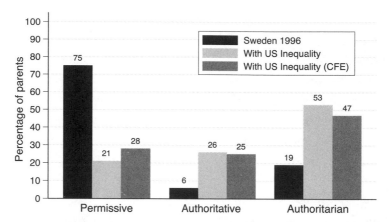

FIGURE 3.3. Estimated distribution of parenting styles for parents with average characteristics for Sweden in 1996 (black bars) versus hypothetical distribution in Sweden if inequality rose to the level of the United States in 2011, measured using model without (light gray) or with (dark gray) country fixed effects

identical to the actual difference in the fraction of permissive parents between Sweden and the United States (see fig. 3.2). This suggests that inequality, rather than individual characteristics or country-specific factors, accounts for most of the parenting gap between Sweden and the United States. Going forward, these results suggest that a continuing trend of increasing income inequality might dramatically increase helicopter parenting in the world.

Two qualifications are in order here. First, even though we control for a number of potential explanations for the choice of parenting style, such as individual socioeconomic characteristics of the parents and country-specific effects, we cannot be sure that we are including all potential factors affecting parenting styles. Hence, we cannot be certain that the link between inequality and parenting is not partially driven by factors that we do not measure. Second, by allowing inequality in Sweden to become as large as in the United States in the aforementioned comparison, we are considering a large change, much larger than that experienced within any individual country in the period considered. In other words, it is unlikely that we will observe in a given country as dramatic a change in parenting styles as in our illustrative example during, say, the next decade.

The statistical analysis also reveals which countries feature an unusual parenting behavior relative to what their level of inequality would predict. Germany and Sweden (two countries with low inequality) turn out to be even more permissive than what should be expected from the negative statistical association between inequality and permissive parenting. Likewise, the proportion of authoritarian Japanese parents is exceptionally low. In contrast, relative to income inequality, very few parents in France and Spain are permissive, and instead many parents are authoritative or authoritarian, a fact that we have already noted and to which we will return. Italian parents stand out for being authoritative rather than authoritarian or permissive. Finally, the authoritarian trait is especially strong (over and above what one might expect from their high level of income inequality) in Great Britain, Turkey, and the United States. In terms of global trends, our analysis identifies a clear increase over time in the popularity of the authoritative parenting style, in line with the global rise in inequality discussed in chapter 2.

What about education? Our estimates indicate that relative to parents who did not complete high school, parents with a high school diploma, and to a greater extent parents with a college degree, are more likely to adopt a permissive parenting style. Parents with a college degree are especially unlikely to be authoritarian, in other words, to believe that obedience is a cardinal value to instill in a child. The finding that less-educated parents are more likely to be authoritarian will be discussed in more depth in chapter 4.

Finally, one might wonder about the effect of economic development on parenting style. When we look at cross-country differences across OECD countries, we find rather small effects. An increase in GDP per capita (a standard measure of economic development) slightly increases the appeal of a permissive style. Overall, in our sample of advanced OECD countries, the effect of income inequality is far stronger and more robust than that of the development level. We return to this discussion in chapter 5, when we consider a larger sample of countries, which also includes developing economies.

THE ROLE OF PUBLIC POLICY: HOW TAXATION AND REDISTRIBUTION AFFECTS PARENTING STYLES

So far, we have only considered the effect of pretax earnings inequality. However, people actually care more about their disposable income, that is, the income that is available to them after paying taxes. Moreover, people's well-being is also affected by public policies that provide public goods (parks, public hospitals, law and order) and safety nets (public pensions, unemployment benefits, health insurance). If parenting styles are determined by parents' expectations about children's future prospects, one should also expect the popularity of different parenting styles to vary with taxation and social expenditure. For instance, in countries with generous welfare state policies, parents may be more relaxed and less obsessed with their children's educational success because they know that the children can rely on state support should they encounter economic difficulties.

Progressive taxation is a powerful policy instrument. A tax code is progressive if the tax rate becomes higher as the taxable income increases. The goal of progressive systems is to redistribute income in favor of poor people with lower earnings, at the expense of rich people with higher earnings. The more progressive a tax system is, the smaller the difference in disposable income between high- and low-income earners.

Our theory predicts that parents are more prone to adopt an intensive parenting style if taxation is less progressive. Conversely, we should observe many permissive parents in countries where taxation is highly progressive. We use a measure of tax progressivity developed by the Andrew Young School of Policy Studies.[31] Figure 3.4 shows that the evidence lines up well with our predictions: in countries with more progressive tax systems, parents are more permissive, less authoritative, and less authoritarian.

Consider, next, the aggregate social expenditure as a percentage of GDP.[32] Social expenditures tend to help poor people and to reduce effective inequality. Therefore, we should expect that in countries that spend more on social policy, parents are more permissive and less au-

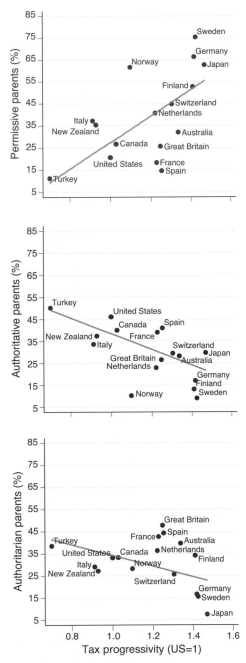

FIGURE 3.4. Tax progressivity and percentage of parents adopting each parenting style across OECD countries

thoritative. This is again confirmed by the empirical evidence. The relationship between social expenditure and the authoritarian parenting style is also negative, although this relationship is weaker and not significant in a formal statistical sense.

One might object that the different results highlighted above have a common root, as countries with a low pretax inequality might have systematically high taxation and high social expenditure, such as in Sweden, and vice versa in countries such as the United States. However, it turns out that each of the three variables discussed in this chapter has a separate effect on the choice of parenting style. In a multiple regression analysis, we find that each one—low pretax earnings inequality, a highly progressive tax system, and high social expenditure—makes parents more permissive.

More precisely, if we take two parents with the same socioeconomic characteristics, the one living in the country with less inequality and/or more progressive taxation and/or more generous social expenditure is more likely to be permissive and less likely to be authoritative and authoritarian. To make this argument more concrete, consider two parents with the same age, education, and so on, living in Germany and Turkey, respectively. Suppose that for the Turkish parent the probabilities of being permissive, authoritative, and authoritarian are 10 percent, 45 percent, and 45 percent (fig. 3.5). Then, based on our analysis the otherwise identical German parent would have probabilities of being permissive, authoritative, and authoritarian equal to 49 percent, 22 percent, and 29 percent. Hence, even though individual characteristics are the same, the German parent is much more likely to be permissive. The difference is explained in part by lower inequality and in part by the more generous welfare state that Germany has in place. To disentangle the two parts, let us imagine a fictitious country where all metrics are the same as those of the actual country of Turkey, except that it has the same pretax inequality as Germany. Let us call such a country pseudo-Turkey. Then, a parent in pseudo-Turkey would have probabilities of being permissive, authoritative, and authoritarian equal to 39 percent, 27 percent, and 34 percent. The gap relative to actual Turkey is smaller in this case: high pretax inequality alone moves the probabil-

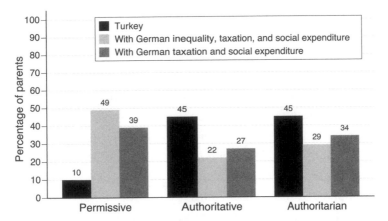

FIGURE 3.5. Estimated distribution of parenting styles for parents with average characteristics for Turkey in 2007 (black bars) versus hypothetical distribution in Turkey if inequality, taxation, and social expenditure (light gray) or just taxation and social expenditure (dark gray) were at the level of Germany

ity of being permissive from 10 percent to 39 percent.[33] For the remaining 10 percent to reach the 49 percent probability of being permissive for the German parent is then due to the more progressive tax system and the more generous welfare state in Germany.

Overall, we see that government policy explains some variation in parenting style, even after accounting for differences in pretax inequality. This implies that changes in economic policy are likely to affect the way in which parents raise their children, which is a theme we will return to in later chapters.

THE EFFECT OF THE RETURN TO EDUCATION

Arguably, the most important effect of different parenting styles is on a child's educational achievement. Since our thesis is that the choice of parenting style hinges on children's economic prospects, we should expect the intensity of parental intervention to increase with the size of the financial stakes. In particular, we expect parents to be less permissive and, especially, more authoritative in countries where the return to education is high. The return to education is related to, but different from, the degree of inequality in a country. If the return to education is high, workers with the highest education earn a lot more than others, which contributes to inequality. At the same time, there are also other sources of inequality (such as the initial distribution of wealth) that have a less direct effect on parenting. Hence, by looking at the return to education rather than just general inequality, we may be able to focus more sharply on the incentives that underlie parenting.

Unfortunately, comparing returns to education across countries is more complicated than one might imagine. The standard ways economists calculate returns to education are by either comparing the earnings of college-educated workers to those with less education, or, alternatively, by looking at the effect of one additional year of education on earnings. However, both of these measures have limitations if one wants to capture differences in economic stakes across countries. In some countries (e.g., Switzerland), vocational training is important. There is sizeable inequality between workers who received different types of vocational training, and admission to different academic tracks is competitive, which is not reflected in the return to the number of years of education. Similarly, in countries such as the United States, there are large earnings premia attached to attending elite colleges relative to low-ranked institutions. The additional gain from being admitted to high-ranked universities is not included in the standard measures of the returns to education, which matters because in other countries (e.g., Germany) differences between universities are much smaller.

Despite these limitations, the cross-country correlation between the return to education and parenting style still lines up well with our theory. We use data on returns to education collected in a recent study by the World Bank.[34] Figure 3.6 shows that in countries where the return to education is higher, parents are more authoritative and authoritarian, while in countries where the return to education is lower, parents are more permissive.[35] Interestingly, the return to education can help explain why in France and Spain so few parents are permissive. As previously noted, this observation was puzzling since neither of these two countries has a very high level of inequality. Here, we see that the returns to edu-

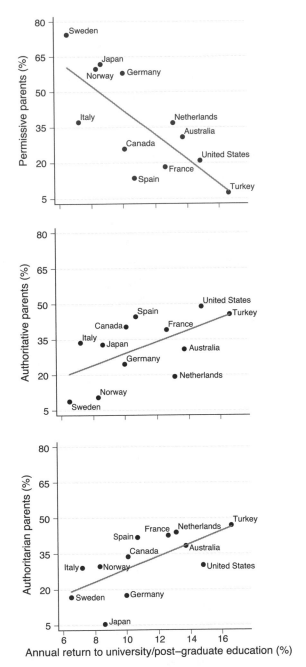

FIGURE 3.6. Return to university and postgraduate education versus percentage of parents adopting each parenting style across OECD countries

cation in France and Spain are among the highest in Europe. The return to education may be among the reasons why French and Spanish parents are pushier than parents in other European countries with lower stakes in education, such as the Scandinavian countries or Italy, a country that shares many cultural similarities with France and Spain.

POLITICAL INSTITUTIONS AND CIVIL LIBERTIES

The factors we have considered so far—inequality, redistribution, and the return to education—all relate to parents' expectations of their children's economic prospects. But aspirations and fears about children's future are not just about money. Consider parents living in a country with repressive institutions where individuals who freely speak their mind are at risk of being attacked or imprisoned without the usual protections of the rule of law. In such a country, parents will be more likely to insist that their children follow conventions and not stand out in any way, which may lead the parents to adopt an authoritarian parenting style. In contrast, in a country where freedom of speech prevails and protections of civil rights are strong, parents will feel encouraged to let children's natural inclinations prevail. In such a country, imagination and independence may be more useful insofar as they foster the development of critical and unconventional thinking that can be a driver of innovation. We would therefore expect permissive parenting to be more widespread.

This discussion suggests that the choice of parenting style should depend not just on economic factors but also on the nature of political institutions, such as the strength of civil rights protections and the quality of the judiciary system. To check whether this is the case, we consider three indicators. The first is an index of human rights and rule of law from the Quality of Government Institute at the University of Gothenburg. The index includes measures related to press freedom, civil liberties, political freedoms, human trafficking, political prisoners, incarceration, religious persecution, torture, and executions. As expected, figure 3.7 shows that countries with better civil rights protections tend to have more permissive and fewer authoritative or authoritarian parents.

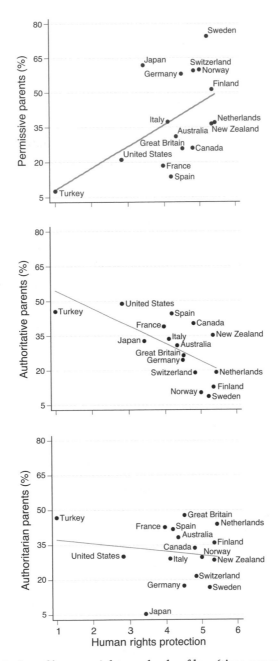

FIGURE 3.7. Index of human rights and rule of law (time average over available observations) and percentage of parents adopting each parenting style across OECD countries

We also consider a measure of corruption from Transparency International, an organization that considers itself independent and politically nonpartisan. The measure ranks countries based on how corrupt their public sector is perceived to be by its citizens.[36] In high-corruption countries, formal institutions are weaker and informal hierarchies can be more important than merit. In such societies, critical and independent thinking may get people into trouble rather than make them thrive. In the ranking, the Scandinavian countries, New Zealand, and Switzerland score highest—in other words, are the countries perceived to be least corrupt. Italy and Turkey are by far the most corrupt countries in our sample (sad, but plausible according to one of the authors of this book). We find that low corruption is strongly positively associated with a permissive parenting style, and negatively associated with an authoritative and (somewhat more weakly) authoritarian parenting style.[37]

Finally, we consider a measure of rule of law from the World Bank (Worldwide Governance Indicators), which combines the views of businesses, citizens, and expert survey respondents. The measure captures perceptions of the extent to which people have confidence in and abide by the rules of society. In particular, it focuses on the quality of contract enforcement, property rights, the police, and the courts, as well as the likelihood of crime and violence. A higher number means a better rule of law. In line with the other measures of institutions, we find that countries with stronger rule of law tend to have more permissive and fewer authoritative or authoritarian parents.

As emphasized before, one should not interpret these cross-country correlations as causal effects. First, the same factors that make citizens support a stronger defense of civil liberty may drive a taste for permissive parenting styles. Second, the three measures of institutional quality discussed in this section are highly correlated with each other. Scandinavian countries have low corruption, strong rule of law, and strong protection of individual liberties, for instance. Nevertheless, these observations are powerful indications that institutions are associated with parenting style according to the patterns predicted by the economic theory of incentives.

TAKING STOCK: WHY THERE ARE DIFFERENT PARENTING STYLES IN THE WORLD

In the previous chapter, we linked the rise of helicopter and tiger parents to the rise in economic inequality that has occurred in advanced economies in recent decades. We argued that when inequality is high, parents have a stronger incentive to push their children toward high achievement in education. Consistent with this interpretation, we were able to show that more intensive parenting is associated with higher test scores and higher educational attainment of children.

In this chapter, we turned to the bigger challenge of explaining differences in parenting styles across countries. Why is it that American, Swedish, or Chinese parents raise their children in distinct ways? Here the conventional wisdom used to be that deeply rooted cultural differences play a key role. In contrast, we find once again that economic incentives can explain much of what we observe.

We started by showing statistical evidence from the WVS on which values parents from different countries consider most important in raising children. As in our discussion of the rise of helicopter parenting, inequality turns out to matter a lot: in unequal countries, parents tend to stress the virtue of hard work over imagination and independence. We also took a closer look at what matters for parenting choices in a set of specific countries. Here we find at least some role for cultural factors, such as the antipermissive tendency of parents in Catholic France and Spain and the great importance that Japanese culture attaches to independence. Nevertheless, the general pattern fits with our economic theory: high inequality and a high return to education foster an intensive parenting style.

We then expanded our analysis of the WVS data by assigning each respondent to either the authoritarian, authoritative, or permissive parenting style (based on their parenting values) and using additional individual-level data. We find that our conclusions are confirmed even after holding constant social and demographic characteristics such as the education of the parents. In addition, the predictions of our theory also hold up when we focus on the effect of changes in income inequality within each country, instead of on the differences in inequality levels across countries. As inequality grows, parents turn more authoritative and less permissive. This observation provides additional evidence against the conventional wisdom that cross-country patterns simply reflect cultural differences. For instance, one might think that Scandinavians live in a more homogenous society, and this induces more cooperation and less inequality, on the one hand, and a more relaxed parenting style, on the other. If this was the whole story, we should see no systematic pattern in the change in parenting over time within each country. Instead, we see that changes in inequality over time are reflected in changes in the intensity of parenting.

We also consider a number of additional variables that should matter for the incentive to engage in intensive parenting. Returns to education affect the choice of parenting style in the direction predicted by our theory: higher returns to education make parents less permissive. Similarly, everything else (including pretax inequality) being equal, parents are more relaxed (i.e., permissive) in countries with more progressive taxation and more generous safety nets. Other than economic factors, the quality of institutions is also important. In countries with strong protections for civil liberties, low levels of corruption, and an independent and efficient judicial system, parents know that their children are better protected, and hence they are able to relax and be more permissive.

We emphasize once again that we entertain no value judgment. Hard work may be valuable for economic growth. However, high stakes in education and intensive parenting styles may well have undesirable effects on society by limiting spontaneity, creativeness, and overall child welfare. Interestingly, Switzerland and Sweden, two countries with strong institutions and civil rights protections where the permissive parenting style is popular, top the 2016 Global Innovation Index.[38]

All of these observations are consistent with the general thesis of this book that when it comes to parenting, incentives matter big time.

CHAPTER FOUR

Inequality, Parenting Style, and Parenting Traps

Parenting styles differ not just across, but also within countries. The parenting choices of the rich differ systematically from those of the poor; for example, psychologists have long noted that authoritarian parenting is more prevalent in families with low income.[1] Other socioeconomic characteristics such as education, ethnic background, and even political views are also related to parenting. Economic analysis can help explain why different parents in the same country choose different parenting styles and what this might imply for income inequality and social mobility in the future.

The impact of socioeconomic factors on parenting has become an increasingly pressing issue recently, due to the large increase in inequality, especially in the United States, which we noted in the previous chapter. This inequality is particularly stark in the major metropolises such as New York, Los Angeles, Chicago, Miami, and Washington, DC, where poverty and conspicuous wealth exist in close proximity. Big cities have always been characterized by great diversity, but income inequality has shot up in recent years. Today, Manhattan is the most unequal county of significant size in the United States, with a level of internal income inequality comparable to the five most unequal countries in the world.[2] As recently as 1980, Manhattan was only the seventeenth most unequal county in the United States.

Increasing inequality goes together with a waning middle class and increasing residential segregation. A study by the social scientists George Galster, Jackie Cutsinger, and Jason Booza based on census data for the one hundred largest metropolitan areas finds that "only 23% of central-city neighborhoods in the 12 large metropolitan areas had a middle-income profile in 2000, down from 45% in 1970. A majority of families (52%) and neighborhoods (60%) in these cities had low or very low incomes relative to their metropolitan area median in 2000."[3] The study also documents an increase in segregation between 1970 and 2000, which means it is becoming less and less common to find low-income families living in high-income neighborhoods, or high-income families living in low-income neighborhoods. A mere 37 percent of lower-income families lived in middle-income neighborhoods in 2000, down from 55 percent in 1970.

In times of rising inequality and segregation, the poor may be left behind not just in terms of income and employment but also in terms of parenting. That is, whereas upper- and middle-class parents respond to increasing inequality and higher returns to education with more intensive parenting, the ability of disadvantaged groups to undertake the same investments may be deteriorating. Indeed, we show in this chapter that there are substantial differences in the parenting choices of parents from different social classes, and that these differences have been widening during the recent phase of rising economic inequality. The increase in the parenting gap further exacerbates inequality and creates a persistent barrier against social mobility.

Our argument here complements Robert Putnam's analysis in his book *Our Kids: The American Dream in Crisis*.[4] As we do, Putnam draws on personal experience. Taking his high school class of 1959 in Port Clinton, Ohio, as an example, Putnam shows that there was a limited social divide at the time. Children from different social backgrounds did not have identical opportunities, but the differences were not huge. Most families were stable, schools were relatively similar, and children lived in socially mixed neighborhoods. Most of the students from his high school class enjoyed better lives as adults than their parents did. Children from today's generation, by contrast, face very different conditions. Privileged families work hard to give their children a leg up in society and segregate themselves in upper-middle-class neighborhoods with good schools, while poor children suffer diminishing opportunities.

Our analysis in this chapter puts the spotlight on the constraints that inequality and poverty place on parenting. In the preceding chapters, we have argued that the recent growth in the popularity of intensive parenting strategies is primarily due to a change in the perceived returns to intensive parenting, and thus is ultimately related to the parents' objectives. When we compare parenting strategies across social classes, these objectives are broadly similar. In line with this finding, the trend toward more intensive parenting can be observed across the social spectrum, just more strongly so in the more advantaged classes. However, the constraints that parents face vary a lot with their income and education.

Some of these constraints are of a financial nature. Certain aspects of intensive parenting are expensive, such as high-quality childcare, music, sports, and enrichment classes, or private tutoring to prepare kids for college entrance exams. A straightforward effect of rising inequality is that it exacerbates the gap in resources available to households from the bottom and the top of the income distribution, making intensive parenting relatively cheap for the wealthy and unaffordable for others. The booming demand for the educational and recreational services that richer families consume makes the constraints even more binding for the poor, since tuition fees and prices grow in response to higher demand.

An equally relevant constraint is time. Richer parents can pay for services such as housecleaning to leave more time for child-rearing. In addition, parents working for very low wages sometimes hold multiple jobs to make ends meet, at the expense of spending time with their children. Even more importantly, time constraints also depend on whether both parents live with the child: intensive parenting is more easily implemented if the burden of childcare can be shared between two parents. In many countries, single parenthood is much more common among poor people. Therefore, single parenting has become an important determinant of the parenting gap across social groups.

We focus our discussion of inequality in parenting primarily on the United States, where the recent rise in inequality is particularly pronounced. However, similar trends can be observed in other industrialized countries. We start by documenting how parenting differs across social classes in the United States. We then go on to explore the root causes of unequal parenting and the potential role for policy interventions.

FACTS ON THE SOCIOECONOMIC PARENTING GAP

We rely on the NLSY97 data for the United States that we previously used in chapter 2 to understand the effect of parenting styles on educational outcomes. There, we discussed how the parenting style variables in the NLSY97 are constructed from two questions on parents' "supportiveness" and "strictness/demandingness." We follow the usual categorization into permissive, authoritarian, authoritative, and uninvolved (i.e., neglectful) parenting.

The data show that parents with different levels of education differ substantially in the parenting strategies they employ. Table 4.1 breaks down the parenting styles of the mothers and fathers in the dataset by education, where "Up to HS" corresponds to parents who have completed up to twelve years of schooling (i.e., completed high school), and "More than HS" are parents with at least some college education. The table shows that for both mothers and fathers, more-educated parents are less likely to be uninvolved or authoritarian, and more likely to be permissive or authoritative. These differences are larger when we break down education into finer categories. Among mothers with a PhD in the sample, none are uninvolved, and half are authoritative.

The broad parenting styles described in the table give an incomplete picture of socioeconomic differences in parenting. For example, even among generally authoritative parents, some may be more intensively involved and spend much more time on their children than others. One way to quantify such differences in the intensity of parenting is to look at time use, as we did in chapter 2.

Figure 4.1 shows how the time use for parenting has changed for less- (up to high school) and more-educated (more than high school) parents in recent decades. We already noted the upward trend that started in the 1980s, corresponding to the recent popularity of more

TABLE 4.1. Parenting style by education of the parent (NLSY97)

Parent's education	All parents		Mothers		Fathers	
	Up to HS	More than HS	Up to HS	More than HS	Up to HS	More than HS
Uninvolved	18%	11%	16%	11%	19%	11%
Permissive	32%	35%	35%	37%	28%	32%
Authoritarian	18%	15%	14%	13%	21%	18%
Authoritative	33%	39%	34%	39%	31%	39%
	100%	100%	100%	100%	100%	100%

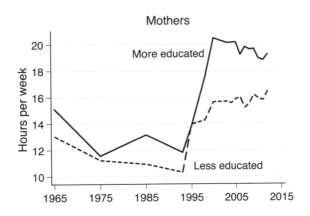

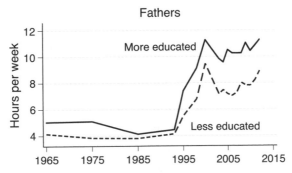

FIGURE 4.1. Time use for child-rearing by mothers and fathers in the United States

intensive parenting styles. Together with this change in the average behavior, we also observe a widening gap between the parenting time of more- and less-educated parents. In recent years, more-educated parents have spent about two hours more per week with their children than their less-educated counterparts. The differences in parenting effort by education level are even more pronounced when we focus on parents who have completed (rather than just started) higher education. Between the years of 2003 and 2006, mothers with a completed college education (bachelor's degree) spent on average four hours more on childcare per week compared to mothers with only a high school education. Mothers with postgraduate education (professional degree or PhD) spent yet another half hour more each week. The sociologist Annette Lareau also documents differences in the quality of time spent with children. While educated upper-middle-class parents engage in time-intensive "concerted cultivation" of their children, parents from humbler backgrounds are often less engaged.[5]

The differences in the time spent on child-rearing do not arise because women with more education are more likely to be homemakers. In fact, the opposite is true: on average, more-educated women both work more hours for pay and spend more time on childcare. Rather than reflecting differences in hours worked in the formal labor market, the higher childcare effort among more-educated mothers is explained by differences in leisure. Women with at least a completed college education enjoy about four hours less leisure per week compared to women with at most a high school education, which lines up with the differences in childcare time. This observation suggests that the gap in childcare time by education level is not simply driven by time constraints, although constraints are clearly important for some subgroups such as low-income single mothers.

The observation of a gap in child-rearing time that corresponds to education level is not restricted to the United States. The economists Jonathan Guryan, Erik Hurst, and Melissa Kearney document that highly educated mothers spend more time on childcare than mothers with less education in fourteen different industrialized countries.[6]

PARENTING AND SOCIAL MOBILITY

Our economic theory of parenting suggests that parents use an intensive parenting style to increase their children's chances of success later in life. One way to measure success and social mobility is to look at children's educational achievement. Table 4.2 breaks down the educational achievement of children (measured by the likelihood of obtaining more than a high school education) by the education of the parents and parenting style, for couples where both parents have the same parenting style.

The table shows that there is strong persistence in education level across generations: regardless of parenting style, the children of more-educated parents have a higher likelihood of being well educated themselves. Nevertheless, parenting style does matter even across parents of equal educational attainment. Parenting style is particularly important for upward mobility, that is, the probability for a child from a home where just one or neither parent is highly educated to end up with higher education. Unsurprisingly, the probability that a child climbs up the educational ladder relative to her parents is the lowest if parents are uninvolved. If both parents have little education, the probability of upward mobility is the highest with authoritative parenting, which increases the probability of success by 13 percentage points relative to uninvolved parenting. Interestingly, children with at least one highly educated parent do as good (and even slightly better) under a permis-

TABLE 4.2. Fraction of children receiving more than a high school education, by education of parent and parenting style, for couples where both parents have same parenting style (NLSY97)

	Neither parent has higher education	One parent has higher education	Both parents have higher education
Uninvolved	36%	52%	79%
Permissive	40%	68%	85%
Authoritarian	43%	62%	78%
Authoritative	49%	67%	84%

sive compared to an authoritative parenting style. This observation points to the possibility that the role model provided by an educated parent and the soft skills that educated parents possess can reduce the need for strict parenting that is a necessary condition for parents to be labeled authoritative by the NLSY97.[7]

The effects of parenting style on upward mobility are substantially larger if upward mobility is defined in terms of the likelihood for a child to move to the top of the education ladder, that is, to obtain a post-graduate degree (such as a degree in law or medicine or a PhD). In households where both parents have at most a high school education, a move from uninvolved to authoritarian parenting increases the likeli-hood that the child will obtain a postgraduate degree by almost a factor of three. In families where one parent has more than a high school edu-cation, a move from uninvolved to authoritative parenting increases the same likelihood by almost a factor of five. Even with authoritative parenting, the probability of a child from such a family receiving a higher degree is only about 10 percent. Still, this result is telling us that intensive parenting is almost a necessary condition for a child with less-educated parents to attain a top-level education.

Taken on its own, the statistical association between intensive par-enting and upward social mobility does not prove that there is a causal relationship between parenting and children's success. In particular, it is possible that children's success depends primarily on some other fac-tor, such as parents' income or wealth, which happens also to be cor-related with parenting style. While this possibility cannot be fully ruled out with our data, it is telling that the association is robust to multiple regression analysis where we control for various factors such as race and ethnicity, the parents' education, household net worth, and house-hold income.[8] This means that if we take, for example, two families with the same household income, one choosing an intensive parenting style and one choosing a nonintensive parenting style, the children of the former family are more likely to climb up the social ladder. The same is true for parents of the same race and education.

It is also interesting to distinguish between the effect of the mother's and the father's parenting style, which do not have to coincide. First, we find that the parenting styles of both parents matter. In a regression that explains the child's educational attainment (years of education, where twelve years corresponds to a high school degree, sixteen years to a college degree, etc.), for both mothers and fathers the authoritative parenting style is associated with the highest educational attainment of the child. Second, moms matter more than do dads. After controlling for other factors, the child of an authoritative mother has about eight months more education compared to a child of an uninvolved mother. For fathers, the advantage of authoritative parenting comes down to only four extra months of education. This likely reflects the persistence of traditional family roles in which mothers play a stronger role in pushing children toward success in education.

Interestingly, authoritarian parenting has opposite effects, depending on the parent: having an authoritarian mom has a positive effect on education (compared to an uninvolved mother), but having an authoritarian dad actually lowers educational attainment.[9] This finding suggests that mothers and fathers may be authoritarian in different ways, with mothers more likely to be strict and demanding about issues related to success in school (such as children doing their homework) and fathers focusing on other dimensions of behavior (such as obeying the parents).

PARENTING STYLE AND UPWARD MOBILITY IN THE UNITED KINGDOM

The United Kingdom provides another particularly interesting example of the effects of socioeconomic inequality on social mobility. Unusually, the United Kingdom has had a fairly stable political system since the Glorious Revolution of 1688 and has been spared revolutions and foreign occupation for centuries. Partly as a result, there has been less social upheaval than in other countries, and the differences between classes continue to have greater relevance than elsewhere.

The data show that, as in the United States, there are substantial differences in parenting choices across socioeconomic classes in the United Kingdom. Recent empirical evidence on variation in parenting across

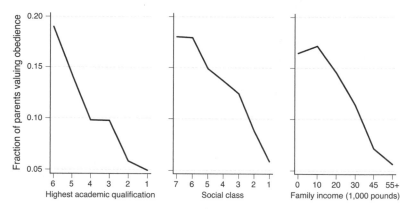

FIGURE 4.2. Fraction of parents in the United Kingdom who consider "obeying parents" to be important for children, by parents' academic qualification, social class, and family income

social classes can be obtained from the Millennium Cohort Study, a survey that tracks the lives of around nineteen thousand children born 2000–2001 throughout their childhood. Figure 4.2 uses this survey to show how the fraction of parents who consider "obedience" an important value in raising children varies across classes.[10] Given that expecting obedience is a defining feature of an authoritarian parenting style, we can interpret the figure as representing the fraction of authoritarian parents across classes. The figure shows that regardless of whether class is defined in terms of education, socioeconomic characteristics (such as blue- vs. white-collar employment), or income, authoritarian parenting is much more prevalent in the lower classes. While the same pattern is observed in the United States (see table 4.1), the class differences are more pronounced in the United Kingdom. For each measure of class, the fraction of authoritarian parents in the lowest class is more than three times as large as in the highest class.

In the US data, we saw that parenting choices have important consequences for social mobility. The same is true in the United Kingdom. We can analyze social mobility using the British Household Panel Survey (BHPS), a data set that provides information comparable to the NLSY97 data for the United States. In this survey, we categorize parents and their (adult) children into seven social classes defined by occupa-

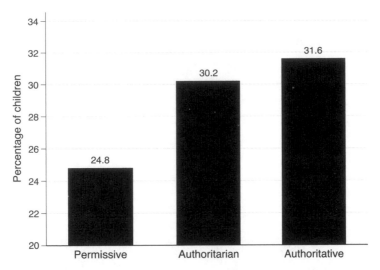

FIGURE 4.3. Share of upwardly mobile children by parenting style in the United Kingdom

tion, ranging from unskilled manual workers to the "higher salariat," which includes managers in large enterprises and upper-level administrators and officials.[11] Now consider the effect of parenting style on upward social mobility, where parenting styles are classified using the methodology proposed by the sociologists Chan and Koo.[12] Figure 4.3 depicts the share of upwardly mobile individuals by parenting style. Upward mobility corresponds to the child ending up in a higher socioeconomic class than the parents.

In the United Kingdom, we find that authoritative parenting is associated with the highest likelihood of upward social mobility. The children of authoritarian parents (the other intensive parenting style) also have a higher likelihood of moving up in the social scale, whereas children of permissive parents are less likely to advance. We can use regression analysis to separate the effect of parenting style from the direct effect of the social class of the parent, which is correlated with both parenting style and social mobility. Here we find, holding fixed the social class of the parent, that authoritarian parenting increases the probability of upward social mobility by 7 percent relative to permissive parenting, and authoritative parenting increases the probability of moving up on the social scale by 13 percent. The effects are even stronger (10% and 14%, respectively) when we look at larger upward movements, where the child is at least two rungs higher on the class scale compared to the parent.[13] An example of such an upward movement would be a family where the parent was a foreman in a factory, and the child became a skilled administrator in government or a big business.

There are both similarities and differences in the analysis of the NLSY97 and BHPS data. The main common result is that in both data sets the authoritative parenting style is conducive to upward social mobility in both education and occupational choice.

SINGLE-PARENT HOUSEHOLDS, MARRIAGE, AND DIVORCE

In the United States, today about one-third of children grow up in single-parent households, and single parenting is particularly pronounced in disadvantaged socioeconomic groups.[14] For example, single parenting is much less common among college-educated mothers compared to high school–educated mothers. For single parents, both financial and time constraints acutely affect their parenting decisions.

Growing up in a single-parent household can imply special challenges, which start with lower resources (due to having the income of only one parent) and continue with greater difficulties in arranging childcare and being able to spend "quality time" with children. These challenges are especially severe for low-income parents, for whom market-based childcare may be unaffordable and who sometimes have to carry multiple jobs to make a living. A single parent who is neither rich enough to afford a lot of childcare services (day care, nannies, etc.) nor has easy access to help from others (such as close family nearby) may simply be unable to be a "helicopter" parent and supervise a child's every move.

Indeed, in the NLSY97 data for the United States, we find that, controlling for age and education, single moms are more likely to be uninvolved or authoritarian and less likely to be authoritative compared to moms who live with the father.

Public institutions that support parents, such as the free public nursery schools in Scandinavian countries, can mitigate the disadvantages of being a single parent. Fabrizio met a number of single parents in Sweden who were doing just fine. However, in countries like the United States where childcare services are offered at market prices, many single parents would have to work long hours just to pay for childcare. For low-income parents, this can be a daunting challenge.

Single-parent households arise when parents either do not marry or choose not to live together in the first place, or when couples separate and divorce. A recent study by three economists from the US Bureau of Labor Statistics, based on an earlier version of the NLSY data (NLSY79), documents a number of facts about the socioeconomic divide in marriage and divorce in the United States.[15] There is substantial variation across education groups, races, and ethnicities. For instance, 19 percent of adults with less than a high school diploma in the NLSY79 cohort (who were born between 1957 and 1964) were never married by age forty-six, while the corresponding percentage of college graduates is 11 percent. The marriage gap between educational groups has increased sharply over time. In the earlier 1950–55 birth cohort, there was no difference at all between more- and less-educated people.[16]

The evidence on the divorce gap is similar. In the cohort born 1957–64, 60 percent of first marriages ended in divorce for those with less than a high school diploma, versus only 30 percent for college graduates. Overall, the probabilities of getting married, staying married, and even of remarrying after a divorce are much higher for adults with more education. Moreover, the gap is larger for the cohort born 1957–64 compared to earlier cohorts. The likelihood of nonmarriage and divorce also varies a lot across races and ethnicities, an issue to which we return in later pages. The rising marriage and divorce gaps between parents of different education levels and socioeconomic backgrounds affect the choice of parenting styles and amplify the inequality in parenting.

Single parenting matters not just because single parents have fewer resources but also because the quality of the relationship between the parents can affect children. There is evidence that children of divorced or separated parents tend to underperform in school relative to children living with two parents.[17] The economist Thomas Piketty has shown that the separation itself need not be the prime cause of the problem.[18] Parents who decide to separate are typically not getting along well to start with. Piketty documents that the school performance of children living with only one of their parents already suffers two years before the separation. In addition, he finds that the large increase in separation rates following a 1975 legal reform in France that made divorce easier increased the number of separations but had no significant impact on the intensity of family conflict. These observations suggest that the turbulence of living in an unsettled family where parents fight frequently is an important determinant of children's poor school performance. Given that they have more stable relationships, highly educated men and women may be better, on average, at establishing harmonious partnerships and handling conflict. This can spill over into parenting style and, ultimately, to the success of children in school.

Among married parents who do raise their children together, it also matters who is married to whom. A general observation about marriage is that spouses tend to be similar to each other in terms of socioeconomic background, a phenomenon that social scientists refer to as "assortative mating." In the United States, people from the major different race and ethnic groups are much more likely to marry a spouse from their own group than someone with a different background. Interracial marriages have become more common over time, but are still the exception: in 2015, 17 percent of newlyweds were married to someone of a different race or ethnicity, compared to only 3 percent in 1967.[19]

Given the recent rise in inequality, how spouses match up in terms of education is also important. For example, if most high school graduates were married to college graduates, a rising college premium would not necessarily increase inequality across families. In reality, however, people tend to marry their like in terms of education as well. This trend has gotten stronger over time, in part in response to the rising level of average education for women. Until a few decades ago, there were many more male than female college graduates. As a result, many men who went to college married someone with less education. In 1980, among married men of ages twenty to sixty with a college degree, 54 percent had a spouse with a lower level of education. By 2007, only 31 percent did.[20] It has become especially hard for the less educated to marry up. A recent study by the economists Lasse Eika, Magne Mogstad, and Basit Zafar finds that "in 1980, [Americans without a high school degree] were three times as likely to be married to one another as compared to the probability of random mating; in 2007, they were six times as likely."[21] Assortative mating by education can amplify the effects of rising inequality on parenting: there is an increasing divide between families with two well-educated parents who enjoy high earnings and stable careers, and others where both mother and father face stagnant wages and uncertain employment prospects.

THE ROLE OF RACE, ETHNICITY, AND NATIONAL ORIGIN

In many countries, an important aspect of socioeconomic inequality is inequality between people from different backgrounds in terms of race, ethnicity, and national origin. The United States is a case in point. According to the US Census Bureau, in 2015 median household income was $77,000 for Asian families, $63,000 for non-Hispanic white families, $45,000 for Hispanic families, and $37,000 for black families. Median income for families with a native-born household head was $57,000, compared to $45,000 for families with heads of household who were not citizens.[22] Gaps in terms of wealth are even larger than income gaps: in 2013, median net worth (the difference between the value of all assets owned, including housing and financial assets, and debt) for non-Hispanic white families was $142,000, compared to only $14,000 for Hispanic families and $11,000 for black families.[23] In part, these differences are related to gaps in educational attainment. In 2015, among the population aged twenty-five and older, 36 percent of non-Hispanic white people held a bachelor's degree or above, compared to 54 percent of Asian, 16 percent of Hispanic, and 23 percent of black people.[24] Given that workers who have completed higher education have substantially higher average earnings, these education gaps contribute to the income gaps between different groups in society. Having high income, in turn, enables households to save more for the future and build wealth. While the income and wealth gaps between these groups were even greater a few decades ago, the progress in closing these gaps has slowed down in recent years.

The disparities in educational outcomes for families from different social backgrounds represented in the national data are readily apparent in Matthias's current hometown of Evanston, Illinois, the home of Northwestern University. Evanston is a suburb of Chicago, located immediately north of the city alongside Lake Michigan. The neighborhoods next to the lake are wealthy, and the average level of education is high. However, unusually for a wealthy American suburb, Evanston is also diverse. A mile inland from the lake, mansions give way to more modest single- and multifamily homes, and there is a sizeable historically black neighborhood. In the 2010 Census, the population of Evanston was 66 percent white, 18 percent black, 9 percent Asian, and 9 percent Hispanic (the sum exceeds 100 percent because the categories are not mutually exclusive), which makes Evanston broadly similar to the United States as a whole (the breakdown for the United States that year was 72 percent white, 13 percent black, 5 percent Asian, and 16 percent Hispanic).

Evanston has well-regarded public schools that are attended by children of all backgrounds. Nevertheless, there are striking variations in educational outcomes across different socioeconomic groups. In fact, a recent study found that in middle school the Evanston public school system has one of the largest achievement gaps between students of different races. White students (who, on average, come from relatively wealthy families) perform almost four grade levels (i.e., years of schooling) above the national average, whereas Hispanic students are at the national average, and black students half a grade behind.[25] These achievement gaps are associated with racial and ethnic differences in parental income and parental education. There are several reasons why the gaps are unusually large in Evanston. First, Evanston is a diverse town with a mix of wealthy and low-income neighborhoods. Such diversity is rare in the United States, where outside of big cities income segregation occurs predominantly between communities—there are "rich" and "poor" towns and suburbs with separate governments and separate schooling systems. A second factor is that Evanston is a university town. The gaps in starting conditions across socioeconomic groups are therefore further amplified through the presence of highly educated university faculty and researchers, groups where minorities continue to be underrepresented. This helps explain why the other cities in the United States with the largest achievement gaps within schools are also university towns, namely Berkeley, California (University of California), and Chapel Hill, North Carolina (University of North Carolina).

The achievement gaps that open up in elementary school persist until students finish high school, at which point these disparities translate into unequal opportunities for further education and careers. Evanston's only public high school is the Evanston Township High School, which has an enrollment of over three thousand students and is regularly ranked among the top high schools in the United States. Of students graduating in 2014, 84 percent went on to attend college. Within the school, however, there are large achievement gaps. The enrollment at the high school reflects Evanston's diversity, with 43 percent white students, 31 percent black students, 17 percent Hispanic students, and 4 percent Asian students.[26] The white and Asian students receive considerably better grades than the other groups, with an average grade point average in 2014 of 3.71 and 3.66 (on a 1–4 scale), respectively, compared to 2.62 for black students and 2.71 for Hispanic students. White and Asian students also take considerably more advanced placement classes, which cover college-level material. There is also a sizeable gap in achievement on the standardized tests that play an important role in applying for college. In 2014, the average ACT score at Evanston Township High School was 27.5 for white students, 17.9 for black students, and 19.5 for Hispanic students (separate results for Asian students are not available). This compares to a national average of 21.0 (out of a maximum of 36) for all students.

The large gaps in scholastic achievement observed in Evanston and more broadly in the United States are concerning; an important step toward reducing differences in income and wealth across racial and ethnic lines would be to provide the best possible education to children, regardless of background. To understand how these differences could be addressed, it is important to know their roots. The largest part of the differences across the aforementioned groups of children can be linked to socioeconomic differences in the adults who look after them, such as gaps in income, wealth, and education. Indeed, it is in towns such as Evanston where these gaps are especially large.

In Evanston, the income per capita of the non-Hispanic white population in 2014 was $53,492, which compares to $24,296 for the black and only $17,939 for the Hispanic populations.[27] Disparities in educational attainment are equally stark, with 79 percent of the white adult population having at least a bachelor's degree, compared to 29 percent for the black, 33 percent for the Hispanic, and 92 percent for the Asian populations. Still, the fact that different outcomes for children correlate with other measures of inequality does not provide a final answer: it is also important to find out exactly why socioeconomic inequality affects children.

One of the dimensions of inequality across racial and ethnic lines is parenting style. In the United States, the data from the NLSY97 show that Asian parents are the most authoritarian (22 percent of Asian mothers are authoritarian, compared to 11 percent of white moms), white parents are the most permissive, and black parents are more authoritarian than Hispanic or white parents. Some patterns differ for mothers and fathers; for example, black mothers are less likely to be uninvolved compared to white or Hispanic mothers, but, for black fathers, it is the other way around. Given the correlation of parenting style with children's success, these differences could explain some of the variation of outcomes for children across groups. Yet the differences in parenting styles across racial groups are small overall and certainly insufficient to explain the large outcome gaps. Moreover, the effect of parenting style may not be uniform across groups. For example, Asian parents are more likely to be authoritarian, a parenting style generally associated with poor outcomes, yet Asian kids often do well, as discussed in chapter 2.

MARRIAGE MARKET AND GENDER IMBALANCE

We mentioned the importance of single parenting as a constraint on the choice of parenting style. The prevalence of single parenting varies not only across education groups but also across racial lines. In 2014, 66 percent of black children (under the age of eighteen) lived with a single parent, compared to 42 percent of Hispanic children, 25 percent of non-Hispanic white children, and only 17 percent of Asian children.[28] These are large differences that can potentially play an important role in accounting for achievement gaps. While there are many reasons for the incidence of single motherhood and the corresponding low marriage rates in some minority groups, poverty is one important factor. Marriage and committed relationships are easier to maintain when the spouses are economically secure. Lack of economic opportunities and high unemployment make this a bigger challenge for minorities.

When it comes to what economists call the *marriage market,* another issue that is especially important for racial minorities is gender imbalance. One factor that favors high marriage rates is a roughly equal "supply" of eligible women and men in the marriage market. Yet, especially in the most disadvantaged urban areas, the balance between the genders is already off because of historically high incarceration rates for young black men. In 2009, 4.7 percent of black males were in prison, compared to 0.7 percent of white males.[29] What is more, many of the men in prison are young and hence at an age where they would usually marry. For black men ages 25–29, the incarceration rate in 2009 was 11 percent overall, and 32.2 percent for those with less than a high school education.[30]

The challenges do not end here. We discussed previously the phenomenon of rising assortative mating, that is, the tendency of well-educated and high-earning spouses to marry each other. A young black woman wishing to give the best opportunities to her children would benefit from attending college herself, while also marrying a spouse who is a fellow university graduate. The challenge for such a woman is that in addition to the overall imbalance in the marriage market, there is also a gender education gap. On average, today women of all races outclass men in terms of educational achievements, but the gap is particularly large for some minorities. In 2012, 69 percent of black women graduating from high school were enrolled in college the following October, whereas the same was true for only 57 percent of black men, giving rise to a gap of 12 percent. The gap was even larger for Latinos. In contrast, it is significantly smaller for white and smallest for Asian graduates, where the gap was only 3 percent.[31]

The college-attendance gap also becomes larger as we consider schools that target less economically advantaged groups of students. Consider the Chicago area as an example. Northwestern University, the school where Matthias works, is a highly selective private university that is regularly ranked among America's top colleges. The cost of attendance is high, with a tuition rate above $50,000 and a total cost of attendance in excess of $65,000 per year (although need-based scholarships are available). The college also displays almost perfect gender balance; in 2015, 1,978 men and 1,993 women were enrolled for undergraduate studies, so that women made up 50.2 percent of the student population.[32] The numbers suggest that the admissions office may be conscious of the role of college as a dating market, and thus aims to provide almost perfect gender balance. The same is true for most other elite undergraduate institutions in the United States; the overall gender imbalance in college enrollment would not be apparent to students attending an elite college.

Located a few miles south of Northwestern University in central Chicago, DePaul University is a large Catholic university with a total undergraduate enrollment of 16,707 students. DePaul is a private institution and the cost of attendance is lower compared to Northwestern, with a tuition rate of $37,000 for students entering in 2016 and a total cost of attendance in excess of $50,000.[33] Compared to Northwestern, the student population at DePaul is more representative of US colleges as a whole. Of the first-year students admitted in 2015, 56 percent were women and 44 percent were men, or roughly five women for every four men.[34] Of course, there are places other than one's college to meet potential dates or spouses, and many college students marry long after graduation. Still, we would expect such a sizeable mismatch to have a noticeable impact on the dating and, ultimately, marriage market opportunities on campus.

Moving further south, Chicago State University is a public college serving primarily the economically disadvantaged South Side of Chicago. Chicago State is substantially more affordable, with a tuition rate in 2015 of $8,800 and a total cost of attendance (including housing) of just above $20,000 per year.[35] Many of the students served by Chicago State are eligible for federal financial aid. Chicago State also primarily serves minority students, with black students alone making up 83 percent of the student body in 2012. The gender imbalance in enrollment is much more pronounced than at Northwestern or DePaul. In 2012, women at Chicago State made up 72 percent of undergraduates, implying that there are more than 2.5 women for every man.[36]

When many more women than men receive higher education, it is inevitable that some of them will be unable to find an equally educated long-term partner. The former "first family" of Barack and Michelle Obama and their daughters (one of whom is now attending Harvard University) has shown what is possible in America. Michelle Obama grew up on Chicago's South Side, neither of her parents went to college, and she was educated in Chicago's public schools. From this start, she went on to attend Princeton University and Harvard University and worked for a major law firm before meeting Barack Obama. Without doubt, she is a role model who offers inspiration to many young women growing up in similar circumstances today. Yet unless the gap in educational attainment between black women and men starts to shrink (or rates of interracial marriage increase substantially), the odds for black women of ultimately marrying and raising children with an equally educated man will be lower compared to white and Asian women who, on average, already benefit from other advantages such as higher family income.

Of course, unlike in an earlier era, making a "successful match" is far from the only or even the main purpose of education today.[37] Still, when it comes to parenting and committed relationships between mothers and fathers, the capabilities and aspirations of one's partner matter, implying that the gender imbalance in education adds to the challenges faced by women from a minority background today.

THE PARENTING GAP AND PERSISTENT POVERTY

Economists refer to *poverty traps* to describe situations where poverty is both the cause and the effect of a persistent bad outcome from which an individual or a society cannot break free. For instance, a country may need investments in physical and human capital to develop. But if the people are so poor that they must consume most of their income to satisfy their basic survival needs, saving and investment will be low and poverty will persist. Another example is a poor homeless person who cannot find employment without a home address because potential employers are suspicious of her or his homelessness. However, a jobless person cannot afford to pay rent. In both examples, poverty leads to poverty.

The facts documented in this chapter show that in addition to inequality in income, wealth, and education, there is also a growing "parenting gap" between different groups in the population. Under some circumstances, such a gap can become a link in a chain going from prosperity to prosperity for some families, but from poverty to poverty for others. In other words, the parenting gap can be the source of a "parenting trap." More intensive, achievement-oriented parenting practices have by now become the norm among groups that are already advantaged in other ways. For example, highly educated parents are more likely to raise their children together, to spend more time on childcare, and to engage in parenting styles that are conducive to their children retaining or improving their position on the social ladder. Conversely, parents in already disadvantaged families face more and more binding constraints that prevent them from engaging in the same achievement-oriented practices. The parenting gap therefore adds to the challenges faced by children from less advantaged backgrounds and can be a hindrance to social mobility in the population.

The time-use data we discussed previously indeed provide evidence of a widening gap between the parental investments of more- and less-educated parents. Figure 4.1 shows that over the past few decades all

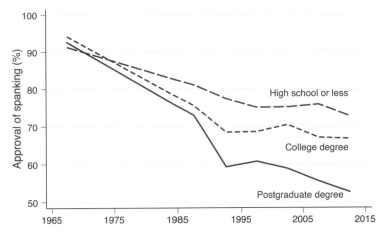

FIGURE 4.4. Approval of use of corporal punishment in the United States by education (percent of adult population)

parents have increased their investment in parenting, but the increase is larger for more-educated parents, suggesting that the parenting gap has gone up.

Other measures of parenting and parental attitudes point in the same direction. The rise in inequality and the return to education that occurred in recent decades has been accompanied by a higher prevalence of parenting styles that are conducive to children acquiring education, in particular, authoritative parenting. In contrast, there has been a decline in more "old-fashioned" methods such as strict authoritarian parenting, which, among other features, is characterized by the regular use of corporal punishment.

Figure 4.4 shows how attitudes toward corporal punishment have evolved over time in the United States for different educational groups in the population.[38] The figure displays the fraction of adults in each group who approve of the use of spanking for disciplining children. In the 1960s, approval of spanking was near universal in the population, and there was little difference in the attitudes of adults of different education levels. Since the 1970s, the approval of spanking has declined substantially, in line with the decline in the popularity of authoritarian parenting. This is a theme to which we return in greater detail in chapter

5, where we discuss international evidence on this point. What interests us here is the growing divide in the approval of spanking between different educational groups. The decline in approval is dramatic among the most highly educated adults (those with postgraduate degrees). Among adults who had attained up to a high school education (i.e., the "Less Educated" in fig. 4.4), the decline in the approval of spanking is only about half of what we observe for the most-educated group. Assuming that the approval of spanking mirrors its use, we see once again a growing gap in parenting practices within the population.

FROM PARENTING GAP TO PARENTING TRAP?

To the extent that the widening parenting gap we document magnifies the differences in opportunities for children from different socioeconomic backgrounds, the possibility of a parenting trap is very real. To understand whether the parenting gap can turn into a trap, a particularly important question must be addressed: How do socioeconomic differences in parenting respond to changes in the economic environment? In particular, if inequality increases (as it has in the United States and many other countries in recent decades), does the parenting gap also grow wider? If yes, this reveals the possibility of a self-reinforcing mechanism that propagates high inequality and persistent poverty. For example, if the parenting gap increases in response to higher inequality, the spread between the average educational attainments of children from the two ends of the social spectrum will also increase. This would lower social mobility and propagate high inequality in the next generation.

To assess the risk of a parenting trap, we need to consider the potential root causes of the parenting gap and then ask what will happen if inequality goes up. Our theory of incentives suggests that there are two classes of explanations for differences in parenting across families in a given society. One possibility is that socioeconomic differences in parenting are primarily driven by the aspirations and expectations that parents from different backgrounds have for their children's future lives. According to this explanation, parents rationally foresee that their children will take different paths and adjust their parenting accordingly.

The sociologists Melvin Kohn and Carmi Schooler proposed a theory of this kind. They conjectured that working-class jobs are often monotonous, and thus a "questioning mind" can only be a hindrance in such an occupation.[39] Hence, parents who expect their children to join the working class may have a lesser incentive to use a parenting style that emphasizes reasoning and discussion, namely, authoritative parenting, and instead revert to the authoritarian approach of unquestioned authority.

Today, this specific idea may appear somewhat outdated. The few remaining jobs in the manufacturing sector are less likely to be routine jobs, as throughout the (post)industrial economy the most repetitive jobs have either been taken over by machines or computers, or have been outsourced to other countries. Nevertheless, the theory may still be relevant, partly because many routine jobs continue to exist in the service sector. As table 4.2 shows, children of parents with relatively little education are less likely to become highly educated themselves, even when the parents choose a parenting style conducive to educational attainment. Part of this may be due to the higher average income of more-educated parents, inheritability of skills, and the transmission of human capital, knowledge, and noncognitive skills such as diligence and patience within the family. Either way, less-educated parents may rationally anticipate that parenting investments that are geared toward children's educational excellence are less likely to pay off for them compared to more-educated parents. Hence, such parents may rationally choose to invest less in parenting, or to invest in a different way.

The second possibility for explaining the parenting gap is that the difference is not in objectives or expectations, but in the constraints that parents face. One such constraint is that parents from different economic backgrounds may have different capabilities in terms of implementing each parenting style.[40] A working-class parent who grew up with authoritarian parents may be less familiar with the concept of authoritative parenting. Molding children's preferences or attitudes, a key ingredient of authoritative parenting, may require soft skills that more-educated parents are more likely to possess. As previously discussed in this chapter, other differences in constraints concern the availability of money and time. Some aspects of intensive middle- and upper-class parenting, such as expensive extracurricular activities, may simply be unaffordable for parents with fewer means. Moreover, parents who struggle economically may be forced to work long hours or to work multiple jobs, leaving less time for parenting.

Yet another facet of inequality goes beyond the family and concerns the wider environment in which children grow up. Education researchers have long recognized the importance of peers: children learn a lot from each other, and ambitious children are likely to do well (say, in terms of education) if they are surrounded by other children with whom they share similar aims and objectives. If parents' investments and the influence of peers mutually reinforce each other, parents whose kids are surrounded by strong peers have an incentive to step up their own parenting effort.[41] Residential segregation implies that children from richer families tend to grow up in neighborhoods with relatively more well-off, highly educated authoritative parents. Equally important is the exposure to positive and negative role models.[42] Residential segregation reduces the probability that disadvantaged children will interact with adults from other social backgrounds who can offer role models different from those observed inside the family.

With these potential explanations for the parenting gap at hand, we can now consider how parents are likely to react to changes in the economic environment, and particularly to an increase in inequality as observed in recent decades. Consider the impact of a rise in both inequality and the return to education on the objectives of parenting, that is, the hopes and aspirations that parents have for their children. In terms of their objectives, the increase in inequality raises the stakes in parenting: parents will be more concerned about their children's position on the social ladder and hence have an incentive to invest more. This can explain why the rise in economic inequality has been accompanied by more intensive parenting overall. Regarding the parenting gap, the question is whether objectives have changed in the same way for parents at different positions on the socioeconomic ladder.

In principle, a rise in inequality raises the stakes for everyone no matter what the background of the parent, so changing objectives do not necessarily imply that the gap in parenting across socioeconomic groups will increase. However, different parents may have different perceptions of the extent to which they can influence their children's outcomes. Rising inequality may spur on parents who think that their children can do well if pushed, but are likely to fail if left to their own devices. By contrast, we can also imagine a parent at the top of the socioeconomic ladder who is confident that their children will do well no matter what they do; for such a parent, a rise in inequality does not change the stakes in parenting. Similarly, if a parent at the bottom of the ladder feels the cards are stacked against her children to such an extent that they will fail to succeed no matter what the parent does, there is little incentive for her to put much effort into parenting. She may then just give up, even if inequality continues to increase. The impact of economic changes is likely to be larger in the middle of the spectrum, where the parents perceive that a wide range of outcomes are possible for their children, and their actions as parents truly matter.

Overall, then, a rise in inequality raises the stakes of parenting, but it does so to different degrees at the different rungs of the socioeconomic ladder. The effect is likely to be largest for midranking groups and smallest for those at the extremes of the distribution who feel that their children's paths are set, regardless of their actions.

Let us now turn to the constraints. As far as money and financial constraints are concerned, increasing inequality clearly widens the parenting gap. By definition, higher inequality and rising returns to education imply that the incomes of those at the bottom of the socioeconomic scale decline relative to those at the top. To make things worse, the increased demand from the wealthier class increases the price of high-quality educational services, cutting off an even larger proportion of low-income families. Rising inequality in terms of income and wealth also translates into rising inequality in terms of time. Low-income parents cannot afford to pay for babysitting, day care centers, and other services that replace their own time, leaving less time and less flexibility for dealing with both work and parenting. For low-income parents, the rise in inequality, even if it provides additional motivation for intensive parenting, may make their aims seem increasingly out of reach.

The differences between more- and less-educated families are magnified by the growing involvement of parents in their children's schooling. Educated parents can help their children do their math and science homework, and assist them in the execution of school-related research projects. Helping with preparing applications to elite schools (such as essay writing) is another area where more-educated parents can be effective, while others may feel helpless.

We have also touched on the growing marriage gap between the rich and the poor. While well-off and highly educated individuals are increasingly likely to be married to someone in the same group and to raise children together, those with lower income and less education are less likely to be married, more likely to divorce, and more likely to raise their children alone. This is unlikely to change in the near future. Even today, marriage is in part about economic security. Men and women with little education face low earnings and a high risk of unemployment, making them less attractive as potential spouses. Rising inequality also feeds back to the marriage market, emphasizing the handicap of disadvantaged groups. If, as we argue, rising inequality raises the stakes in parenting, it also raises the stakes in finding a partner who will make a good parent. The most-educated individuals will try to pair up with partners who are highly educated themselves, increasing the assortativity of the mating process.[43] In plain words, poor people find it harder and harder to climb up the social ladder through marrying up. This, in turn, further increases the gap between the opportunities of children from the two ends of the socioeconomic spectrum.

Finally, we have discussed the evidence of increasing residential segregation in cities. This means that children from rich and highly educated families tend to interact more and more with children from the same background, most of whom are exposed to ambitious authoritative parents. Peer effects reinforce the direct effect of parents. The children of poorer families are instead increasingly cut off from this virtuous loop. Residential segregation also has a negative effect on social mobility through marriage: young men and women from the lower ranks of society are simply less and less likely to bump into a wealthy Prince (or Princess) Charming.

The upshot of this discussion is that rising inequality will likely further exacerbate the parenting gap in society. In turn, the parenting gap will generate more inequality. This raises the uncomfortable prospect of an ever-growing gap in opportunities between children of subsequent generations. The parenting gap turns into a parenting trap.

POLICIES TO ESCAPE THE PARENTING TRAP

Even though the mechanisms described in this chapter all contribute to the risk of a parenting trap, this outcome is not inevitable. The parenting gap and the possibility of a parenting trap can be curtailed by policy interventions. As usual, "there ain't no such thing as a free lunch," and it is ultimately up to voters and governments to decide how much should be done to curtail rising inequality and preserve the cohesion and inclusiveness of society. Social science research can provide guidance on which policies are likely to be effective in addressing these challenges.

There are two types of policies that could help. One class of policy interventions would address the underlying inequality that is at the root of the parenting gap. Given that differences in parenting across socioeconomic groups are primarily due to the constraints that parents face, interventions that relax constraints for less-advantaged families should also reduce the parenting gap. The second class of policy interventions would specifically focus on supporting disadvantaged children.

The first class of interventions comprises traditional fiscal and social policies such as progressive taxation and general transfers aimed at reducing after-tax inequality. If rising inequality widens the parenting gap, redistributive macroeconomic policies could be expanded to create a counteracting force. We saw in chapter 3 that redistributive fiscal policies affect parenting, namely, they reduce the need for intensive parenting and thereby contribute to shrinking the parenting gap. For the specific purpose of addressing the socioeconomic differences in parenting, policies could be targeted toward families with young children. In fact, most industrial countries already have policies in place that reflect the desire to decrease inequality in opportunities for children, for example, through programs that provide income support to families with young children or provide targeted help in areas such as health insurance.

Another important policy area is public provision of or subsidies to nursery schools. An improved availability of childcare provides incentives for poor parents (especially, single mothers) to enter the labor force, while offering children of different socioeconomic backgrounds the opportunity to spend time together. In an increasingly segregated society, the exposure of children to a socially diverse environment may be a powerful tool to curtail the parenting gap. While the idea of free or highly subsidized nursery schools financed by general taxation may sound far-fetched to some readers, it is precisely the recipe that Scandinavian and other European countries have adopted for years. Even though such policies are costly, there is value in children interacting with children of different socioeconomic backgrounds: Fabrizio and Maria found the experience of Nora in a Swedish public nursery school to be much more formative than any elite preparatory school in Great Britain would have been.

The second set of policies focuses on the education of disadvantaged groups. Research conducted by the Nobel laureate James Heckman in cooperation with a team of coauthors has documented the crucial importance of the skills acquired by children in the very first years of life.[44] There is by now a large body of research documenting the efficacy of specific Early Childhood Intervention (ECI) programs targeting disadvantaged families. Interventions such as subsidized provision of high-quality, center-based childcare and in-home support for parents have proven highly effective. Interventions that aim to provide better information and awareness about child development to parents can also be important.[45] The benefits of ECI programs extend not just to future educational attainment and labor earnings but also to health and marriage market outcomes. In addition, these policies have been shown to lower children's future propensity to commit crimes and to become dependent on welfare policy.

One of the best-known ECI programs is the Perry Preschool Project, which provided high-quality preschool education to African American children living in poverty during the years 1962 to 1967. The cost of the program was about $11,000 per child per school year (in 2007 dollars). The Perry Preschool Project was a randomized control trial, meaning that the treatment (i.e., preschool education) was provided only to a subgroup of children, selected through random assignment. This feature has allowed researchers to compare the future lives of children assigned to the program to the outcomes of children with equivalent characteristics who were not selected. In a joint study with the economists Rodrigo Pinto and Peter Savelyev, Heckman documents that the program resulted in a 65 percent reduction in lifetime violent crime, a 40 percent reduction in lifetime arrests, and a 20 percent reduction in unemployment.[46] Other ECIs yield similar results. For instance, the economists Eliana Garces, Duncan Thomas, and Janet Currie study the effects of the Head Start program, which was a public preschool program for disadvantaged children serving more than 800,000 children.[47] They found that participation in Head Start led to improved educational outcomes and reduced crime.[48]

The mechanisms through which these programs work are also interesting. The primary channel is not an improvement in the academic (or cognitive) skills of the kind that can be measured by IQ tests. Children from families that receive help through ECI programs do make some progress on IQ scores, but the gains are small and tend to fade away over time. Rather, the main mechanism through which ECI programs achieve results is by improving what economists call noncognitive skills. These skills comprise attitudes and behaviors that make people succeed in social interactions in both school and the workplace, such as motivation, patience, perseverance, self-control, and the capacity to evaluate the consequences of today's action on future outcomes. Several studies show that such skills are crucial for success in life, more so than cognitive skills measured by IQ tests.[49]

Such ECI programs help build noncognitive skills in two different ways. On the one hand, disadvantaged children benefit from exposure to qualified teachers, better role models, or smaller class groups. On the other hand, the programs affect parents' investments and parenting style. The impact of ECIs on parents' investments hinges on the details of the programs. For instance, some ECIs aim to reduce welfare dependency by providing incentives for parents to work, under the expectation that working parents will have access to more financial resources to provide for their children's needs. A potential downside of this approach is that when parents work more, they may have less time to interact with their children. The economists Francesco Agostinelli and Giuseppe Sorrenti study the effect of the Earned Income Tax Credit (EITC) in the United States, which is a program that gives income support to parents, conditional on employment.[50] Indeed, they find that for low-income families who cannot access high-quality childcare services (because they are unavailable or too expensive), the program has a negative effect on child development because children end up interacting less with their parents. In contrast, the net effect of the EITC is positive if parents have sufficiently high wages, both because of the direct effect of higher earnings and because these families are more able to afford replacing their own child-rearing time with market services. These findings suggest that while ECIs can be effective in reducing the parenting gap, they must be designed carefully and take into account both direct effects on children and indirect effects through parents' behavior.

An additional class of policies that may contribute to lowering the parenting gap concerns the organization of the education system. Children today spend much of their childhood in school, and what happens there matters a great deal for socioeconomic differences in parenting. We will discuss this issue in detail in chapter 9.

How costly are these policy interventions? Many of the policies we have discussed are less expensive than one might expect. Subsidizing day care reduces the burden of other welfare policies and generates tax revenue by increasing labor participation. Intervention programs for disadvantaged families reduce crime and hence lower the need to spend money on police and on building prisons. The long-run benefits of increasing social cohesion are harder to quantify but may well be substantial. In short, in addition to moving societies closer to the ideal of equal opportunity for all, policies that reduce the parenting gap have a higher rate of return than is apparent at first sight.

PART TWO

Raising Kids
throughout History

CHAPTER FIVE

From Stick to Carrot

The Demise of Authoritarian Parenting

"Spare the rod, spoil the child." This old adage summarizes what was viewed for centuries as the natural approach to child-rearing. Corporal punishment came in various forms and guises, be it "spanking," "slapping," "smacking," "paddling," "belting," or "birching," and was once routinely practiced both at home and in school. In contrast, nowadays condemnation of corporal punishment is nearly universal. On his web page, William Sears, a pediatrician and author of a number of popular parenting books, provides ten reasons not to hit one's children. The list starts with the story of a mother who used to spank her preschool daughter, until she saw her hitting her little brother. "When confronted, her daughter said, 'I'm just playing mommy.' This mother never spanked another child."[1] Sears continues by asserting that spanking creates emotional distance between parents and children, is linked to child abuse, and simply does not work to modify children's behavior.

Attitudes toward corporal punishment have radically changed in just a couple of generations. We have never hit our own children as a matter of principle, yet during our own childhood, occasional slaps were still widely accepted. One generation back it was much worse. Matthias's parents report how teachers routinely beat children in the 1950s. Fabrizio's father was subject to physical disciplining and humiliation by his school teachers even for minor misdemeanors. This would be unthinkable (and indeed criminal) today.

Going back even further in time, parents saw nothing wrong with corporal punishment, and adopted a firm-handed approach as recommended by the experts of the day. Parents from all social classes regarded asserting their authority as an essential part of their parental duty. The notion that one should convince children that what adults say is right would have sounded strange if not bizarre to our grandparents. Their view was that children are just children: too young to understand, but as soon as they grow up, they will be grateful to their parents for their strict upbringing.

In this chapter, we explore how parenting practices and views of childhood have evolved over the course of history. Given that until fairly recently strict parenting and an emphasis on obedience was the norm, we focus in particular on the incentives that underlie the authoritarian parenting style. We also examine the historical role that religion has played in shaping views of parenting and the impact that religiosity has on the choice of parenting style even to the present day.

PARENT-CHILD RELATIONS THROUGHOUT HISTORY

The moral authority of religion has long supported the use of the cane to discipline children. For instance, the Bible takes the view that children are intrinsically unable to make their own judgments: "Folly is bound up in the heart of a child, but the rod of discipline will drive it far away."[2] Moreover, physical punishment is thought to be cathartic: "Blows and wounds scrub away evil, and beatings purge the inmost being."[3] In the Islamic tradition, corporal punishment is admitted under some circumstances. In one Hadith, one reads: "Order your children to perform prayer when they are seven years old and beat them (for neglecting it) when they are ten."[4] There are echoes of similar principles in African cultures, like the Bangubangu proverb: "The parent who corrects his son with a rod does not sin."[5]

Religious authority was not alone in advocating a strict discipline regime: most intellectuals and philosophers endorsed the same view. The Greek biographer and philosopher Plutarch was one of the few exceptions. In his "De liberis educandis," he writes: "Children ought to be led to honorable practices by means of encouragement and reasoning, and most certainly not by blows or ill-treatment, for it surely is agreed that these are fitting rather for slaves than for the free-born; for so they grow numb and shudder at their tasks, partly from the pain of the blows, partly from the degradation."[6] Yet, Plutarch's position is unusual. Based on a sample of autobiographies and diaries, the British historian John Plumb documents that among "200 counsels of advice on child-rearing prior to 1770, only three, Plutarch, Palmieri, and Sadoleto, failed to recommend that fathers beat their children."[7]

Social historians still debate the roots of the rough methods of the early days. One view is that parents used not to care much about their children. In his pioneering work *Centuries of Childhood*, published in 1960, Philippe Ariès argues that before the sixteenth century parents were emotionally detached from their children, in part because child mortality rates were high.[8] In support of his point, Ariès claims that people in the Middle Ages did not keep any memento of a dead child. "No one thought of keeping a picture of a child if that child had either lived to grow to manhood or had died in infancy. . . . It was thought that the little thing which had disappeared so soon in life was not worthy of remembrance."[9] Ariès quotes the philosopher Montaigne: "I have lost two or three children in their infancy, not without regret, but without great sorrow," adding, "I cannot abide that passion for caressing new-born children, which have neither mental activities nor recognizable bodily shape by which to make themselves lovable."[10] Such indifference was allegedly the cause of the widespread mistreatment or even abandonment of children.

The literature of the 1960s and 1970s is heavily influenced by Ariès's thesis. The psychohistorian Lloyd De Mause goes as far as defining the history of child-adult relations as a "nightmare" from which humankind has only recently started to awake.[11] In his introduction to the collected essay volume titled "The History of Childhood," he offers a telling periodization of the modes of parent-child relations: infanticidal mode (until the fourth century), abandonment mode (fourth to thirteenth century), ambivalent mode (fourteenth to seventeenth century), intrusive mode (eighteenth century), and finally helping mode (since the mid-twentieth century).[12]

More recent research has pushed back against this view. The social historian Hugh Cunningham relies on evidence from diaries, figurative art, and funerary monuments, and concludes that parents in ancient societies loved their children just as we do today.[13] While institutions of the time absolved parents who abandoned or sold their children, already in the classical era, parents were affectionate toward their children. Parents also grieved over the loss of young children, even though in times of high mortality the death of a young child was a common event. Cunningham discusses a number of studies by medievalists that refute the claim that the idea of childhood was alien to medieval society. Overall, the current consensus among historians lines up well with our view that even in the past, most parents loved their children and had what they believed to be their best interests in mind. This does not mean that children received a lenient treatment. In his book *Adults and Children in the Roman Empire*, the historian Thomas Wiedemann documents that even though children had an important role in the Roman society, they were subject to harsh discipline from their teachers and educators.[14]

Among philosophers, the view that parenting should be strict was dominant well into the Age of Enlightenment. John Locke (1632–1704), the Father of Liberalism, himself a Baptist, thought that parents should not be concerned with making their children happy.[15] Rather, they should attempt to elevate them quickly out of immaturity, with the aim of forging a strong adult personality. Strict parenting works best, in his view, to achieve this goal: "If you would have him stand in awe of you, imprint it in his infancy. . . . For liberty and indulgence can do no good to children; their want of judgment makes them stand in need of restraint and discipline."[16] At the same time, Locke acknowledged childhood as a critical formative period. "The little and almost insensible impressions on our tender infancies have very important and lasting consequences. . . . Of all the men we meet with, nine parts of ten are what they are, good or evil, useful or not, by their education."[17] He also recommended that parents soften their stance as children grow up. Children should gradually be treated as reasoning beings, since "imperiousness and severity is but an ill way of treating men, who have reason of their own to guide them."[18]

While Locke viewed childhood as merely instrumental to the formation of an adult personality, another great political philosopher and a leading intellectual figure of the Enlightenment, Jean-Jacques Rousseau (1712–78), took a radically different position in his celebrated treatise *Emile, or on Education*.[19] According to Rousseau, childhood is an important phase of human existence in its own right. Educators should refrain from interfering with children's freedom and happiness. Instead, they should accommodate children's distinct preferences and inclinations, and let children learn from experience at the speed and in the form that fits them.[20] In Rousseau's ideal world, there is no role for external discipline: "Children should never receive punishment merely as such; it should always come as the natural consequence of their fault."[21] Put in modern terms, Rousseau advocated a permissive parenting style, on the grounds that children learn best through their own experience, rather than through instruction and discipline by adults.

Given that he abandoned his own children to orphanages, many view Rousseau as a hypocritical authority on raising children. Nevertheless, Rousseau's views influenced generations of educational reformers, including Pestalozzi, Froebel, Montessori, and Dewey. For instance, Maria Montessori (1870–1952) believed that children have a spontaneous drive toward learning and developing from a young age.[22] Her pedagogic theory underscores the value of guided independence: "The conquest of independence begins from the first commencement of life. As the being develops, it perfects itself and overcomes every obstacle that it finds on its way."[23] The main task of teachers is to guide this process by creating an environment that offers opportunities for independent learning. Unlike Rousseau, Montessori argues that teachers should be responsive and correct children when mistakes are made, but their intervention should be constructive and friendly rather than punitive.

The ideas of Maria Montessori and other education reformers have gained influence in the course of the twentieth century, and today there are many schools that are based on her pedagogical approach. The transition was a slow one, however; in European countries, methods that rely on strict discipline and corporal punishment were the norm in schools until after World War II. The United States presents a similar picture. The American education reform movement of the 1800s led by Horace Mann, which campaigned for universal state-sponsored public education, brought new approaches to education in the New World that were in part modeled on the experiences with state-run education in Prussia. However, this reform movement still embraced some authoritarian principles and emphasized the importance of discipline and obedience. Authoritarian methods also long enjoyed popularity in the home; in the previous chapter, we mentioned that over 90 percent of American adults approved the spanking of children as late as 1970 (fig. 4.4).

THE DEMISE OF THE AUTHORITARIAN PARENTING STYLE

In the last few decades, the approval rate of spanking has plunged, especially among educated parents. This is true in the United States and even more so in Europe, where corporal punishment is now illegal in many countries. Since the evidence for the United States was discussed in the previous chapter, here we focus on the trends in Europe, Australia, and Japan.

According to the comparative study of Austria, France, Germany, Spain, and Sweden mentioned in chapter 3, far fewer parents report spanking their children today than report having been spanked as children themselves.[24] In Sweden, 24 percent of people born before 1962 say that they were beaten by their parents (already a much lower proportion than in the United States at the time). The number falls below 16 percent for people born between 1968 and 1973. Today, surveys indicate that no more than 6 percent of Swedes still find it acceptable to slap children even mildly. In Austria and Germany, the incidence of corporal punishment started out higher than in Sweden (above 50 percent for children born before 1962) but has also declined sharply over the years, both as a practice and as an accepted social norm. A longitudinal study of German parents between 1996 and 2008 shows a strong growing opposition to any form of corporal punishment.

We have already noticed that authoritarian parenting continues to be popular in some Catholic countries such as France and Spain. It is therefore not surprising that corporal punishment is more resilient there—70 percent of the population born in the 1960s and 1970s report being smacked by their parents during childhood—and that there is widespread use of corporal punishment even today.[25] In Italy, also Catholic, a recent survey finds that half of parents report having smacked their children in exceptional circumstances, a quarter hit them a few times a month, and more than 3 percent do it almost every day. Although corporal punishment is still relatively widespread, only a minority of Italian parents claim to approve it. More than half of all parents actually think that smacking is a bad educational practice, while only around a quarter of them voice some support.[26] Approval has also been falling over time. Compared to a similar survey in 2009, the proportion of parents supporting corporal punishment is substantially lower in a survey carried out in 2012.

The falling approval of corporal punishment is closely connected to the general decline in the authoritarian parenting style. Interestingly, the decline in authoritarian parenting continued even after the peak of permissive parenting in the 1970s. In other words, while parenting has become more intensive, we do not observe renewed popularity of the traditional principle that children should blindly obey their parents. We can see the persistent decline of authoritarian parenting in the data from the WVS, at least in countries for which information is available for a sufficiently long time span. Recall that our classification of an authoritarian parenting style in the WVS data hinges on the parental emphasis on the value of obedience. In Australia and Japan, the share of authoritarian parents was cut in half between 1981 and 2012 (from 59 percent to 30 percent in Australia, and from 10 percent to 5 percent in Japan). In contrast, the share of authoritative parents during the same period increased from 11 percent to 40 percent in Australia, and from 22 percent to 37 percent in Japan. This pattern is not exclusive to the Pacific region. Take Spain and Sweden, the two European countries that have, respectively, the largest and smallest share of authoritarian parents in Europe. In spite of the difference in levels, the changes over time follow a similar pattern. In Sweden, the share of authoritarian parents fell from 19 percent to 11 percent between 1996 (first available year) and 2011, while that of authoritative parents doubled. In Spain, the share of the authoritarian parenting style fell from 46 percent (1990) to 34 percent in the most recent survey, offset again by an increase in the share of authoritative parents. Overall, the decline in authoritarian parenting and the growing popularity of the authoritative parenting style is widespread across the whole set of OECD countries.[27]

TRADITIONAL SOCIETIES AND THE VALUE OF INDEPENDENCE

Are there economic factors that can explain, first, the secular persistence of the authoritarian parenting style, and then its quick demise in the second half of the twentieth century? Our theory highlights the importance of economic incentives. Loving parents weigh the costs and benefits of different approaches to parenting. Changes in the economic environment affect the relative appeal of different parenting styles. As we saw, the prevailing parenting style remained the same for many centuries. Economic historians point out that the world in general did not change much in that period, at least relative to the extraordinary pace of transformation during the two last centuries. With regard to the popularity of authoritarian parenting, we believe that the most important characteristic of the preindustrial environment was that it provided few incentives for endowing children with a sense of independence.

Before the onset of industrialization, societies were largely rural and characterized by far more rigid social hierarchies than today's world. The living standards of the vast majority of the population also did not change much between the fall of the Roman Empire and the British Industrial Revolution. As emphasized by the classical economist Thomas Malthus, technology improvements allowed societies to feed more people over time, but population growth ultimately caught up with the increase in resources (we will return to this theme in chapter 7). As a result, living standards stayed close to the subsistence level throughout the preindustrial era. Urbanization was low, and although the material living standards in cities were a little higher than in the countryside, disease rates and mortality were also higher.

A common trait of the preindustrial world is that parents and children were tied together more closely than what is common today in terms of work, education, and mutual support. All family members would provide services to the family as a productive unit, with different tasks assigned according to gender and age. Likewise, the transmission of knowledge and skills was largely confined to the family: most of what children needed to learn they picked up from their parents and older siblings. Families also entailed strong implicit obligations, such as taking care of the elderly. A child abandoning the family in order to pursue success on his or her own would be stigmatized both by the family and by the wider society.

This discussion points to the fact that in preindustrial society, the benefits of independence were low. Independence is especially important when a child must succeed in a world that is different from that through which their parents can guide them. A strong sense of independence is less valuable, or even dangerous, where children live together with their parents for most of their lives and follow in the parents' footsteps in terms of occupational choice. In that case, parents can teach children all they need to know and monitor them closely, preventing them from shirking on what parents view as the children's duties. Through encouraging them to adhere to social norms and overseeing their actions closely, parents can also reduce risky behavior in their children, such as premarital sex or fighting.

In the traditional world, a sense of independence may be a particularly dangerous asset if it implants in the youngsters' minds ideas such as abandoning the family and breaking social norms. The Italian writer Giovanni Verga develops this theme in his novel, *The House by the Medlar Tree*, first published in 1881.[28] The novel follows a family of poor fishermen who live in the Sicilian village of Aci Trezza. The main source of income is a small fishing boat. At the outset of the novel, 'Ntoni, the eldest of the five children, leaves for military service. When a storm destroys the family's boat, a long sequence of misfortunes ensues. After returning from war, 'Ntoni rejects the perspective of going back to the traditional lifestyle of the family and embarks on a series of risky enterprises that all come to a bad end. First, he leaves the home village to seek his fortune. Then, frustrated, he turns to alcohol, idleness, and crime. He is imprisoned, leaving his family in financial ruin, unable to pay back a debt incurred before the boat was destroyed. Having ended his prison term, 'Ntoni tries to go back to the village and resume the old family life. But it is too late; he faces rejection from his own family. His attempt to break free from the traditional lifestyle has ended in disaster, ruining his life and excluding him forever from his traditional community.

The author summarizes the moral of the novel as follows: "Whenever one who is weaker, or less careful, or more egoistic than the others wants to detach himself from the group due to a desire to explore the unknown or a lust for betterment, the world, this voracious fish, will swallow him."[29] According to Verga, the independent spirit that lures a young person away from the beaten path can only lead to self-destruction. In such a world, obedience is a safer value than imagination or independence.

THE RISING RETURN TO INDEPENDENCE IN THE MODERN ECONOMY

The downside of the authoritarian strategy is that constraining children's choices hampers their ability to discover the world and their own innate talents and predispositions. As Rousseau noted, by making independent choices and experiencing both the positive and negative consequences of their own actions, children acquire maturity, become more assertive, and can eventually discover more easily their own path in life. Yet finding one's personal path is less important in traditional societies characterized by low social and occupational mobility. For instance, in a class-based society where farmers' children are going to be farmers, and the children of aristocrats are going to be rich rentiers, there is little left for children to discover independently. Life has its "natural" course, and everybody must learn to stay in her or his own place. Some of the great geniuses had to fight hard to subvert this order: Georg Friedrich Händel became a musician against the will of his father, who wanted him to be a lawyer.[30] According to Händel's biographer, he practiced the clavichord in the attic where his father could not see or hear him. He also had to enroll in a law course to appease his father before he was able to drop out and pursue his passion.

Our argument implies that authoritarian parenting is more appealing in societies characterized by limited technical progress, where human capital is mostly acquired within the family, usually from parents teaching children their own profession. This approach works well for preindustrial society. Until the onset of industrialization, most people in the Western world were engaged in agriculture, a sector where children could work with their parents. There was more social and occupational mobility among city dwellers working as artisans or craftsmen, but even there, most skill acquisition took place within the family, and families that were already engaged in those professions were often protected formally through guilds. In such a setting, the authoritarian parenting style ruled.

Instilling a sense of independent responsibility in children is more attractive in dynamic societies where young people are called to make important decisions on their own. The continuous increase in the division of labor in industrialized societies increases the number of occupations, making it more likely that a child will find an occupation that fits her or his talents better than the parents' occupation. New opportunities often arise in new sectors. For instance, few workers in today's software industry have parents working in the same area. Even within occupations, rapid technical change makes traditional knowledge obsolete, which reduces the effectiveness of children learning from their parents even if they work in the same profession.[31] In agriculture, traditional practices and techniques lost value when agriculture was mechanized. A parent who works as an accountant may lack the computer skills that are necessary for young people who start today in the same occupation. Fabrizio's father was a skilled technician working in Italian state television. His specialized knowledge was made obsolete by satellite and digitalization. His mother was a fashion designer, but had no familiarity with computers, an essential tool for today's designers. In sum, technical progress changes the rules of the game in parenting, making authoritarian parenting itself obsolete.

In line with this view, social historians document a gradual change in attitude toward children and parenting during the period of time when industrialization upended the traditional economic order. The historian Linda Pollock argues that changes first began to appear in the late eighteenth century, mostly in the middle and upper ranks of society.[32] According to historians Carl Kaestle and Maris Vinovskis, the first generation of reformers was an intellectual elite that adopted many of Rousseau's views on childhood.[33] Their influence was initially limited to the more progressive sectors of society, but was set to become pervasive as economic conditions evolved.

An important factor that changed the relative appeal of different parenting styles is the expansion of higher education in the twentieth century. When children studied at home, parents could still rely on the force behind the persuasion of the cane. Yet, as children move to colleges offering ample opportunities for fun and games, parents can no longer hope to monitor them. Rather, children must be able to succeed on their own. Authoritarian parenting declined progressively as close-knit patriarchal families were replaced by a new model where children receive formal education outside the home, and few children continue in their parents' occupation. Yet, this change was still slow in the first half of the twentieth century. The social historian Antoine Prost reports the results of a survey conducted by the magazine *Confidences* in France in 1938, finding that almost one-third of the readers agreed to the principle that parents should choose a career for their children and steer them toward the chosen path from early childhood.[34] The idea that parents know what is best for their children and should make the important calls concerning life choices was still broadly accepted before World War II.

It was in the 1960s that traditional authoritarian parenting collapsed. As discussed in chapter 2, a low return to human capital investment made permissive parenting attractive in that period. Here we see that a waning advantage of working in the same occupation as the parents, which we will refer to as a low *incumbency premium*, also contributed to the demise of authoritarian parenting at that time. Since the 1970s, the evidence suggests that the incumbency premium has fallen even more. A team of economists has recently documented that over the last few decades occupational mobility has continued to increase in the United States.[35] Meanwhile, wage inequality across workers of the same education level also has increased, reflecting the growing importance of people finding jobs that match well with their individual talents and skills.[36] In this world, it is more and more important for young people to discover their natural comparative advantage rather than learning one of their parents' occupations.

In summary, our view is that the decline of authoritarian parenting is related to the demise of traditional, rigid societies where independence was of limited value and where parents could easily assert their authority and control their children's choices. Of course, we do not suggest that an economic cost-benefit consideration was the only reason why parents were authoritarian. In the preindustrial era, a system of cultural and religious values and practices had developed that helped legitimize the authority of parents. Yet, this cultural superstructure did not survive the blow of modernization: in a modern, highly mobile economy, the value of independence is too high for a culture of pervasive authoritarian parenting to be sustainable.

OBEDIENCE AND ECONOMIC DEVELOPMENT

Consistent with our view that a modern economy is incompatible with widespread authoritarian parenting, figure 5.1 shows that the fraction of parents emphasizing obedience, which is the typical trait of an authoritarian parenting style, declines with an increase in economic development, as measured by the GDP per capita.[37] Obedience is most popular in rural sub-Saharan African countries (with the notable exception of Ethiopia); it has an intermediate level of popularity in Central Asia and Latin America; finally, it is least popular in Europe, North America, and in the richest East Asian countries. The latter group consists of

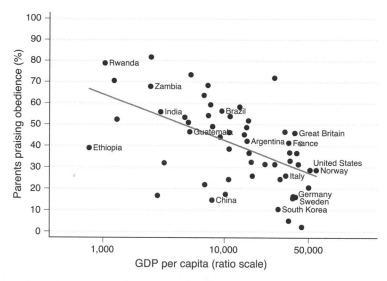

FIGURE 5.1. Share of parents emphasizing obedience and GDP per capita across countries

economies with high occupational mobility, a small agricultural sector, and a large proportion of young people receiving higher education. Conversely, figure 5.2 shows that the fraction of parents emphasizing independence increases with GDP per capita.[38]

In a nutshell, parents in poor countries tend to be authoritarian, whereas in rich countries authoritative and permissive parenting styles are widespread. Since economic development goes hand-in-hand with the rise of occupational mobility and with a decline in the traditional role of families in the transmission of knowledge and productive skills across generations, this observation is consistent with our arguments.

The case of Brazil is especially telling and illustrates well our point. Brazil is an emerging economy with a lower GDP per capita than the OECD economies and a notoriously high level of income inequality. According to our theory of incentives, given the large economic disparity, we should expect few Brazilian parents to be permissive and most to choose an intensive parenting style. Given the lower level of development compared to the OECD economies, we should also expect that most of this intensive parenting should come in the form of the authori-

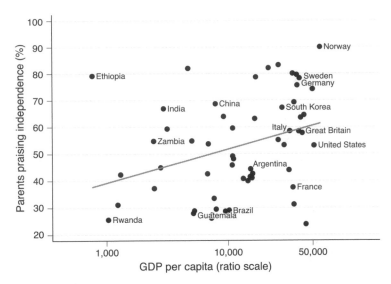

FIGURE 5.2. Share of parents emphasizing independence and GDP per capita across countries

tarian rather than the authoritative style. The data confirm these expectations. In the most recent WVS (2014), 55 percent of the parents in Brazil are authoritarian, 35 percent are authoritative, and less than 10 percent are permissive. Only 24 percent of them single out imagination as an important value in child-rearing. The share of permissive parents is significantly lower, not only than in Europe but also relative to the United States. The share of authoritarian parents is substantially higher than in both Europe and the United States.

RELIGIOSITY AND PARENTING STYLE

Brazil has another distinctive feature: it is a very religious country. According to a Gallup poll, 86.5 percent of Brazilian respondents report that religion is important in their daily life, compared with 65 percent in the United States, 40 percent in Germany, and less than 20 percent in Scandinavian countries. In this section, we discuss the effect of religiosity on parenting style. We show that in religious countries like Brazil parents tend to be more authoritarian. Why should this be the case?

The thesis of this book is that loving parents wish to prepare their children for the world that awaits them. We argue that parents' views of what is in store for their children depends on the speed of social and economic change. However, if the actual speed of these transformations matters, parents' *perceptions* of the speed of change are no less important. Different people have different beliefs about the future. Some think that the next generation will live in a society much different from ours; perhaps they expect that robots will replace humans in many occupations, that the information technology revolution will open new frontiers, and that even norms and moral values will change. Such parents would be unlikely to view the family as the main source of learning and be more inclined to let their children discover the new world independently as it evolves.

The opposite should be true of parents who believe that the world is regulated by a never-changing order and that the duty of educators is to transmit to children an immutable set of values and truths. This is where religion and religiosity come into play. For instance, a recent study argues that conservative Protestants in the United States "consider the Bible to be without error, providing reliable and sufficient insights to guide the conduct of all human affairs, including child rearing," and believe that "all human relationships . . . are shaped by specific patterns of divinely ordained authority relations."[39] In such a stable world, it is unnecessary, and possibly inadvisable, to encourage children to be independent and imaginative.[40]

A related point is that many fundamentalist Christians believe humans to be born sinful and that only a strict religious upbringing can purify children's souls. Kaestle and Vinovskis report that "the early Puritans had stressed that children were innately evil. . . . The only proper response for parents was to watch their children closely and to discipline them at very young ages."[41] According to the sociologists John Bartkowski and Christopher Ellison, conservative Protestants (either evangelical or fundamentalist) do not believe that good parenting is about emphasizing self-confidence, creativity, and intellectual curiosity.[42] Instead, they believe that "to succeed in adult roles, children must be trained to embrace the divinely-ordained principles of authority and hierarchy."[43] Authoritarian parenting is a natural implication of this parenting strategy. For instance, according to the psychologist Irwin Hyman: "Truly authoritarian societies emphasize unquestioning loyalty to leaders, reflexive obedience to authority, and the foolishness of dissent. Children are taught at home and school that they must not question requests by authorities, including parents, and that punishment will invariably follow disobedience."[44]

EMPIRICAL EVIDENCE ON THE ROLE OF RELIGIOSITY IN THE UNITED STATES

Is there an empirical connection between religiosity and an authoritarian parenting style? To answer this question, we turn to data for the United States. We use data from the Child Development Supplement (CDS) of the Panel Study of Income Dynamics (PSID), a popular dataset that follows a cohort of children and their parents. In the initial survey of the PSID-CDS in 1997, parents were asked whether they have ever spanked their children. In addition, they were asked whether religion is very important in their life. Religious parents have a more positive attitude toward corporal punishment: 70 percent of religious parents report spanking their children, compared to 58 percent of nonreligious parents.

As usual, one may worry that the difference may be driven by other socioeconomic characteristics, such as income or education, that may be related to both religiosity and the use of corporal punishment. As we did earlier, we can use logistic regression analysis to determine the relationship between religiosity and parenting style while holding constant other characteristics, which here are income, education, age, the sex of the child, and race. Neither income nor education turn out to have a significant effect on spanking in this dataset. African Americans are more likely to have spanked their children, while Hispanic parents have a below-average propensity for spanking. Religiosity has a large effect, more than all of these other characteristics: it increases the relative probability (the odds ratio) of spanking versus not spanking by a factor of 1.72. For example, if a nonreligious parent with given socioeconomic characteristics spanks her children with a probability of 20 percent, the probability of a religious parent with the same characteristics is 30 percent. This is a large difference.

One may also wonder whether specific religious denominations, rather than just religiosity in general, matter in the choice of different parenting styles. To answer this question, we go back to the WVS data for the United States. We classify respondents into four categories: nonreligious, Catholic, Protestant, and other religions (this group includes all religious minorities). Respondents are classified as nonreligious if they do not identify with any religious denomination and, in addition, do not regard religion as a "rather" or "very" important matter in life.[45]

A number of interesting patterns emerge from the analysis.[46] First, nonreligious parents are significantly more permissive than religious ones. Among religious parents, when we look at the division between authoritative and permissive parenting, there are no significant differences across denominations.[47] Important differences do emerge when we consider the authoritarian parenting style. In the United States, Protestants are significantly more likely to be authoritarian than any other group.

To get an impression of the differences across the groups, consider three fictitious mothers whom we name Libertad (nonreligious), María Purificación (Catholic), and Margarita (Protestant). The three mothers are assumed to have identical socioeconomic characteristics (age, education, etc.). Suppose that, based on these characteristics, nonreligious Libertad has a 50 percent chance of being permissive, and a 25 percent chance of being authoritative and authoritarian, respectively. According to our estimates, for María Purificación the likelihood of being permissive, authoritative, and authoritarian is 35 percent, 25 percent, and 40 percent, respectively; the same probabilities are 30 percent, 25 percent, and 45 percent for Margarita (see fig. 5.3). Interestingly, in this example, religion has almost no effect on the probability of the three mothers being authoritative. However, religious mothers like María Purificación and Margarita are more likely to be authoritarian and less likely to be permissive. The effect is stronger for Protestant Margarita than for Catholic María Purificación. These differences are quantitatively large, es-

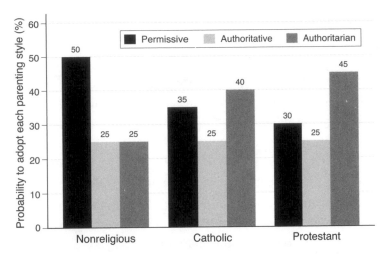

FIGURE 5.3. Probability for a fictitious child in the United States to be subject to each of the three parenting styles if her mother is nonreligious (Libertad, reference group), Catholic (Maria Purificacion), and Protestant (Margarita)

pecially if one considers that our analysis compares parents with identical socioeconomic characteristics other than religion.

RELIGIOSITY AND PARENTING ACROSS COUNTRIES

The WVS data allows us to extend the analysis of the role of religiosity to more countries. This is interesting for two different reasons. First, we can investigate the importance of religiosity for explaining variation in parenting styles, in addition to the country-specific factors such as inequality, which we have already discussed in chapter 3. Second, the characteristics of different denominations may vary across countries. In the United States, evangelicals are more conservative than the rest of the population. In contrast, European Catholics tend to be more conservative than Protestants.

We start by analyzing the effect of religiosity irrespective of denomination. As before, we categorize respondents as religious if they regard religion as either "very" or "rather important," and as nonreligious otherwise. In the entire WVS sample, which includes both developed and developing countries, the total number of respondents is 274,504.

Of them, 72 percent are classified as religious and 28 percent as nonreligious. Religiosity is clearly associated with different propensities to adopt each of the parenting styles. Among the parents adopting a permissive parenting style, 59 percent are religious; among those adopting an authoritative parenting style, 70 percent are religious; and among those adopting an authoritarian parenting style, religious parents make up 81 percent of the total. Compared to their overall population share of 72 percent, religious people are overrepresented among authoritarian and underrepresented among permissive parents. Hence, religious people are more authoritarian and less permissive than nonreligious people, whereas there is no significant deviation from the population average when we consider the authoritative parenting style.

Consider next the sample of OECD founders we studied in chapter 3. Restricting attention to these countries allows us to categorize religious people according to their denominations. In the full sample, this is complicated by the large number of affiliations that exist in the world. The OECD sample includes 53,328 responses, 51 percent of whom are classified as religious. Among the parents adopting a permissive parenting style, 37 percent are religious; among those adopting an authoritative parenting style, 57 percent are religious; and among those adopting an authoritarian parenting style, religious parents make up 62 percent of the total. Compared to their overall population share of 51 percent, religious people are again overrepresented among authoritarian and underrepresented among permissive parents. The main difference to the full sample is that the percentage of religious people is lower in the industrialized OECD sample, reflecting the secularization that accompanies the process of economic development.

Looking at the average effect of religiosity across respondents from all OECD countries may be problematic for reasons we have already discussed in this book. For instance, it may be more informative to compare the propensity to adopt different parenting styles between religious and nonreligious Swedes (with given socioeconomic characteristics) and between religious and nonreligious Turks, rather than comparing, say, religious Turks to nonreligious Swedes. Even when focusing on intranational comparisons, we still find that religiosity affects the choice of parenting styles. Consider two otherwise identical parents living in the same country. Suppose that the nonreligious parent has a probability of 50 percent, 25 percent, and 25 percent of being permissive, authoritative, and authoritarian, respectively (like Libertad in fig. 5.3). Then, for the religious parent the probabilities of being permissive, authoritative, and authoritarian are 42 percent, 24 percent, and 34 percent.[48] Once again, the main finding is that religious parents are more authoritarian and less permissive than nonreligious parents.

We can use the data from the WVS to break down the effect by religious denomination. Relative to the analysis for the United States alone, the WVS data allow us to distinguish five denominations: Buddhists, Catholics, Muslims, Protestants, and "other religions" as a residual category (note that in the US sample, we had too few Muslims and Buddhists to separate them out). To describe the findings, consider five fictitious mothers from different religiosity categories who have otherwise identical characteristics. Using French names, we call them Marianne (nonreligious), Jeanne (Catholic), Marguerite (Protestant), Farah (Muslim), and Caihong (Buddhist). Let us assign to Marianne the usual reference probabilities of 50 percent (permissive), 25 percent (authoritative) and 25 percent (authoritarian).

Figure 5.4 summarizes the estimated probabilities of each parenting style for the different denominations. Muslim mothers like Farah are significantly less permissive and more authoritarian than those in any other religious denomination. They are also more authoritative.[49] Christian mothers like Jeanne and Marguerite come next, with a similar pattern. They are more authoritarian and less permissive than Marianne-like nonreligious parents, albeit not to the same extent as Muslim parents. Buddhists mothers like Caihong are the least authoritarian among all denominations and are about as authoritarian as nonreligious mothers; they are instead strongly inclined to be authoritative. Contrary to the sample of US parents, there is no significant difference between Catholics and Protestants. This is perhaps not surprising: the international sample includes many European countries where Protestants (mostly Lutherans or Anglicans) are today less socially conservative compared to both European Catholics and evangelical Protestants in the United States.

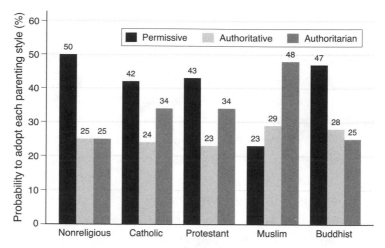

FIGURE 5.4. Probability for a fictitious child in the OECD to be subject to each of the three parenting styles if her mother is nonreligious (Marianne, reference group), Catholic (Jeanne), Muslim (Farah), and Buddhist (Caihong)

POLITICAL ORIENTATION, ECONOMIC CONSERVATIVISM, AND OTHER DIMENSIONS OF SOCIAL CONSERVATIVISM

Religion is only one dimension of conservativism. Some people are religious and liberal, while there are others who are conservative and nonreligious. The WVS also reports information about the political preferences of respondents. It is interesting to note how these preferences correlate with parenting styles. Moreover, we can also check whether religiosity has an effect on parenting style across people with the same political inclination.[50]

We classify voters into left, right, and center, relative to the political spectrum of each country.[51] Consider again our preferred reference individual (here, assumed to be a left-wing voter) with a 50 percent probability of being permissive, a 25 percent probability of being authoritative, and a 25 percent probability of being authoritarian. We compare this with an otherwise identical person who is in the center or on the right. The centrist voter would be permissive, authoritative, and authoritarian with probabilities of 40 percent, 28 percent, and 32 percent.

For the rightist voter, these probabilities amount to 33 percent, 29 percent, and 38 percent. As one moves from left to right, there is a mild shift from the permissive to the authoritative parenting style, and a more pronounced shift from the permissive to the authoritarian parenting style. In addition, the political views do not appear to change the effect of religiosity on parenting styles. Take, for example, the group of center voters. The association between religiosity and parenting style is the same as that in the entire population (namely, religious people are more authoritarian and less permissive). The same is true if one restricts attention to the left-wing or the right-wing voters. This indicates that religiosity and political preferences have almost independent effects on parenting styles.

We can also consider a more economic dimension of conservativism by looking at a question about the attitude toward inequality. People are asked to state their own attitude toward income inequality on a 10-point scale, where 1 is "incomes should be more equal" and 10 is "we need larger income differences as incentives." We categorize an individual as proequality if their answer is between 1 and 3, as middle between 4 and 7, and as proinequality between 8 and 10. We find no significant differences in parenting style between the proequality and the middle group. Instead, proinequality people are more permissive than the average of the population, although the difference is small, suggesting that economic conservativism is less important than religiosity and social conservatism in determining parenting styles.

TAKING STOCK

In this chapter, we have examined the historical persistence and recent decline of the authoritarian parenting style. We documented that both economic factors and cultural attitudes, specifically religiosity and conservatism, contribute to explain changes in the popularity of authoritarian parenting over time and differences in the prevalence of this parenting style across socioeconomic groups.

First, there are fundamental economic factors that affect the attractiveness of authoritarian parenting. In societies where technical change is slow and occupational mobility is low, most children follow in the parents' footsteps in terms of career choice. This enables parents to teach children what they need to know and to exert direct control over them. Moreover, children have little to gain, and often a lot to lose, from breaking free from the control of their parents. In such societies, obedience is more highly valued than independence and imagination. A low rate of technological change and low occupational mobility were characteristic of all societies throughout the preindustrial period. In contrast, in modern economies, with a high occupational and social mobility, children benefit more from being independent. Thus, authoritarian parenting becomes less useful as modernization and development proceed. Accordingly, we have documented that the popularity of an authoritarian parenting style declines with an increase in the level of economic development.

Second, religiosity also matters. In our view, religion matters because it shapes parents' beliefs about the world in which their children will live. Parents who believe that values, aspirations, occupations, and technologies will change rapidly hold children's independence in high regard. Such parents may also praise hard work, but do not insist on obedience and the principle of adult authority. By contrast, conservative religious principles are associated with a view of the world whose order is immutable, where the parents' duty is to teach children absolute truths. Consistent with our arguments, we have shown that religious parents are more authoritarian and less permissive, and are more likely to engage in corporal punishment.[52]

Overall, the results suggest that the secularization of societies may have concurred with technological trends in determining the decline of the authoritarian parenting style. It will be interesting to see the extent to which this conclusion holds up in the future. Despite being generally conservative, religion itself is not immutable, but changes alongside society. For instance, the progressive Pontificate of Pope Francis is introducing reforms that may affect the perception of the world. As time goes by, conservativism may detach itself from religiosity, at least for some denominations. According to a study of the Pew Research Center, three-quarters of adult Catholics in the United States are in favor of same-sex marriage in 2017 (up from 36 percent in 2004), although this is still opposed by the official doctrine of the Catholic church.[53] Support for same-sex marriage remains lower among white evangelical Protestants (35%) but has also increased significantly since 2004 (11%). Ultimately, these transformations are likely to affect the choice of parenting style of religious believers. Consistent with this view, we have shown that the effect of religiosity on parenting today varies across more or less conservative denominations.

We also considered the effect of political and economic conservativism. The effect of political conservativism is similar to that of religion: right-wing parents are more prone to be authoritarian. Interestingly, the effect is much smaller when we considered a measure of right-wing views on economic issues, namely, the attitude toward redistribution. This suggests that right-wing orientation on political versus economic issues are fundamentally distinct concepts. In particular, a right-wing economic orientation could stem equally well from a libertarian rather than conservative worldview.

Another aspect that we have not emphasized but that might play a role is social norms, which also form part of the environment that determines the incentives for the adoption of different parenting styles. For our grandparents, spanking children was not only a natural thing to do; it was also socially acceptable. If a neighbor had witnessed them wielding the cane, they could expect that he or she would approve and perhaps even support them in admonishing the badly behaved child. Today, one would get a different reaction. María and Fabrizio recall trying to control a temper tantrum their young daughter had on a walk in Stockholm. While they were far from using anything close to corporal punishment, they were chiding their daughter with a certain energy. At that moment, a passerby approached them and urged them to stop, saying, "Otherwise your child will hate you when she is an adult." Clearly, social norms have changed, and this can feed back into parents' behavior.

Social norms can help explain the speed of change in parenting styles in recent decades. As parents moved away from authoritarian practices, a social stigma attached itself to corporal punishment. Changing social norms can induce rapid changes in attitudes, so that even parents who otherwise would have been authoritarian may swim with the tide and become more permissive or authoritative. Social norms may also be part of the reason why in some countries (e.g., Spain) and in some regions (e.g., the southern United States) the authoritarian parenting style proves more resilient. When parents interact with many others who approve of the use of corporal punishment, this lowers the pressure to shy away from authoritarian methods. In contrast, in some communities (such as many American university campuses), the notion of hitting children is so heavily disapproved of that no parent would risk being discovered dispensing corporal punishment.

CHAPTER SIX

Boys versus Girls

The Transformation of Gender Roles

A favorite topic of discussion among parents is the difference between raising boys and girls. To be sure, parents in Western countries now routinely question gender stereotypes, and many strive to raise their children in a gender-neutral way. For example, rather than giving dolls to girls and cars to boys, such parents may seek out toys that are not associated with traditional gender roles. Yet in practice, boys and girls do develop differently in the early years and confront their parents with different challenges.[1]

In their own lives, Fabrizio (father of a daughter) and Matthias (father of three sons) have experienced opposite sides of the girl-boy divide. Marisa and Matthias often struggle with the frequent outbursts of aggression and (moderate) violence their three boys exhibit toward one another. Such problems go beyond sibling rivalry: boys are also more likely to display physically aggressive behavior in school or day care than girls are.[2] Marisa and Matthias's boys proved no exception to the rule. When their first child, Oskar, attended a preschool for two-year-old children in Los Angeles, he was one of only two boys in the class—and the only one who seemed to take great pleasure in "pushing" other children, throwing sand at them, and engaging in other forms of mischief. The preschool teachers were greatly concerned about this, and Marisa and Matthias were called in for a number of uncomfortable meetings to discuss what could be done to change his behavior. When

Oskar started to attend the German School in Chicago the following year, history appeared to repeat itself. At the first school meeting, other parents brought up that one particular boy was causing trouble by frequently picking fights with the others, resulting in some kids coming home from school with scratches on their faces. Marisa and Matthias were worried their child was once again going to be singled out. However, the school director cheerfully put the blame on another boy, making Marisa and Matthias proud that Oskar was, at worst, the second-roughest child in school for once. Similar stories can be told about their younger sons, Lukas and Nico.

In contrast, Nora never pushed anyone and instead was occasionally the injured party. Fabrizio and Maria still recall with horror an occasion in Stockholm when a small friend of hers chased her with a homemade sword. Then, a couple of years later, she was in tears after being pushed down into her chair at kindergarten with such force that she hit her head on the wall. Again, the perpetrator was a wild boy. Things did not get any better when Nora moved from Sweden to Switzerland: she and a group of girlfriends became the target of a vicious group of local teenage boys whose families had apparently transmitted anti-immigrant sentiments to them. In the end, none of these episodes had a long-lasting effect on Nora, and hurt feelings more often arose from arguments with other girls, which were never violent but at instances psychologically painful.

These anecdotes fit into a wider trend. Boys are relatively more likely to get "into trouble" in educational settings than girls are, not just in terms of violence or fighting but also in terms of higher rates of grade repetition and dropping out of school, and higher rates of conditions such as attention deficit disorder. Indeed, concerns are being raised that the modern educational environment, which demands concentration and attention while often allowing for little physical activity, is more suited for girls than for boys.[3]

Part of the reason why the differences between boys and girls have come back into focus is precisely because educational institutions now mostly work under the assumption that there should be no differences at all in how boys and girls are treated. This is a fundamental shift from a few decades ago, when there was much more separation in terms of what boys and girls were supposed to learn, and single sex schools were common.

In parallel with changes in the education system, there also has been a transformation in the parenting of boys versus girls, which is our primary interest here. For most parents in industrialized countries today, if they treat their boys and girls differently, it is usually in response to their different behaviors and needs. Their aspirations for their children, in contrast, tend to be quite similar: for both boys and girls, most parents today hope that their children will receive a good education and be able to make a good living, without necessarily having to depend on a spouse. This was different even a few decades ago, when there was much more separation in gender roles, and parents prepared their boys and girls for entirely different lives. In many developing countries, large gender differences for both children and adults are still the norm today.

Differences in gender roles for adults imply that parents face distinct incentives in their decisions regarding their daughters and their sons. In this chapter, we trace out how parenting differs for boys and girls around the world, and how these differences relate to the economic roles women and men play at each stage of development. In line with our overall thesis, we will show that shifting economic incentives have a powerful effect on parenting, and these incentives can explain why gender differences in child-rearing have transformed in recent decades. Given that gender differences were larger in the past, we start with a historical perspective and lay out how economic change has shaped gender roles and the parenting of boys and girls from preindustrial times to the present.

THE ECONOMIC ROOTS OF GENDER ROLES

In earlier times, women and men had sharply distinct roles. In part, gender roles reflected that most societies were patriarchies, where men held most power and women had little say. We can still see the ramifications of a heavily lopsided distribution of power across the sexes in some developing countries today. In her seminal book *Woman's Role in Economic Development*, the Danish economist Ester Boserup describes a number of societies where most hard work in the field is done by women, while men enjoy ample leisure.[4] Women were also disadvantaged in many other ways, ranging from exposure to violence in relationships to a lack of legal and political rights.

But there is more to gender differences than power and discrimination: the division of gender roles also has economic roots. For example, breastfeeding limits the mobility of a mother with a young child. In a society where women have many children, it makes sense for men to specialize in tasks requiring one to move around a lot (such as hunting), whereas other work that is more easily combined with tending to small children falls to women. Similarly, in a society where certain tasks require superior physical strength, men tend to specialize in these tasks.

The best-known historical example of a specific technology shaping gender roles is the plough. Before the tractor was invented, working with a plough required a lot of strength, which gave male workers a natural advantage. Whether ploughs were used in a specific society depended on soil characteristics and the climate. Boserup describes in her book how in societies that did not use the plough, women did much of the agricultural work, whereas in plough-using societies, men worked the fields. The plough was widely used in the northern parts of Europe and North America. As a result, the "traditional" division of labor in which women take care of the home and children and men do more work in the fields has a long history in these parts of the world.[5]

The division of labor by gender was reflected in differences between how parents raised their boys and girls. In preindustrial times, schooling was reserved for a small elite group, and most children started to work at a young age. The tasks that the children carried out reflected the gendered division of labor in the wider society. In an overview of parent-child relations in Europe in the nineteenth century, the historian

Loftur Guttormsson describes how in Iceland sheep herding was generally assigned to boys as young as seven, while "looking after younger siblings was a typical girls' job."[6]

TECHNOLOGICAL CHANGE AND THE EVOLUTION OF GENDER ROLES

The fact that the gendered division of labor has economic roots suggests that changes to the economic environment will, over time, be reflected in gender roles. And indeed, technological changes over the last one hundred years have revolutionized gender relations and much reduced historical divisions between women's and men's work. One aspect of technological progress is that in many cases machines replaced the need for manual labor, thereby reducing the demand for physical strength. Instead, the labor market has increasingly rewarded cognitive and social skills, thus eroding men's comparative advantage.

Over a longer span of history, however, technological progress has sometimes served to widen gender inequalities. Nowadays, sharp divisions in male and female roles are often thought to be linked to historical norms that go back to this preindustrial era when, in fact, in many ways there was less separation between the genders in preindustrial times compared to, say, the United States in the middle of the twentieth century.

In the preindustrial economy, most families worked in agriculture. Women and men usually performed different tasks, with women often in charge of small animals and gardening for home consumption, while men were responsible for large animals and market-crop production. Even so, both women and men were working, and everyone's work centered on the homestead. With both parents close by, children would spend a lot of time with both mother and father. Women usually had the primary responsibility for small children, but once children reached five or six years of age they would start to work alongside their parents, and both mother and father shared the responsibility of looking after them.

The separation of gender roles reached a peak only after the Industrial Revolution. Both technological and institutional forces worked together to sharpen the division between women's and men's roles in society. According to the economic historian Joyce Burnette, before the Industrial Revolution, tasks such as the operation of a spinning wheel were deemed female-specific jobs because women had greater dexterity.[7] The advent of factories and mechanization changed the picture. In the early phase of industrialization, technical progress actually reduced the importance of dexterity relative to physical strength for certain tasks, such as the operation of a spinning mule, which were then taken over by men. In addition, male-dominated unions became increasingly opposed to employment competition from women. Burnette documents labor disputes in the early 1800s where female mule-spinners and their employers were violently attacked by male spinners in Glasgow. Over the course of the nineteenth century, women faced increasing discriminatory barriers in many segments of the labor market.[8]

The new industrial technologies also encouraged new ways to organize work in factories and large offices, which for the first time introduced a separation between the home and the place of work for most of the population. Men would leave the house to go to the factory, and with the rise of railways and suburbanization, the spatial separation between the home and work spheres further increased. There were some (usually younger) women working in the factories, but given that they still had to take care of young children, married women with children became increasingly isolated within the home sphere.

The new circumstances with separate home and work spheres shaped expectations about what roles women and men should play in society. Among those classes that could afford it, married women no longer participated in the formal labor market. In time, the new gender roles transformed how boys and girls were raised. Guttormsson writes: "While men faced ever increasing opportunities in the business and professional sectors, women were to confine their activity to motherhood and domestic management. Women should dedicate their lives to serving the needs of their husbands and children and express their femininity through their supportive relationships, whether as wife, mother, daughter, or sister. . . . Concurrently, the education of girls should aim at making them good wives and mothers."[9]

The separation of the adult spheres was rapidly reflected in girls' and boys' education. When formal education in reading, writing, and arithmetic became a valuable skill in the labor market, a sizeable gap between male and female education opened up because only boys would be expected to enter the formal labor market. According to Guttormsson, this was "manifested indirectly in a noticeable gender discrimination in educational provision, in school as well as at home, where girls received more limited instruction in writing and arithmetic than boys." For girls, education "should be restricted to their future roles as housewives. Book learning should be kept to a minimum, as it risked diverting them from more useful tasks."

WOMEN'S RISING LABOR MARKET PARTICIPATION IN THE TWENTIETH CENTURY

In the United States, the gender division between labor market and home was at its most pronounced in the decades between World War I and World War II. There were some women in the labor force even during these years, but with few exceptions these were single women, either young women who had not (yet) married or older women who were either widowed or divorced. The convention was that once a woman got married, she would stop working. In many professions, this was not even a choice but a rule, instituted in so-called marriage bars. For example, in most US states, female schoolteachers were required to be single and would lose their job upon marriage. The proper role of a married woman was understood to be the one to look after the household and the children. Marriage bars were widely adopted in the early 1900s and disappeared only in the 1950s.[10]

Women's roles in the labor force started to expand substantially during World War II. While men were in the armed forces and fighting in Europe or Asia, millions of women, many of them married, joined the

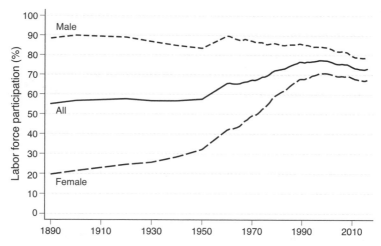

FIGURE 6.1. Labor force participation rate (percent of population aged 16–64) by gender in the United States

labor force to keep up war-time production. After the war, it became increasingly acceptable for women to work, and the female labor force participation rate began to rise.

Figure 6.1 displays the labor force participation rate by gender in the United States from 1890 to the present.[11] Throughout most of the period, more than 80 percent of adult men were working (most of the remainder was made up of men in education or early retirement). For women, the labor force participation rate increased very slowly from 20 percent in 1890 to 28 percent in 1940. After World War II (the war period itself is not displayed because the data is recorded at the frequency of a decade until 1960), female participation increased steadily every decade and reached 70 percent in the 1990s, not far below the participation rate of men.

Like the earlier transformations in the nineteenth century, the expansion of women's labor force participation in the twentieth century was in large part driven by technological change. As already mentioned, one aspect of this change was the demand for specific skills in the labor market, where physical strength became less and less important. The research of economist Claudia Goldin shows that in the 1920s and

1930s the gap in physical strength was still an important reason why women had fewer and less attractive labor market opportunities.[12] Since then, most new jobs have been created in the service sector and in new occupations that do not require physical strength but instead build more heavily on cognitive and social skills. The economist Michelle Rendall argues that this structural change has favored women's comparative advantage and can help explain the rise in female labor supply.[13]

Economists Jeremy Greenwood, Ananth Seshadri, and Mehmet Yorukoglu have pointed out that technological progress also had repercussions for labor done in the home and the organization of family life.[14] In the year 1900, it would have been difficult for a mother to work full-time unless she was able to afford servants. The amount of time required to prepare food, do laundry, clean the house, and care for the children was such that regular work outside the house was simply impossible for many. Technological progress in the household has greatly reduced these time requirements, thereby allowing many more women to pursue careers in the formal labor market. The spread of labor-saving appliances such as the refrigerator, the dishwasher, the washing machine, and the vacuum cleaner played a key role in this shift. A related factor is the development of market-based alternatives to goods previously produced in the home, such as take-out food and center-based childcare. Together, these innovations gave women much more of a choice in how to spend their time.

The changing labor market opportunities for women were also reflected in the gender wage gap. There can be many reasons why women and men are paid different wages, including outright discrimination, but also factors such as differences in education, experience, and physical strength. Figure 6.2 shows how the gender wage gap evolved in the United States from 1890 to today.[15] In 1890, average wages for women were less than half of those for men. Over the following century, the wage gap gradually closed, although in the 1950s and 1960s the upward trend in relative female wages temporarily reversed. Factors that contributed to this temporary widening of the pay gap were the large gap in college education at the time (see fig. 6.5) and the entry of older, relatively inexperienced married women

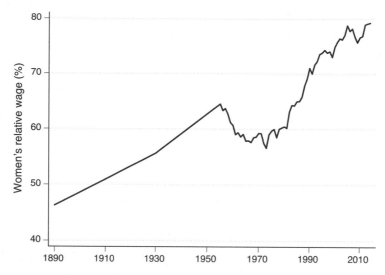

FIGURE 6.2. The gender wage gap (median earnings of full-time, year-round, female workers aged 15 and older relative to men) in the United States

into the labor force. Nowadays, women earn on average 20 percent less than men do.

BEYOND TECHNOLOGICAL FACTORS: LEARNING AND CULTURAL TRANSMISSION

Technological change is not the only driving force behind changes in the role of women in the labor market. Outright discrimination and prejudice against working women also played an important role. The personal story of Marie Skłodowska Curie is a good example of the discrimination to which even great female scientists were subject. Ms. Curie was the first woman to win the Nobel Prize in Physics in 1902 and the first person to be awarded Nobel Prizes in two different disciplines after winning the prize for chemistry in 1911. After winning her first Nobel Prize, only her husband (and colaureate), Pierre Curie, was able to secure a professorship at the University of Paris. She was offered a position and became the first woman to hold a professorship in Paris only after Pierre's tragic death in an accident. Later on, only a few months before receiving her second Nobel Prize, the French Academy of Sciences turned down her application with the explanation that women could not be part of the Institute of France.[16]

Recently, a number of researchers have examined how forces of cultural change have contributed to the erosion of discrimination over time and thereby help explain the rise in women's labor market participation. Economists Raquel Fernández, Alessandra Fogli, and Claudia Olivetti focus specifically on husbands' prejudice against their own wives joining the labor force.[17] They provide evidence that early in the twentieth century, the marriage market was tilted against women with better career prospects. In the cohort born in 1890, the probability for a college-educated woman to remain unmarried was 31 percent, versus only 8 percent for less-educated women. Evidently, many men were looking for a devoted housewife, and education and career ambitions implied more troubles than opportunities. By now, the situation has reversed: as we discussed previously, today college-educated women are substantially more likely to get married than less-educated women. Fernández, Fogli, and Olivetti argue that the evolution of men's attitudes was crucial for the change. Moreover, these attitudes were acquired in men's family of origin. For example, if a man's mother was working during his childhood, it is substantially more likely that as an adult he will end up marrying a woman who works. This example shows that the impact of parents on their children, which we highlight throughout this book, extends to attitudes about gender roles.

Men were not alone in changing their attitudes toward working women: women's views evolved too. Early in the twentieth century, given the dominant gender roles of the time, women may have worried about how their decision to join the labor force would affect their families and in particular their children. In another study, Fernández argues that women learned over time that a different type of life was both possible and possibly more appealing.[18] The beliefs about the desirability of working were transmitted across generations, ultimately giving rise to the initiation of a new norm in society. The learning mechanism can explain how changes in gender attitudes and a rise in female labor supply mutually reinforced each other. Fernández's research provides a powerful example that shows that the transmission of values and attitudes within families are both the cause and the effect of a social change.

CHANGES IN TIME USE AND EDUCATION

Despite the overall convergence in gender roles, some differences across genders still remain. As we saw above, the labor force participation rate of women is still slightly lower than that of men, and there is still a gap between the average wages of women and men. Compared to the labor market, we observe even larger differences in the home. Figures 6.3 and 6.4 display how the time use of men and women is divided between market work (formal employment or self-employment for profit) versus nonmarket work (taking care of the house, cooking, and so on, but excluding childcare).[19]

Men continue to spend most of their time on market work, with only a small decline in market time and an even smaller increase in work in the home. Women have increased their market work and decreased their nonmarket work over time as a result of their entry into the labor force. However, even today women do on average much more work in the home than men.

Our economic theory of parenting predicts that parenting choices for girls and boys will reflect the gender roles prevalent in society because parents desire to prepare their children for the economic circumstances that they will face in adulthood. Given the large increase in female labor force participation in recent decades, we would expect that parenting choices for girls during the same period gradually shifted from preparing them for being homemakers to equipping them for being successful career women. As an example of the shift in such choices, consider patterns in education. The trends in labor market participation suggest that parents of girls before, say, 1940 would have had little reason to expect their girls to have a strong need for the type of education that has a high payoff in the labor market, but from the 1960s onward, such an education would be equally valuable for boys and for girls. Hence, the incentive to provide girls with high levels of education

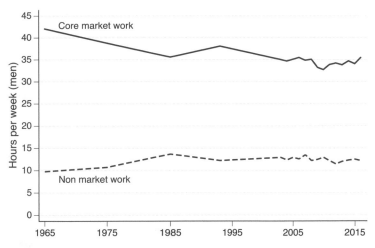

FIGURE 6.3. Time allocation of men in the United States

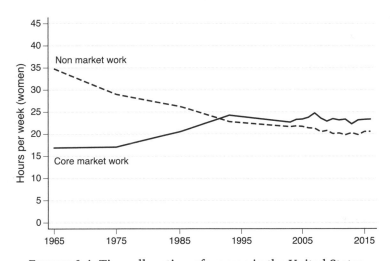

FIGURE 6.4. Time allocation of women in the United States

has risen over time. And indeed, while previously boys received more education than girls, the data show that women's relative education began to catch up with (and ultimately overtake) that of men just as their labor force participation and relative wages were rising.

Figure 6.5 displays the fraction of young adult women and men in the United States who have completed a college education (i.e., at least

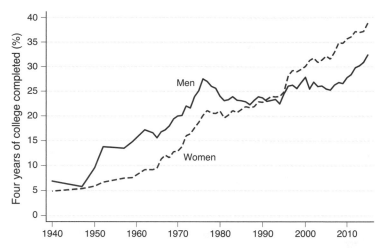

FIGURE 6.5. Share of age group 25–29 who have completed four years of college by gender in the United States

four years of college).[20] Before 1940, college education was rare and confined to a small elite group, with rates of less than 10 percent for both genders. Just after World War II, male but not female education started to rise rapidly (in part, this gap was amplified by the GI Bill, which covered tuition fees and living expenses of World War II veterans attending college). Throughout the 1950s and 1960s, there was a large gap in relative education—almost twice as many men as women completed college. Female education started to expand quickly after the mid-1960s, just as many more women started to work. By the early 1990s, young women had caught up with men, and by today more women than men complete college.[21]

Historically, women and men were also taught different skills. When Fabrizio was in middle school in the late 1970s in Italy, girls and boys would sit together, a relatively recent innovation in the Italian school system. However, there was an exception. When the timetable said "technical applications," boys and girls were separated. Fabrizio recalls his fruitless attempts to build the prototype of a steam engine, while his female schoolmates would learn to sew, cook, and entertain guests. In the fragmented Italian high school system, the adjective "feminine" still featured in the names of some vocational schools. The mission of those vocational schools was to form modern responsible housewives by teaching them proper table manners and home economics. Other schools were preparing girls to become stenographers and typists. Boys would instead attend industrial technical schools where the percentage of girls was tiny.

Gender imbalance is not just a memory of the past. In Nora's class in the Federal Institute of Technology, there are three male students per female student, reflecting the persistent gender gap in science and technology. When Maria, Fabrizio's wife, resigned her professorial appointment at the department of economics of the University of Zurich, not a single female full professor was left in the department. Northwestern and Yale, our current institutions, fare a little better, but gender balance in academia is still some way off.

DO PARENTS OF GIRLS AND BOYS HAVE A DIFFERENT PARENTING STYLE? EVIDENCE FROM THE UNITED STATES

Our theory maintains that altruistic parents respond to their expectations of what their children's lives will be like, and they aim to equip them with values, skills, and attitudes that will help them in the future. As we have seen, in industrialized (or, better, postindustrial) countries, the economic roles of women and men have substantially converged in recent decades, which suggests that differences in how parents treat boys and girls should have diminished also.[22]

The data on parenting styles discussed in previous chapters bears this out. Here we focus on the Panel Study of Income Dynamics (PSID) with the Child Development Supplement (CDS) in the United States (which we already used in chapter 5) because this data set contains a set of questions on gender attitudes in addition to information on parenting styles. We can construct measures of permissive, authoritative, and authoritarian parenting along the lines of the approach that we followed with the WVS.[23] The data allow us to distinguish the parenting styles that are used by parents of girls and boys. The questions on parenting style refer to the year 1997. Overall, consistent with our hypothesis, the distribution of parenting styles is similar for the two genders. Parents of girls are more likely to be authoritative and less likely to be permissive or authoritarian, but in terms of magnitude these differences are small (within one to two percentage points), resulting in almost identical distributions of parenting styles. This is what we would expect: if parents have similar plans and aspirations for their boys and girls, as well as similar perceptions of which values and skills will pay off, they should treat them in similar ways.

Despite the overall convergence in gender roles, there is still a lot of variation in attitudes toward gender today, with some subscribing to a vision of near-perfect gender equality and others continuing to support a more traditional division of gender roles. Our theory suggests that such differences in attitudes should be reflected in parenting: parents who would prefer their daughters to focus on home life and motherhood while their boys should be the primary breadwinners would have strong incentives to assert these views through their parenting choices.

The PSID-CDS data set contains a number of questions on gender attitudes, so we can examine whether this prediction is backed by the data. Consider the following statement: "There is some work that is men's and some that is women's and they should not be doing each other's." A parent who agrees with this statement would appear to favor traditional role models. As a consequence, we would expect that such a parent would strive to prepare daughters and sons for distinct gender roles, and hence treat them differently. In terms of parenting style, in chapter 5 we have linked authoritarian parenting to a low perceived return to children's independence. Parents who believe that women and men should take up narrowly prescribed roles in society rather than follow their own inclinations implicitly place less value on independence, and hence should be more likely to be authoritarian.

The data support this prediction. In the United States, there are now relatively few people who favor a strict separation of gender roles, with more than 80 percent of respondents either disagreeing or strongly disagreeing with the statement above. Those who do agree with the statement are substantially more likely to be authoritarian and substantially less likely to be permissive than the majority. Even when we control for other factors such as household income, education, age, and race, those who agree that women's and men's work should stay separated are almost twice as likely to be authoritarian compared to being permissive.[24]

What is more, the respondents who favor traditional gender roles are not only more authoritarian in general, but they are especially likely to be authoritarian if they have a daughter. Specifically, parents who agree with the statement on the separation of men's and women's work are 5 percentage points more likely to be authoritarian (after controlling for other factors) if their child is a boy, but 8 percentage points more likely if their child is a girl. These are large increases relative to the baseline probability of being authoritarian of about 39 percent.

The gender attitudes of parents are closely linked to economic variables. In particular, individuals who favor traditional gender roles tend to have lower family income and less education than those who favor more gender equality. Low family income can be a direct consequence of supporting traditional gender roles: in the households where respondents favor a strict separation of male and female spheres, the woman is less likely to be working outside the home, hence reducing the financial resources available to the household.

Another explanation for the association of traditional gender roles with household income and education is that mother and father can both work full-time only if they have access to childcare. If the only available childcare takes the form of paid day care or hiring a nanny, this choice will be more affordable for those with more economic resources.

Interestingly, one variable that turns out not to be an important determinant of gender attitudes is gender itself: those who favor traditional gender roles are as likely to be women as men. This suggests that traditional role models are not always remnants of a patriarchal society that men are more likely to support because it benefits them at the expense of women. Instead, in line with the economic theory of incentives, traditional role models may in part reflect trade-offs in organizing life at home and in the workplace, which affect women and men alike.

The PSID-CDS survey also asks a direct question about parenting boys versus girls, namely, whether the respondent agrees with the statement, "Parents should encourage just as much independence in their daughters as in their sons." In the survey, only a small fraction of respondents (6%) disagree with this statement. The few respondents who do not think that girls need as much independence also have more traditional attitudes about gender roles in general. For example, they are more than twice as likely as the others to think that it is more important for a wife to help her husband's career than to have one herself, and more than half of the respondents in this group agree that "it is much better for everyone if the man earns the main living and the woman takes care of the home and family."

Not surprisingly, how the view on girls' independence is associated with the choice of parenting style hinges on whether the respondent is the parent of a boy or of a girl. For parents of boys, agreeing with this statement does not change the likelihood of being authoritarian. For the parents of girls, however, believing that girls should be less independent is associated with an increase in the probability of being authoritarian by 25 percentage points, or close to a doubling of the probability of being authoritarian compared to the average. These correlations are consistent with our hypothesis that parents' expectations and aspirations regarding their children's future are a key determinant of parenting style.

PARENTING BOYS VERSUS GIRLS ACROSS COUNTRIES

Thus far, we have seen that in the United States, while most families raise boys and girls in similar ways, those parents who believe in traditional role models and a gender-based separation of work treat girls and boys differently. We now consider whether this relationship holds more broadly across societies. The theory of incentives suggests that in societies where traditional role models prevail and where men and women carry out substantially different tasks in their daily lives, differences in parenting between boys and girls should be more pronounced. We can examine this hypothesis by looking at other countries with a stronger separation of gender roles.

To determine the relationship between traditional gender attitudes and differences in parenting styles, we can make use of the WVS data set employed in previous chapters, which also includes questions on gender attitudes. We use the full sample, including both industrialized and developing countries. Consider the statement, "Men should have more right to a job than women," which we regard as a good indication of a gender-biased attitude. In the entire sample, about 40 percent of respondents agree with this statement. Within this gender-biased group, 48 percent are authoritarian parents, 39 percent are authoritative parents, and 13 percent are permissive parents. The corresponding proportions for the non-gender-biased group are 40 percent, 37 percent, and 23 percent. Thus, gender-biased respondents are more authoritarian and less permissive parents compared to the average. Religiosity is also closely associated with gender bias: 45 percent of the religious parents are gender-biased, as compared to 27 percent of nonreligious parents.

Table 6.1 shows that both religiosity and gender-biased attitudes are independent predictors of parenting style. Take the category of religious parents. There, as few as 13 percent of the gender-biased parents are permissive, compared to 18 percent of the gender-neutral parents. Conversely, as many as 51 percent of the gender-biased parents are authoritarian, compared to 46 percent of the gender-neutral parents. The pattern is even more striking if one considers the category of nonreligious parents. There, as many as 32 percent of the gender-neutral parents are permissive, compared to 18 percent of the gender-biased parents. Conversely, only 28 percent of the gender-neutral parents are authoritarian, which compares to 34 percent among the gender-biased parents. In the case of nonreligious parents, we also observe that gender-biased parents tend to be more authoritative.

The same pattern emerges if we infer gender bias using agreement with any of the following statements in the WVS: "It is a problem if

TABLE 6.1. Parenting styles, religiosity, and gender attitudes
(World Value Survey)

	Religious		Nonreligious	
	Gender-neutral	Gender-biased	Gender-neutral	Gender-biased
Permissive	18%	13%	32%	18%
Authoritative	36%	36%	40%	48%
Authoritarian	46%	51%	28%	34%
	100%	100%	100%	100%

women have more income than their husbands," "Preschool children suffer with a working mother," "University education is more important for a boy than for a girl," and "Men make better business executives than women do." In all these cases, religious and gender-biased respondents are most likely to be authoritarian, whereas nonreligious, gender-neutral respondents are most likely to be permissive. This pattern is broadly consistent with what we found in the PSID-CDS data for the United States.

Gender attitudes vary also with the level of development. Countries with higher GDP per capita have a much smaller fraction of people agreeing with the statement that men should have more rights to jobs than women. Within countries, education is the strongest predictor of gender attitudes. Respondents with at least a college education are much less likely to agree to the statement, and respondents with less than a high school education much more so. Gender attitudes are also related to political orientation; compared to respondents reporting a left-wing orientation, right wingers are much more likely to agree that men should have more rights to jobs than women, even after controlling for other determinants such as social class, education, age, and gender of respondent.

In rich countries, women's recent progress toward equality is often measured by the increase in female labor force participation. In the United States and the United Kingdom, for example, the women's liberation movement considers achieving equal work opportunities for

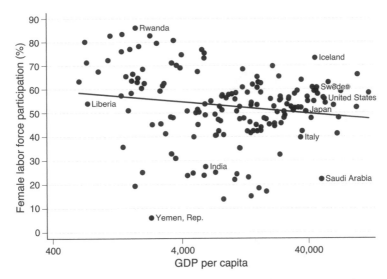

FIGURE 6.6. Female labor force participation and GDP per capita across countries in 2016

women one of its most important aims. Across a broader range of high-, middle-, and low-income countries, the relationship between female empowerment and female labor supply is less clear. In some countries, women do a lot of work precisely because they have little power.

Figure 6.6 shows how the female labor force participation rate varies relative to GDP per capita across countries.[25] The Western industrial countries are in the top-right corner: all of these countries have high income per capita (more than $30,000 in 2016) and a labor force participation rate of close to 40 percent or higher. One of the few rich countries where most women do not work is Saudi Arabia, a country whose wealth is based on extracting oil. Given the mainly resource-based economy, education and human capital are less economically important in Saudi Arabia compared to other rich countries, which arguably makes it less costly for the ruling regime to enforce traditional role models. Nevertheless, we are seeing some changes even in Saudi Arabia, with rising female labor force participation over time and a recently announced decision to rescind a long-standing ban on women driving cars.

Among the poorer countries with a GDP per capita below $4,000, we observe wide variation in female labor supply, with hardly any women working in some cases and in others participation being even higher than in the West. Here high participation of women in the labor market can actually be a symptom of unequal gender rights. This observation relates to our discussion of plough use earlier in this chapter. According to Boserup, in countries with low historical plough use a patriarchal culture can develop where most day-to-day work is done by women.[26] Indeed, many of the high-female-participation countries are places that score low on other measures of women's empowerment, such as political or economic rights or measures of violence against women.

In terms of parenting practices, these findings suggest that we should expect the way boys and girls are raised not to depend just on the country's level of development but also on the specific technologies, institutions, and cultural practices in place and the gender roles that they imply. A particularly relevant institution is marriage. There are still many countries (predominantly in Africa and the Middle East) where polygyny (the practice of men marrying multiple women) is common. Allowing men but not women to have multiple spouses is a form of gender discrimination, and countries where polygyny is common usually score low on various measures of gender equality.

A side effect of polygyny is that it raises the economic value of having daughters. When there is polygyny, brides are in high demand because richer men will be able to have multiple wives. This demand for wives is reflected in the institution of a bride price: the groom pays a price to the father of the bride for the privilege of marrying her.[27] Thus, from a parents' perspective, having daughters is economically valuable. There may be some benefits of this for daughters, as the parents have an added economic incentive to take good care of them. However, there is also a downside: when parents view daughters as an investment, they will also have a desire to have many of them, resulting in high fertility rates and relatively less money left for other forms of investment, such as business entrepreneurship. The economist Michèle Tertilt has shown that this effect leads to faster population growth and substantially lower savings in countries where polygyny is widespread, contributing to poor development outcomes in many of these countries.[28] For example, in Chad, Gambia, Guinea, and Sierra Leone, more than 20 percent of married men have at least two wives. All of these countries are also among the poorest in the word, with a level of income per capita in 2016 ranging from $473 in Gambia to $664 in Chad.[29]

The economic theory of incentives suggests that the economic "desirability" of girls versus boys should be reflected in how parents invest in their children. We can examine this prediction by comparing countries where girls are economically valuable (such as the countries with high polygyny rates) to other cultures where girls (purely in financial terms) are not an investment, but a financial burden. This is true in particular when parents, rather than receiving a bride price, are expected to provide their daughter with a substantial dowry when she marries, which is paid to the family of the groom. When dowries are combined with a patrilineal society (sons stay with the family and take over the parents' farm or business, and daughters join their husband's family), there is little economic upside to having daughters.

The different economic value of having girls versus boys is reflected in the choices that parents make. Most dramatically, in recent decades this has resulted in widespread use of sex-selective abortion in countries where there is a strong preference for male children. In countries such as India and China, many more sons than daughters are born, with an excess in male births of more than 10 percent in recent years. The Nobel laureate and economist Amartya Sen has termed this phenomenon the "missing women," that is, the shortfall in women relative to the natural ratio of about equal numbers of boys and girls.[30] Recent estimates are that there are more than 100 million missing women around the world—a fact that drives home the huge impact that incentives have on parents' decisions.[31] Notably, sex ratios at birth are more balanced or even tilt toward more girls being born in the African countries with high polygyny rates, where bride prices rather than dowries are common.

The unequal treatment of boys and girls does not stop at birth, either. In India, the phenomenon of missing women is not just due to fewer girls being born but also because of the higher child mortality rate for girls than for boys. This is, at face value, surprising because if equally treated, girls are actually somewhat less likely to get sick than boys and have higher survival rates in most societies. The evidence suggests that unequal treatment after birth is responsible for the disparity. One factor is malnutrition. Many children in India are stunted, which is a clear sign of malnutrition. Stunting is much less common for firstborn sons, which are also the children with the highest economic value for parents because, in patrilineal society, these sons will provide for their parents in old age. Another factor is breastfeeding, which tends to be very beneficial for children, especially if the quality of the available water is poor. The economists Seema Jayachandran and Ilyana Kuziemko have found that in India the duration of breastfeeding is shorter for girls than for boys, which contributes to the gap in child health and development.[32] They conjecture that this gap is due to son preferences. Breastfeeding suppresses fertility, and women with only daughters are more eager to try for another child (i.e., a son) than those who already have a boy.

These examples show that how parents think about raising boys and girls is closely tied to the local institutions in terms of gender roles and the economic value of each. The presence of polygyny, bride prices, dowries, and patrilineality all matter when parents make choices about parenting. The close association between parenting practices and such local institutions is another demonstration of the power of economic incentives in determining what parents do.

TEACHING KIDS ABOUT SEX BEFORE AND AFTER THE SEXUAL REVOLUTION

Another dimension of boy-girl differences in parenting relates to attitudes toward sex. Many parents attempt to educate their children about proper sexual activity, while others aim to instill in them that it is a good idea to abstain from sex until marriage. Much of the time, girls are put under much more pressure to preserve their virginity than boys. In some parts of the world, sharp divisions in the expectations that are placed on girls versus boys regarding sexual activity continue to the present day.

Much of parents' behavior in this realm can once again be understood in terms of reacting (more or less consciously) to incentives. In
addition to their personal views on morality, parents are aware that
engaging in premarital sex could have very real consequences for the
youngsters. First, there is the risk of acquiring a sexually transmitted
disease, which can lead to long-term repercussions for health and re-
production. Second, there is the risk of pregnancy. Third, even if the
first risks are avoided, there is a risk of social consequences if the child's
activities become the object of social judgments. There may be shaming
and ostracism, and getting married may become less likely or even
impossible for the child.

To some extent, these risks apply to both boys and girls, but most of
the time, girls are much more vulnerable. In Europe and the United
States during decades past, having a child out of wedlock would have
severe consequences for young women, with many young mothers
being ostracized by society and even their own families. The same was
not true for the fathers, and the identity of the father may not even
be known.

The consequences of being a single mother were severe due not just
to social consequences but also because of economic repercussions.
Before the onset of industrialization, most people were fairly poor and
malnutrition was pervasive. There was also much more exposure to
infectious diseases, and susceptibility to disease depended directly on
nutrition: well-fed children and adults are more resilient. Being a single
mother would often condemn young women to a life of poverty. With
no husband to support them, they and their children were economically vulnerable and hence at high risk of disease or even death. The
situation in many developing countries today is similar. Given these
severe consequences, it should come as no surprise that parents were
strict in enforcing chaste behavior, particularly when their daughters
were concerned.

The themes just discussed are analyzed in a recent study by the
economists Jesus Fernández-Villaverde, Jeremy Greenwood, and Nezih
Guner.[33] These authors argue that economics can explain why not only

parents but also institutions like churches and states have enforced norms and laws that stigmatize sex. On the one hand, parents caring for their daughters' well-being are wary of the economic and psychological harm that girls carrying out-of-wedlock babies could suffer. On the other hand, churches and governments are concerned about the costs associated with providing charity to unwed mothers. For these institutions, strict sexual mores were also a means to control the cost of their charitable activities. The study (in line with the theory of incentives of our book) argues that the costs and benefits of instilling sexual mores responded to changes in the economic environment over time that render the consequences of early sexual activity more benign. For instance, the general rise in income levels and the creation of the welfare state imply that the consequences of single motherhood are now much less severe than for earlier generations. Most importantly, there is no longer a close link between income and survival, so that this issue has ceased to be a literal question of life or death.

One key factor was an improvement in the technology of birth control: condoms greatly reduced exposure to sexually transmitted diseases, and the birth control pill allowed youngsters to engage in sex with minimal risk of pregnancy. In such an environment, parents have little reason to worry about the sexual adventures of their children. This is exactly what we observe. While presumably some parents would still prefer their children to be abstinent, in practice most adolescents in Western countries engage in sex before marriage, and this is not perceived to be a major problem, especially relative to other concerns such as, say, drug use or school performance. While in 1963 more than 80 percent of the population disapproved of premarital sex, data from the General Social Survey show that disapproval of premarital sex in the United States decreased from 34 percent in 1972 to 21 percent in 2012. Europeans are even more liberal. In Sweden, 54.4 percent of the babies born in 2013 had an unmarried mother, and acceptance of premarital sex is almost universal.

As these surveys suggest, in the industrialized countries, both the frequency with which people engage in premarital sex and its social acceptance have changed dramatically. The transformation was particularly fast during the "Sexual Revolution" of the 1960s and 1970s.[34] Changes in birth control technology and legislation that allowed young unmarried women access to the pill without parental consent were especially prominent during the same period. This explains both the changes in behavior and the changing attitudes of parents toward their children's sexual activities during that time.[35]

POLITICAL CONSEQUENCES OF RAISING BOYS AND GIRLS

So far, we have argued that changes at the level of the economy and society affect parents' incentives for how to raise girls and boys. We conclude this chapter by arguing that parents' incentives matter not just in terms of their decisions within the family but can also affect their political views and actions, and therefore feed back into changes in the society at large.

Parents' political views matter wherever government institutions affect children and parenting. This is true not just in democracies: even unelected governments generally find it in their interest to serve at least some of the population's needs. For example, we can understand the rise of public education in the nineteenth and twentieth centuries in part as a response to increased demand for education by parents who wanted their children to gain the skills necessary for success.

In this chapter, we have documented that parents of boys and girls often faced different incentives. Does this imply that parents of boys versus those of girls want different things from their government? There is strong evidence showing that this is indeed the case. Economist Ebonya Washington has shown that in the US Congress, having daughters substantially increases a legislator's likelihood to vote liberally on social issues, and especially on issues directly concerning women, such as reproductive rights.[36] Intriguingly, legislators who have daughters are also substantially more likely to be Democrats rather than Republicans, suggesting the possibility that looking at the world through the eyes of daughters makes politicians more likely to take liberal rather than conservative views on a wider range of issues.

Concern for daughters also played a central role among the political forces that drove the larger changes in women's rights in recent history. Consider the case of the United States and the United Kingdom. Legally and politically, these countries were highly patriarchal during the preindustrial period. Women had no political rights, such as voting or running for office. They also had few other rights, and particularly so if they were married. In fact, under common law, married women had no separate legal existence from their husbands. They were not able to own or inherit property, they could not work without permission from their husbands, they could not obtain a divorce, they could not obtain custody of their own children in case of separation, and marital rape was not legally recognized.

The status quo of legal nonexistence and the lack of legal protections for married women gradually changed throughout the nineteenth and twentieth centuries. Notably, much of the improvement in the legal rights of married women (such as improvements in marital property law, divorce law, and child custody law) occurred long before women gained the right to vote. This raises an interesting question: If only men could vote and run for office, why did they find it in their interest to extend more rights to women?

Of course, part of the answer is that the women's rights movement gained strength throughout the nineteenth century, and women became more effective at lobbying for their cause. However, Matthias has argued in research with Michèle Tertilt that economic forces that raised politicians' concern about their daughters' future also played a central role.[37] While male politicians may have been opposed to limiting their own gender-related privileges, they also liked to know that their daughters had protections against abusive or irresponsible husbands. These concerns became especially pronounced in the nineteenth century, which witnessed increasing problems of alcoholism among men, a situation that often carried severe consequences for their families.

From the perspective of men in their roles as voters and politicians, they faced a trade-off between their own privileges and more rights and protections for their daughters. Matthias and Michèle argue that the rising importance of human capital in the nineteenth century is what tilted the balance and led to the expansion of women's rights. Once getting a good education became a precondition for success, men had reason to worry not just about the well-being of their daughters but also about the education of their grandchildren. Given the division of gender roles at the time, mothers had primary responsibility for looking after children and making sure that they got a proper education. To succeed in this role, they needed rights and protections, which men were willing to guarantee once the education of children became a central concern.

The expansion of women's rights can therefore be understood as a shift in emphasis from the privileges of men to the needs of children, driven by the rising importance of human capital and education in the economy. We can see the increasing concern over the needs of children reflected in the public debate about the expansion of women's rights at the time. The change was remarkably quick. In 1868, an editorial in the *London Times* still made the case for continued patriarchy and argued that "the proposed change would totally destroy the existing relation between husband and wife. That relation is at present one of authority on the one side and subordination on the other. . . . If a woman has her own property, and can apply to her separate use her own earnings, she is practically emancipated from the control of her husband. . . . What is to prevent her from going where she likes and doing what she pleases?"[38] Just a year later, the *Times* had changed its tune and came out in support of women's rights. The needs of children were central to the argument: "It is true that theoretically [the husband] is liable to maintain her, as well as their children. But this liability is practically qualified. . . . As for children, no degree of neglect short of criminal maltreatment brings the father within the penalties of the law. . . . It must, therefore, be admitted that while the Common Law makes the husband master of all his wife's personal property, no equivalent obligation to support her or their children in tolerable comfort is imposed upon him."[39]

In summary, just as the parenting choices of parents of girls and boys line up with economic incentives, so do the actions of voters and politicians who look at the world in part through the eyes of their own children and then respond to their perceived needs.

OUTLOOK

The process of changing gender roles that started with industrialization is far from complete. While in the industrialized countries male and female participation in the formal labor market are now close to equal, large disparities in certain sectors of the economy remain, as does a sizeable gender wage gap. We do not know where this process will lead; women and men are not the same, and as far as parenting is concerned, the basic biology of pregnancy and breastfeeding will continue to play some role in people's choices.

What we do know is that differences in how girls and boys are raised are tightly linked to the incentives faced by their parents. The starkest examples of gender inequality and discrimination against girls can now be found in developing countries. If these countries succeed in transforming their economies such that human capital becomes the key factor of production and the separation of home and work spheres is overcome, we should observe substantial progress toward more equal treatment of girls and boys in the decades to come.

CHAPTER SEVEN

Fertility and Child Labor

From Large to Small Families

Long before parents consider which parenting style to adopt, they have to confront more basic questions, namely, whether to have children in the first place and, if so, how many. The answers that parents in the industrialized world arrive at today are vastly different from those of most parents before them, and also different from those of parents in other parts of the world.

FROM LARGE FAMILIES TO SMALL FAMILIES: BY CHOICE, NOT BY ACCIDENT

The modern ideal is for families to be small. In the United States, a large majority of adults say that the ideal number of children for a family to have is two, and less than 15 percent favor having four children or more, which was still the norm a few decades ago in the time of the baby boom.

Figure 7.1 shows how Americans' views of an ideal family have changed over the past seven decades.[1] Until the mid-1960s, large families were popular: the most desired family size was four children, followed by three-child families, and less than 30 percent of respondents said that having two children was best. From the mid-1960s to the 1980s, the proportions shifted continuously in favor of smaller families, leading to the current norm of two-child families.

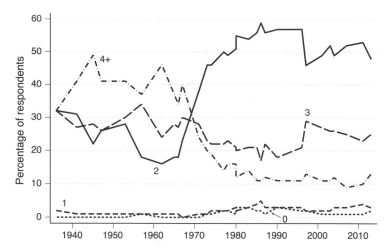

FIGURE 7.1. Desired family size ("What do you think is the ideal number of children for a family to have?") in the United States

If we go further back in history, families were even larger. In the nineteenth century, most families had five or more children, and having just three or four would have been considered the bare minimum.

What explains the trend toward smaller families? Certainly, the availability of birth control plays some role. Starting in the 1960s, the introduction of the birth control pill made it easier for couples to end up with the exact number of children they wanted. Generally, however, researchers working on fertility choice regard birth control technology as a secondary issue. People have long known various ways of influencing how many children are born; important examples are the timing of marriage (later marriage for girls reduces the potential lifetime number of children), breastfeeding practices (breastfeeding suppresses menstruation, though it is not an infallible method of birth control), and basic methods of birth control such as coitus interruptus. Many of the major changes in fertility behavior took place long before modern methods of birth control such as latex condoms or the pill became widely available.[2]

A study by the development economist Lant Pritchett corroborates our view that fertility is mostly determined by choice. Pritchett documents that across countries the total fertility rate closely tracks the desired fertility rate. The correlation coefficient between actual and desired fertility is very high, indicating that the main determinant of differences in fertility across countries is the number of children people claim to desire.[3]

Having ruled out that fertility outcomes are mainly a matter of chance, the economic perspective suggests that if people choose to have fewer children, incentives for having large versus small families must have shifted. Applying this hypothesis to the choice of the number of children, the implication is that either the benefits from having more children have gone down, or the cost of having many children has gone up. On the cost side, the trend toward more intensive parenting that we documented in previous chapters may be an important part of the story: if parents desire to invest a lot in their children and spend a lot of time with each and every one, having additional children becomes more costly both in terms of money and time.

In this chapter, we apply the theory of incentives to understand parents' fertility choices across countries and over time. We will argue that changes in the cost of raising children play a key role in explaining the data. The intensity of parenting is one part of the cost of children, but it is neither the only nor the most important one. Three additional components of the cost of children play a key role: the economic returns to child labor, the cost of investing in human capital, and the value of women's (i.e., mothers') time. We will show how changes in these costs can explain much of the evidence on how many children people choose to have.

FERTILITY CHOICE THROUGHOUT HISTORY AND ACROSS COUNTRIES

Consider first the basic facts of fertility choice. Throughout most of history and much of the world today, people have had many more children than the one or two common in today's rich countries. The fertility choices made by people in a country are commonly summarized by the so-called total fertility rate. The total fertility rate is the sum of age-specific fertility rates (i.e., the number of births to mothers of a given

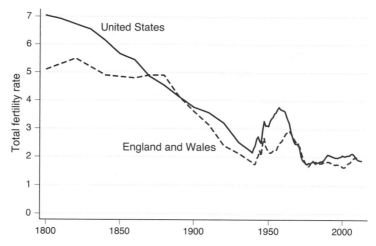

FIGURE 7.2. Total fertility rate in the United States and England and Wales

age, divided by the number of women of this age) across all ages. The total fertility rate gives the total number of children a woman who survives throughout the entire childbearing period will have over her lifetime, provided that age-specific fertility rates stay constant over time. Hence, the total fertility rate can be interpreted as an approximation of the average number of children per woman. A total fertility rate of around 2.1 (sometimes called the population replacement rate) is consistent with a constant population in the absence of migration. Today, the total fertility rate is below the population replacement rate in almost all industrialized nations, while it is above the replacement rate in a large number of developing countries.

Figure 7.2 shows how fertility rates have changed in the United States and the United Kingdom (specifically, England and Wales) from 1800 to the present.[4] In the early nineteenth century, families were large, with about five children per woman in England and Wales and almost seven in the United States. Over the course of the nineteenth century, fertility rates started to decline, gradually in the United States and rapidly in England and Wales after about 1880. By the early twentieth century, fertility rates had fallen to less than half of their initial values; typical families had two or three children, not much different from today.

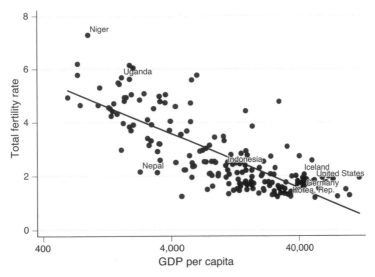

FIGURE 7.3. Total fertility rate and GDP per capita across countries in 2015

During the twentieth century, fertility rates initially continued their downward trend. By the mid-1930s, just after the Great Depression, the total fertility rate had reached about two children per woman in both countries. The trend toward low fertility was briefly interrupted after World War II, when the baby boom period saw rising fertility across industrialized countries. The baby boom was especially strong in the United States, where fertility returned to nearly four children per woman in the late 1950s. However, soon the downward trend in fertility reestablished itself. The low fertility rates of the 1930s were reached again in the 1970s, with little change since.

Apart from the baby boom period, the dominant pattern in the last two hundred years has been one of declining fertility during a time of economic growth: the higher the income, the fewer children were born. This negative relationship between income and fertility also holds across countries today. Figure 7.3 displays the relationship between GDP per capita (measuring economic development) and the total fertility rate across countries in 2015.[5] The picture shows that, on average, the number of children is lower when GDP per capita is higher. In most of the richest countries of the world, the total fertility rate is between one and two children per woman. At the other end of the scale, countries with a GDP per capita of less than $1,500 all have fertility rates above four. In the poorest countries of the world today, women have between five and seven children in their lifetime, similar to what was observed in the United States and England two hundred years ago.

The most striking pattern in the data is that the richer people are, the fewer children they have. However, while this pattern holds both within and across countries in the current era of industrialization and economic growth, the picture is quite different if we consider earlier history. In fact, the decline in fertility observed in the United States, England, and other countries during a time of improving conditions amounts to a sharp reversal of a stable relationship between living standards and fertility that had prevailed throughout most of human history. Before about 1800, the relationship between living standards and fertility was positive: when times were good, people responded by having more children. At the same time, good economic conditions led to lower mortality rates, mostly because of improved availability of food. Both factors implied that good economic times led to faster population growth.

It was this positive relationship between income levels and population growth that led economist and demographer Thomas Malthus (who died in 1834, just before the onset of the fertility decline) to make dire predictions for the fate of humanity. Malthus argued in his famous book *An Essay on the Principle of Population* that any increase in the supply of food accelerates population growth, until there are so many extra mouths to feed that the food surplus is used up. At that point, famine and poverty will set in. This crisis will reduce the size of the population until the food supply has caught up, and the cycle starts anew. According to Malthus, outside of short periods of surplus, this cycle condemns humanity to persistent poverty, with no prospect of an improvement in living standards that can be sustained for the long term.[6]

Today, we know that most of the world ultimately escaped from the Malthusian cycle. Still, Malthus's theory provides a broadly accurate description of the relationship between income and population in the preindustrial era. Even in earlier times, there were large differences in the level of productivity and in technological progress around the world. In our era, people who live in technologically advanced countries experience higher living standards. In contrast, if the Malthusian mechanism is in place, an increase in productivity (say, the introduction of a crop rotation system that increases the food harvest per acre) primarily results in higher population growth. Over time, the population growth outruns the increase in food production, due to the progressive crowding of productive land and the diminishing returns to labor in agriculture, the main productive activity in Malthus's time. At this point, living standards (measured as food per person) will have returned to the previous level, and the only permanent result of the increase in productivity will be higher population density.

Consistent with this prediction of the Malthusian theory, productivity differences in the preindustrial era were primarily reflected in population density, but not in income per person. Living standards in most countries around the world were similar and close to the subsistence level, but more productive places had more people. For example, China was technologically the most advanced country for many centuries, including in agriculture, where labor-intensive rice farming produced much higher yields than European agriculture. Yet the average Chinese farmer was not much better off than the average European one. Instead, China experienced a larger population growth and an extremely high population density, making China the world's most populous country, which it still is today. Similarly, Western Europe experienced relatively high productivity growth in the centuries leading up to industrialization. While this growth did bring some improvements in living standards, its primary effect was to increase population density and to drive up the share of Western Europe in world population.

In the first decades of the industrialization era, just when Malthus was developing his theory, the prediction of a positive relationship between economic growth and population growth still held up. The population in England grew rapidly as factories started spreading in the cities, leading to the crowded conditions and widespread poverty familiar from Charles Dickens's writings. Just a few decades later, the relationship between income and population growth reversed, bringing the Malthusian era in world history to an end.

The reversal in fertility behavior that we observe in the United States and England in the nineteenth century is also known as the *demographic transition*. Apart from fertility decline, the demographic transition is also characterized by declining mortality: in parallel with families having fewer babies, life expectancy rose, and infant and child mortality fell. The demographic transition is a universal feature of economic development: each and every country that successfully escaped preindustrial stagnation also experienced a large decline in fertility and mortality in the course of industrialization. Generally, countries that start to grow later undergo the demographic transition with increased speed. It took multiple generations for the fertility rate to be cut in half in the United States and England, but less than twenty years in the "Asian Tiger" economies of Hong Kong, Singapore, South Korea, and Taiwan.

THE "QUALITY" OF CHILDREN AND THE ECONOMICS OF FERTILITY

For a long time, economists used to view fertility choice as being outside the purview of their field and left explanations behind fertility rates to other disciplines, such as sociology and demography. Today, however, we regard fertility as just another choice people make that can be analyzed with the same economic toolset that applies elsewhere.

The economic perspective is that parents' decisions on how many children to have can be explained by the incentives they face. Incentives depend on what parents' objectives are in having children and on what the costs of having children are. Start with the objectives. Why do people have children? A simple answer is that evolution has programmed people to want to have children: after all, childless parents do not pass on their genes, so natural selection should favor individuals who like to have children. However, a general desire for children cannot explain the basic facts of fertility choice that we have described. Parents would then like to have as many children as possible, subject to the constraint of being able to afford the cost of raising the children.

A poor family close to the subsistence level would be able to afford only a small number of children. In contrast, a millionaire should have no trouble supporting a very large number of children. Hence, if all people cared about was the number of kids they have, we would expect that just as richer people tend to buy more food and more cars than others, they should also end up with more children. But as we have seen, at least over the last two hundred years, we observe precisely the opposite: the richer people are, the fewer children they choose to have.

The puzzle posed by the negative income-fertility relationship was first tackled by the Nobel laureate Gary Becker, who did more than anyone else to apply economic thinking to understanding why parents make the decisions they do.[7] Becker's basic insight was that while parents enjoy having children in general, they also enjoy what he called the "quality" of their children. Child quality can be interpreted in different ways, but generally this means that parents enjoy their children being successful and prosperous, that is, they altruistically care about the welfare of their children. This, of course, is the same assumption on which we base our analysis of parenting styles.

Parental concern for child quality implies that parents face two related but distinct decisions regarding their children: how many to have and how much to invest in each of them. Fertility choices then depend on income (or, more generally, the resources available to the parents), on the costs of children, but also on the relative attractiveness of investing in child "quantity" (i.e., a large number of children) rather than quality. From this viewpoint, a decline in fertility during a period of rising incomes could be due either to an increase in the cost of children or to a shift in the relative attractiveness of child quantity and quality.

We believe that the drop in fertility that accompanied economic growth reflected a shift from investing in child quantity to child quality, driven by economic incentives. The most important form of child quality is education. When we talk of investing in child quality, we mean the choice to send children to school rather than making them work, and perhaps to pay for a good private school rather than sending them to a mediocre public school. Schooling is not an end in itself; when parents invest in children's education, they do it with the expectation that this is an investment that will bear returns in terms of better economic prospects for the kids.

In the view of economists working on the interaction of economic development and fertility choice, the economic trend that was largely responsible for the demographic transition was an increase in the return to investments in human capital, that is, rising returns to education. In particular, the seminal contribution by the economists Oded Galor and David Weil argues that high returns to education incentivized parents to invest more in child quality and, to make such investments affordable, to have fewer children than earlier generations did.[8]

In the preindustrial economy, for most parents there was no economic reason to provide their children with formal schooling to acquire literacy, math skills, and the like. Most of the population was illiterate, and that was just fine, as most occupations did not require literacy skills. Literacy was only required for some very exclusive professions, such as the clergy and scholars at the early universities. Such occupations were not open to most of the population, so there was little reason to desire such an education for one's children. We thus see that the lack of an economic return to education explains the lack of investment in child quality.

The flip side of a low return to education is that child labor is more attractive. Children who were not occupied in school could work and help support the family from a young age. Hence, a low return to education also explains why child labor was widespread in preindustrial times. In fact, the possibility of child labor arguably had an even larger effect on the cost of having children than the education choice: working children mostly support themselves and are thus "cheap" from the parents' perspective. This is why when children are working, it makes sense to have a lot of them.

CHILD LABOR

When it comes to child labor, one may wonder whether we are stretching the concept of altruistic parents who care about the welfare of their children a bit too far. After all, among the social evils that raise the most concern in industrialized countries today, child labor ranks high on the list. On college campuses, there are regular protests against the use of "sweatshop" labor, and boycotts are maintained against producers of shoes and clothing who are thought to exploit child laborers. Does it make sense to ever conceive of child labor as the well-considered choice by an altruistic parent who cares for her children?

Clearly, there are cases of child labor that are not due to a parent's choice, such as in cases of child abduction or, more commonly, when orphaned children are involved. But both now and in the past, most child labor ultimately is the result of choices made by a parent. For many parents today, sending their children to work at a young age is simply unimaginable. Yet even in rich countries the time when child labor was common is not that far in the past. In fact, child labor, not as a main occupation, but as a part-time activity, can still be found in many parts of the economy. This is particularly true for farming, where many children are still expected to help out with the "family business" from a young age.

This was also Matthias's experience. While Matthias's father was primarily a civil servant, the family also ran a small farm on the side, and there was no question that the children had to help out when necessary, performing tasks ranging from feeding the animals to weeding the fields in the summer. Matthias was not an enthusiastic child laborer and tried to get out of it whenever possible, but it never occurred to him (or presumably anyone else) that there could be anything wrong with him working.

Indeed, even when child labor is made illegal, there is usually an exception for employment on family farms, for example, by making laws specific to manufacturing or factories. In Germany, teenagers can obtain a driver's license for cars only at age eighteen, but children on a farm can be licensed to drive huge tractors from the age of fifteen, and they are not even required to pass a driving test.

In the past, child labor was not the exception, but the norm. Before the rise of mass education in the nineteenth century, child labor was expected of all but the most advantaged children. Child labor was not just common; it was not stigmatized in any way. If anything, it was the opposite: child labor was considered to be beneficial for children, whereas the opposite of child labor, namely idleness, was considered harmful, leaving them unprepared for adult life and potentially leading them to a life of crime. Well before the creation of modern schools that taught literacy and numeracy, there were so-called "work schools," in which otherwise unoccupied children would be put to productive use. Unlike modern-day "sweatshops," these work schools were not primarily designed to make a profit off children, but rather to prevent otherwise unoccupied children from getting into trouble.

Even today, when child labor is generally considered immoral, and the source of exploitation and abuse, many people may regard some work experience to be useful for children. This is certainly true for older children, who may use summer jobs to get a first glimpse of "real life." And on farms, it continues to be common (and legal) for children to help out with the family's work.

Of course, the conditions of child labor in preindustrial times and in developing countries today are quite different from, say, helping out for a few hours on a modern farm once in a while. But the decision to send children to work also has to be put into the perspective of the overall situation of families, which, in places where child labor is common, is usually one of poverty. When feeding the family is a daily challenge and schooling is not a realistic option anyway, having the older children contribute to the family's income is a natural choice.

An interesting, and perhaps also alarming, example of the role child labor opportunities play in determining fertility rates can be found in the early industrialization period.[9] Before industrialization, child labor in the vast majority of cases meant that children were working with their parents. Even after factory work became the norm, hiring entire families as workers (parents and their children together) continued to be common.[10] But there also arose some new forms of child labor that specifically took advantage of children's smaller bodies. One important example of this is mining. The Industrial Revolution was built on coal, and thus, coal mining became a major growth industry during industrialization.

Coal mines were hazardous places, but given the small spaces miners often had to work in, they were also ones where children could be put to especially productive use. In mining regions, children received high wages, and having many children working could be lucrative for parents. It should then be no surprise that throughout the early nineteenth century, mining regions were characterized by extraordinarily high fertility rates. This was true not just in England, but across the whole of Europe: mining areas had the highest fertility rates, followed by rural areas, whereas urban fertility rates were lower and also started to decline earlier.[11] These observations support the conjecture that the incentives provided by the potential returns to child labor had a substantial impact on parents' fertility decisions.

EDUCATION, CHILD LABOR, AND FERTILITY DECLINE

Now consider the relationship between child labor, education, and fertility choices in the specific example of England, the birthplace of the Industrial Revolution. Early industrialization lowered the demand for skilled workers because specialized artisans could be replaced with machinery operated by unskilled workers. Moreover, industrialization initially also increased the demand for child labor, not just in mines but also in factories. The dominant industrial sector early on was textile production, and just like in the mines, there was demand for children: small hands can be an advantage in weaving, for example.

Over time, however, industrialization created a much higher demand for human capital. The creation of larger industrial enterprises led to the rise of administrative departments with a need for literate and numerate clerical workers. The increase in wealth also swelled the size of governments and led to the creation of the welfare state, which created an additional demand for clerical workers in the public sector.

From the parents' perspective, the rising returns to education suddenly made sending children to school a much more attractive option. This explains why schooling rates started to rise sharply in the mid-nineteenth century, well before public, compulsory schooling was introduced. As it does today, schooling started to hold the promise of a

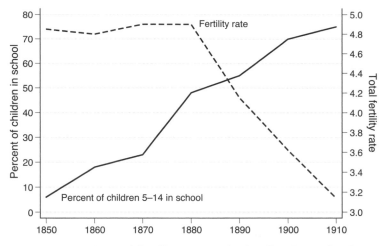

FIGURE 7.4. Total fertility rate and schooling in England

better economic life for children, and altruistic parents responded by taking their children out of work and putting them into school.

Figure 7.4 shows that even in 1850, the fraction of children who attended school was very small.[12] However, in the following decades, schooling rose quickly, with close to half of children attending school in 1880 and more than 70 percent in 1910. Thus, it was precisely during the phase of rapid fertility decline when more and more parents decided to send their children to school.[13]

The converse of the increase in schooling is the decline in child labor. Before the rise of mass schooling, most children would perform labor of some form, often by helping out their parents on the family farm, in the workshop, or at home. There were also many children in formal employment, including factory work. Figure 7.5 shows that in 1850 more than a quarter of children aged ten to fourteen were in formal employment. In the following decades, as schooling rose in popularity, child labor started to be crowded out, and in the twentieth century, formal child labor became increasingly rare in Britain.[14]

The rise in schooling and the decline in child labor explain why children started to become much more expensive from the parents' perspective. School fees had to be paid; even more importantly, the children no longer contributed to household income through their labor. These

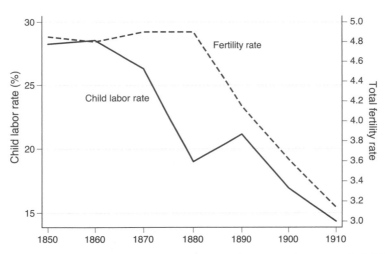

FIGURE 7.5. Total fertility rate and child labor rate (fraction of children aged 10–14 working) in England

factors shifted incentives toward having smaller families. Thus, the economic change of a higher demand for human capital created the modern, education-oriented, middle-class family and thereby explains some of the most important social trends in the industrialization period.

The close association between child labor, education, and fertility that characterizes the demographic transition period in England can also be observed across countries today. Figures 7.6 and 7.7 display how schooling rates and child labor rates relate to fertility across countries in more recent times. In figure 7.6, we see that in all countries where children's expected education is below four years of schooling, the fertility rate is well above four children per woman.[15] Conversely, there is not a single country with expected schooling of ten years or more with a fertility rate at that level. Similarly, figure 7.7 shows that in countries where child labor is widespread (measured by the percentage of children aged seven to fourteen who work), fertility rates are also high.[16]

In the industrialized world, outside of agriculture, child labor is now a distant memory. Instead, social concern about child labor is focused on children working in "sweatshops" in developing countries. Nevertheless, the basic trade-off between work and education is still present

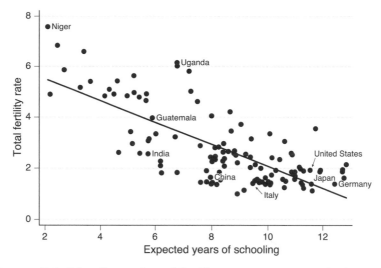

FIGURE 7.6. Schooling and total fertility rate across countries in 2010

today and may well continue to affect fertility choices in the future. In Germany, for example, the school system in most states has separate academic and vocational tracks. For children on the vocational tracks of *Hauptschule* and *Realschule*, formal schooling generally ends after nine or ten grades, usually at ages fifteen to sixteen. Subsequently, many of these children start formal apprenticeship programs in which they earn a salary. If they continue living at home (as most do), they are often expected to contribute some of their income to help with overall household expenses. Just a few decades ago, working-class children were expected to take up apprenticeships and start earning money even if they were academically gifted. For Matthias's mother, who grew up in a small farming village in Northern Germany, being allowed to continue even through *Realschule* (that is, through the tenth year of school) was a privilege that was highly unusual for the time.

Nowadays, education has expanded yet again, and more parents desire their children to remain in school at least until the completion of high school if at all possible. But similar trade-offs can arise even for higher education. In the United States, as the cost of college has risen disproportionately to growth in average incomes, children from poorer

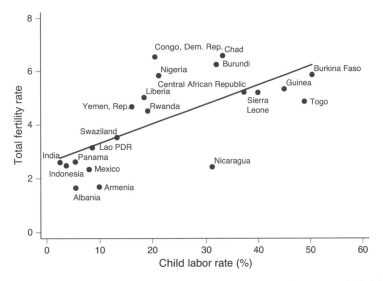

FIGURE 7.7. Total fertility rate and child labor rate (fraction of children aged 10–14 working) across countries in 2010

families are increasingly constrained in their education choices by their parents' ability to pay. Conversely, families who want to provide the best possible education to their children are acutely aware of the high potential cost of doing so, which may well discourage them from having another child.

THE ROLE OF MORTALITY RATES

Another factor that plays a role in determining fertility rates is the second aspect of the demographic transition, namely mortality. Before the late nineteenth century, infant and child mortality rates were universally high around the world. In England, for example, in the early nineteenth century about one in three children would not live to see their first birthday. Mortality rates were especially high among the children of the poorest parents, who struggled to feed their children and provide good shelter, and often lived in unhygienic conditions; the lack of access to clean water was especially deadly. But the richest families were not immune to the misfortune of losing young children: vaccinations for

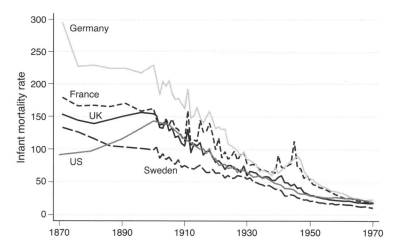

FIGURE 7.8. Infant mortality rate (mortality per 1,000 live births before first birthday) in United States and European countries

various potentially deadly diseases were not yet available, and before the discovery of antibiotics, even routine infections could end up being fatal for young children. In biographies from the preindustrial era, the specter of death was an ever-present danger for children. For instance, Johann Sebastian Bach had twenty children with two wives, but only half of them survived to adulthood. His children and grandchildren were no luckier, and by the end of the nineteenth century, there were no remaining descendants of the great composer.

Figure 7.8 shows that infant mortality rates remained high until the end of the nineteenth century.[17] In the United Kingdom, for example, in 1900 more than 15 percent of children would not survive to their first birthday. However, survival rates improved gradually as a result of improved hygiene, better nutrition, the introduction of vaccinations, and the availability of antibiotics.

Knowing that losing a child at a young age was a likely possibility must have weighed heavily on parents in earlier times. What is less clear is whether this anticipation shifted parents' incentives toward wanting more or fewer children. On the one hand, one might argue that high child mortality and the grief that comes with it increases the cost of having children, which may lower the desire to have additional children. On the other hand, if parents feel that having at least a few surviving children is essential, it may also be that in the face of high mortality rates they decide to have more of them in order to improve the odds that at least some of them will survive. From this perspective, high child mortality may be expected to increase the desire for large families. However, any such effect was likely to be limited by the fact that even in the preindustrial era, most of child mortality was concentrated at young ages (i.e., infant mortality before the first birthday). Once a child had survived the first year, the odds of reaching adulthood were good. This implies that couples could ensure a high likelihood of having surviving children by having an additional baby whenever a child died during the first year, that is, so-called *replacement fertility* as a reaction to infant mortality. A number of empirical studies find evidence supportive of replacement fertility, but generally the effect is less than one-for-one, in the sense that, on average, additional births do not fully make up for the loss of a child.[18]

Overall, the evidence suggests the decline in mortality rates may have been a contributing factor to the overall decline in fertility during the demographic transition.[19] At the same time, mortality alone can account for only a minor portion of the change in fertility. Given the evidence on replacement fertility, a decline in mortality should trigger a less than one-for-one decline in fertility, implying that the number of surviving children would actually go up. In the course of the demographic transition, however, fertility declines much more than mortality, so that the average number of children per family surviving into adulthood falls substantially. This suggests that other factors must be responsible for most of the decline in fertility.[20]

Another indication of a relatively minor role for mortality is the timing of the fertility decline: In the major industrialized countries, rapid fertility decline started decades before the major reductions in infant mortality in the twentieth century and is more closely aligned with changes in schooling rates and child labor compared to changes in child mortality (see figs. 7.4 and 7.5).

THE POLITICAL CONSEQUENCES OF THE
TRANSFORMATION IN PARENTING

The term "Industrial Revolution" suggests that the economic and social transformation that first started in late eighteenth-century Britain and later took hold all around the world was primarily about a switch in the methods of production. But as we have seen in this chapter, the Industrial Revolution did much more than replace farms and small workshops with factories; it also resulted in a complete transformation of family life, from large families living in poverty with working children toward the modern ideal of two parents with only a few children who spend their youth in school and are put on a path toward future prosperity. The most important driving force of this transformation was not so much the creation of the factory system but the growing importance of human capital. Where previously most people's income was primarily based on the returns to their physical strength, after about 1850 human capital in the form of education and knowledge became the main economic factor. In response, successive generations of parents decided to have fewer and fewer children, and to devote more and more time and resources to providing them with the best education possible.

Yet another dimension of the transformations that came with industrialization is political: the same phase of development that brought about the modern family also brought about the modern state. What we mean by this is that the large states that are now well established in all industrialized countries (usually democratic, raising a lot of taxes, heavily involved in education and regulation of the labor market, and providing broad social insurance) did not exist before industrialization, but were almost fully formed by the early twentieth century. We are discussing these changes here because some of the forces that changed parents' incentives to have many versus few children also changed parents' incentives to act in their roles as voters and, more generally, political actors. This is particularly relevant because some of the key aspects of the modern state are intertwined with the modern family.

We already discussed in the previous chapter how the increased importance of education contributed to the expansion of women's rights in the nineteenth century. A central motive underlying reforms in women's rights was the protection of married women from the whims of irresponsible husbands, so the women could, in turn, protect and provide for their children and make sure they receive a proper education. Another example is the public provision of old-age insurance (such as social security, public pensions, and health care for the elderly), which became an increasingly important issue after falling family sizes and higher mobility meant that the elderly became less able to rely on their children living with them and supporting them.

An even more direct link between changes in the family and political change can be found in the area of public education. In the United States and England, the government did not play an appreciable role in education until the late nineteenth century. The formal schooling that had been available generally consisted of Sunday schools provided by churches, which did not teach much beyond basic literacy skills (and, of course, the Bible). When the demand for human capital rose and education increasingly became an important factor of production, parents who wanted their children to be educated provided a natural constituency in favor of public provision of education. Another part of the coalition consisted of employers: owners of modern enterprises wanted to meet their own needs for a skilled workforce and thus also had an interest in supporting an expanded state role in public education.[21]

Given these forces, England moved from a laissez faire approach in the education sector to state-funded, compulsory education within the space of a few decades at the end of the nineteenth century. Education reform started around the same time in the United States. Given that education is primarily a state (not federal) responsibility, the spread of compulsory, public education was slower compared to England, but even the laggards had introduced comprehensive education reform before World War I. Tellingly, the most industrial states were also at the forefront of expanded education.

Another instructive example is the regulation of child labor, which we examined from an economic perspective in our earlier research.[22] The first child labor laws were passed in Britain in the 1830s. These were mostly driven by humanitarian concern for working children and specifically targeted the abuses of children in industrial sectors such as mining. Much wider regulations of child labor (imposing minimum-age laws for all of manufacturing) came decades later, during the same period when public schooling was also introduced.

The main political force that advanced broad child labor restrictions was the labor movement, namely, unions and their associated political parties. Unions strive to look after the workers' interests, and this may involve seeking to restrict potential sources of competition that could undercut workers' wages. This explains why, even to the present day, unions are often skeptical of free trade and sometimes support limits on immigration. The drive to restrict child labor can be understood in the same terms: if children are prevented from working, there is less competition for adult union workers, which tends to increase labor demand and push up wages.

There is a crucial difference between this and other forms of labor regulation, however, that explains why child labor appeared on the union agenda only when mass education was also taking off. In the case of, say, restricting immigration, the trade-off is clear-cut: there is competition for jobs between union workers and foreigners who the union does not represent. In the case of child labor, in contrast, the potential competition (working children) often comes from the same families that are represented by unions. Union workers who rely on child labor for a sizeable part of their family income are unlikely to support restrictions.

This observation explains why in the early industrialization period, when child labor was common, restricting child labor was not high on unions' agendas. What made the difference was that in the late nineteenth century, the rising demand for human capital prompted many working-class parents to send their children to school. As a result, there was now a constituency that no longer relied on their own children's labor, but could still benefit from restricting other parents from sending their children to the factories. Hence, it was only in the age of mass education that the labor movement identified restricting child labor as a key objective.

The influence of the labor movement can also be observed in the fact that child labor was specifically restricted where children were competing with adult workers, namely in manufacturing. In contrast, child labor continued to be legal in family agriculture, where assigning light work to children could make the overall business run more efficiently. Hence, while humanitarian concern about children also played some role (especially early on), unions' drive to limit competition is what explains the widespread adoption of general restrictions on child labor.

Similar political and economic forces are at work in developing countries where child labor is still widespread today. Many Western activists motivated by humanitarian concerns attempt to push back against child labor through product boycotts, the imposition of international labor standards, and public campaigns against "sweatshop" labor. Such measures may backfire if they displace working children into informal employment and lower direct competition between adult and child workers. If adult workers have less reason to be worried about competition from children, political support within developing countries for the introduction of a comprehensive ban of child labor will fall. Against their original intentions, such campaigns may then delay the ultimate eradication of child labor.[23]

EXPLAINING THE BABY BOOM

The long-term trend toward low fertility rates in industrialized countries has been fairly continuous for more than a century, except for one major interruption: the baby boom period after World War II. Fertility shot up in the 1950s and 1960s, not just in the United States, but also in war-ravaged European countries and in Japan. As figure 7.9 shows, the baby boom was especially pronounced in the Allied countries that (for the most part) did not fight on their own soil: in addition to the United States, this includes Canada, Australia, and New Zealand.[24]

So far, our economic explanations for parents' choice of the number of children have focused on the quantity-quality trade-off, that is, the notion that parents had fewer children because forgoing child labor and seeking high-quality education made children expensive. The baby boom period presents a challenge to this interpretation; fertility rose sharply, but education levels continued to increase, and there was no

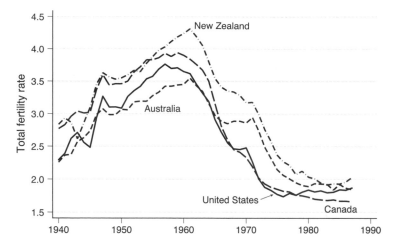

FIGURE 7.9. Total fertility rate during and after World War II in United States and Allied countries

reemergence of child labor. Nevertheless, the baby boom can be readily explained in terms of economic forces.

The first factor to consider when explaining the baby boom is that the main driver behind changes in fertility behavior had switched. Increasing investment in child quality had driven down fertility rates a few decades earlier, but this was no longer an important factor by the early postwar era. By that time, child labor had mostly disappeared in industrialized countries. Schooling was already compulsory and publicly provided in all advanced economies, so that education also ceased to be an important part of changes in the costs of children. While education levels continued to increase, now most of this increase concerned tertiary (college and postgraduate) education. At the time, higher education was much less costly than today and most students attended well-funded public institutions, so that the cost of education had only an indirect impact on parents' decisions.

In contrast, there are other components of the cost of childrearing that did change substantially during the baby boom period. In an era of public education and low food prices, the biggest cost of having children is the time it takes to raise them. The time cost associated with raising children has two different components. First, there is the actual amount of time required to take care of children, and second, there is the economic value of that time. Leading explanations of the baby boom focus on these two factors.

Consider, first, the actual time required to raise children. Some aspects of this time cost have changed little or not at all over time; for example, pregnancy still lasts just about nine months. But there are other costs to raising children that are tied up with more general tasks of running a household, and some of these have been subject to rapid technological progress and corresponding time savings.

One key role here is played by the spread of labor-saving appliances in the household, which we already discussed in the previous chapter. As parents of multiple children can attest, children can generate seemingly unlimited quantities of laundry, and dealing with that still takes a significant amount of time today. Yet compared to earlier times, the burden of doing laundry has been massively lowered by the development of washing machines and dryers. Another task that takes a significant amount of time is food preparation. Here, time requirements have been reduced through the development of technologies such as the refrigerator, the dishwasher, the electric stove, and the microwave oven. By the peak of the baby boom in the late 1950s, a large majority of US households had such appliances, whereas before the 1940s such appliances were rare.[25] There are also complementary innovations such as the increased availability of prepared foods in easy-to-reach supermarkets, which did away with the need to prepare every meal from scratch. The economists Jeremy Greenwood, Ananth Seshadri, and Guillaume Vandenbroucke have argued that these technological changes in home life played an important part in driving up fertility rates in the 1950s.[26]

An equally important factor is the *opportunity cost of time*. During the baby boom period, raising children was still primarily women's work. The opportunity cost of the time a mother spends raising children is the value of her next-best use of time. For example, if having another child means having to give up a lucrative and rewarding career, the mother's opportunity cost of time is high, and her incentive to have another child will be lower. The role of the cost of time suggests that alternative uses of a woman's time, and specifically the opportunity to work in the formal labor market, should matter in her fertility choice.

In the decades before World War II, it was unusual for married women to work outside the home. Indeed, as discussed in chapter 6, in many professions there were so-called marriage bars that precluded women from working once married. In many states, for example, this was true for teachers, who had to be single (if they were female; no such marriage bars existed for men). Today, in most industrialized countries, the majority of married women work even after having children, so that the trade-off between having more children (and spending more time on them) or having more time available for work and career becomes central to fertility decisions.

The long-run trend toward higher female labor force participation discussed in the previous chapter suggests the opportunity cost of time has been rising, which should contribute to a long-run fertility decline. Nevertheless, in his research on the baby boom with the Israeli economists Moshe Hazan and Yishay Maoz, Matthias found that the opportunity cost of time can explain a lot about why fertility first rose and then fell in the 1950s and 1960s.[27] Their work builds on the observation that the trend toward higher labor force participation of married women of childbearing age was temporarily interrupted at the exact time when fertility went up.

Consider figure 7.10, which compares the labor force participation rate of women in the United States aged twenty to thirty-two (the main childbearing years at the time) to those of older women aged thirty-three to sixty.[28] From the late 1940s to about 1960, young women's labor supply is substantially lower than both before and after the baby boom. During the same period, there was a substantial rise in the labor supply of older married women who in the prewar period generally would have been out of the labor force.

According to Matthias and his coauthors, the link between these opposing movements in labor force participation can be found in a major event that shaped female labor supply decisions in this period: World War II. The war affected women primarily though the labor market: as men were fighting in Europe and Asia, millions of American women

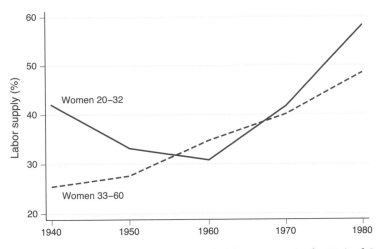

FIGURE 7.10. Labor supply of younger and older women in the United States

responded to urgent calls to join the labor force and started working in offices and factories. For a substantial number of these women, the impact on their labor supply was persistent: they liked the experience and continued working throughout the postwar years.[29]

Now, how is the rise in female employment during the war linked to what happened to fertility rates in the 1950s? Here it is important to recognize that most of the women who had children during the baby boom period were still children or teenagers during the war and hence too young to work. Instead of streaming to the factories during the war like older women, they were still spending their days in school. Nevertheless, the increase in female labor supply during the war did affect them, namely, through their employment prospects after they became adults in the late 1940s and 1950s.

The prewar pattern in the labor market had been that most women would work for a few years when young, between finishing high school and getting married. Then they would drop out to have kids. For the generation of women who became adults just after the war, the issue was that there were millions of women from the war generation still in the labor force. Jobs available to women, however, were limited. As wartime production wound down and men returned to their civilian jobs, the war generation of women was displaced. The labor market still featured substantial segregation by gender, with many women restricted to positions in areas such as retail and clerical work. Matthias and his coauthors argue that many of the positions available to women were taken up by those who joined the labor force during the war and decided to keep on working after it was over. The heightened competition from older women increased labor market competition, depressed wages, and more generally worsened labor market conditions for young women. Put differently, the value of the young women's time in the labor market decreased, which meant that other options, such as getting married earlier to start a family, became comparatively more attractive.

In the data, we can see this effect from a sudden drop in the average age at which women got married during the baby boom, followed by a rapid rise in the age of marriage once the baby boom reached its end. Given that most women started to have children soon after getting married, earlier marriage led to a large, temporary decline in the average age at first birth (fig. 7.11).[30] The baby boom is primarily due to this shift toward women starting to have children at an earlier age, whereas there was little change in fertility rates for mothers above the age of thirty.

Summing up, the most promising explanation for the large postwar baby boom is the decline in the cost of children due to technological changes in the household, together with the repercussions of World War II for the female labor market. One empirical confirmation for the view that the war played an important role comes from comparing the baby boom across countries. Technological changes in the household ultimately affected all rich countries in similar ways, but only those who participated in the war would be expected to have the additional upward push on fertility due to wartime mobilization. Figure 7.9 shows that among Allied countries that mobilized for the war, the baby boom is universally large and similarly timed. Figure 7.12 provides an alternative comparison of the US baby boom with fertility rates in neutral countries.[31] What is apparent is that the neutral countries have much smaller baby booms than the US, explained by the fact that wartime mobilization was not a factor in neutral countries.

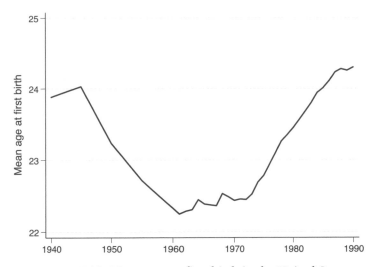

FIGURE 7.11. Mean age at first birth in the United States

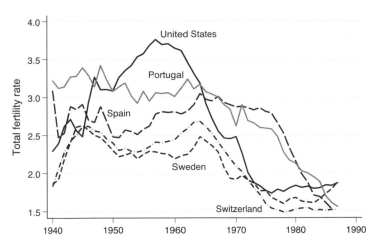

FIGURE 7.12. Total fertility rate in United States compared to countries that were neutral in World War II

THE CHALLENGE OF LOW FERTILITY

For a long time, political concern about population growth focused on populations growing too fast; China's recently abandoned one-child policy is only the most extreme example of a wide range of family plan-

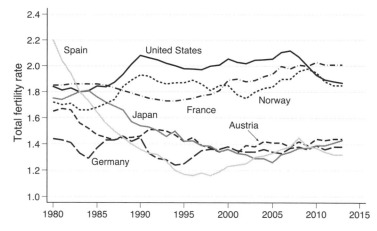

FIGURE 7.13. Total fertility rate in industrialized countries

ning programs that were designed to lower family sizes, with hopes for positive effects on the accumulation of human capital and income growth. But more recently, the tide has turned.

In most industrialized countries, fertility rates are now well below the population replacement level (which, recall, is the level that would result in a stable population size). Figure 7.13 displays the total fertility rate for a number of industrialized countries from 1980 to the present.[32] A fertility rate of two children per woman implies a stable population size in the long run, as there is one child per parent. The figure shows that today some of the industrial countries (such as France, the United States, and the Scandinavian countries) are at or slightly below replacement fertility. However, there is also a group of countries with much lower fertility rates, 1.5 children per woman or lower. Examples include Japan, Germany, Italy, and Spain. If sustained, such low fertility rates will lead to substantial population decline over time. Low fertility also amplifies population aging, meaning that the number of young workers will decline relative to retirees, which puts high pressure on social insurance systems for old-age support and health care. In Germany, for example, the population size is projected to decline from the current 80 million to 67 million by 2060. Already today, substantial areas in East Germany are experiencing rapid population loss; at current fertility rates, such a scenario will increasingly become the norm.

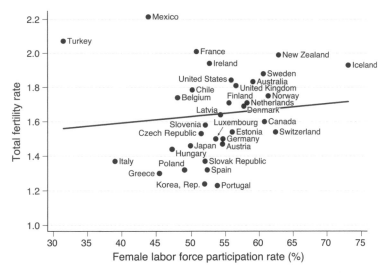

FIGURE 7.14. Female labor force participation rate versus total fertility rate in OECD countries in 2015

What explains ultra-low fertility in a large set of industrialized economies? We have argued that in advanced economies, the time cost of raising children is a key driver of fertility. Some of the overall decline in fertility in the later phases of the demographic transition can be attributed to the large rise in female labor force participation that has been observed throughout rich countries since World War II. However, high female labor force participation does not explain why fertility has fallen much further in some countries than in others. In fact, what is particularly intriguing about current fertility rates in industrialized countries is that the countries with the highest fertility rates are also the ones where the most women are working. Figure 7.14 shows that the relationship between the total fertility rate and the female labor force participation rate among industrialized countries is now positive: the countries where more women work are also the countries where women have more babies.[33] All countries with a fertility rate above 1.8 have a female labor force participation rate above 50 percent, and the low-fertility countries cluster at relatively low participation rates.

The economists James Feyrer, Bruce Sacerdote, and Ariel Stern have argued that this pattern can be understood by realizing that, contrary to the baby boom period, women today do not consider having a career and having a family as mutually exclusive options: most of them want to have both.[34] What varies across countries is the ease with which the two can be combined. In countries where both fertility and female employment numbers are high, it is easy and straightforward to have children without major career interruptions. For example, France and the Scandinavian countries provide accessible and affordable childcare from an early age. Low-fertility countries often lack such a childcare infrastructure, in particular for the youngest children where the demands on mothers are the highest. Another factor experienced more frequently in low-fertility countries is social norms such as expectations that the "appropriate place" for a young mother is at home with her children.

For Matthias, the impact of government policy and social norms on women's ability to have both children and a career is particularly stark when comparing his experience as a child in Germany to his life as an adult in the United States. In 1970s Germany, combining family with a career was a difficult task. Public day care started only at age four; younger children were almost universally cared for by their mothers. Even with school-age children, work could be a challenge, given that school generally took place only during the morning hours, with kids returning home by lunchtime. What is more, even during regular school hours, the school was not a reliable provider of childcare: if lessons had to be canceled because a teacher was sick, the children would simply walk home. It was a setup that made handling child-rearing and a demanding career nearly impossible for women. A good number of the women who did work did so as a last resort because their children's father was absent, unemployed, or even in prison. No wonder, then, that being a working mom with young children carried a certain stigma.

A few decades later, Matthias's experiences as a parent in the United States are of a different kind. Matthias's wife, Marisa, is a casting director and often works on multiple television shows or movies simultaneously. When each of their boys was born, Marisa worked pretty much right up to the time of delivery, with a few final phone calls to arrange work matters straight from the hospital bed. Afterward, she took off from work for just a few weeks of recovery and then started to reengage with her business. Being married to an academic with a flexible work schedule made this easier for Marisa, but so did the easy availability of additional help from day-care centers, nannies, and babysitters. Many of Marisa and Matthias's friends in the United States went about having children in a similar way, with relatively short work interruptions followed by a quick return to full-time work, aided by nannies or day care. To be sure, this approach to having children comes with its own challenges and can be stressful. However, under these circumstances, there is no need to make a hard choice between having a large family and an ambitious career. What is also absent is stigma: different families deal with careers and childcare in different ways, but unlike in 1970s Germany, in today's United States there is no general perception that one approach is inherently better than another.

In recent work with Fabian Kindermann, Matthias has examined which policies are most promising for raising fertility rates in industrialized countries.[35] In line with the arguments already presented, they find that ultra-low fertility rates can be overcome if both government policies and local social norms evolve such that having a family is more easily compatible with both mothers and fathers pursuing careers. In contrast, simply subsidizing children may be relatively ineffective. Notably, some countries with very low fertility rates already highly subsidize childbearing. In Germany, for example, government support for couples with children comes in the form of tax breaks and direct monetary transfers that are much more generous than in the United States, yet Germany's fertility rate is still substantially lower. Rather than just handing out money, policies that specifically support working mothers (such as making day care for young children more widely available) are more promising. Part of the challenge also concerns the division of labor within the household: in many cases, the countries with the lowest fertility rates are also the ones where men do the least amount of work in the home. If men can be convinced to share more of the burden of childcare (for example, by introducing "daddy months," i.e., parental leave specifically for fathers, as practiced in Sweden and a few other countries), women will have an easier time deciding to have more kids.

WHEN LOW FERTILITY IS NOT A CHOICE: THE CASE OF CHINA

While industrialized countries now struggle to raise fertility, many developing countries' family planning policies have the opposite objective, to curtail population growth. The most drastic and at least superficially successful example of such a policy is the one-child policy in China.

Until the 1960s, the Communist Party encouraged large families under the belief that high population growth would make China more powerful. As a result, the population of the People's Republic of China almost doubled in the second half of the twentieth century. The doctrine of the party changed in the 1970s, when the government introduced some family planning policies to limit fertility, including the "later, longer, fewer" campaign to encourage delayed marriage. Eventually, the draconian one-child policy was introduced in 1979. In urban areas, families could have only one child, while in rural areas two children were permitted. The restriction did not apply to ethnic minorities. The policy remained in place until 2016.

The economic and social consequences of the policy are complex. The Chinese economy got a boost during three decades when most of the population was of working age, with relatively few children and retirees to support. However, this period is coming to an end. Today, China (where the total fertility rate is now 1.6) faces rapid population aging, which is leading to challenges in financing pension payments and health care for an increasing number of retirees.[36]

The one-child policy also had important effects inside the family. Early on, the policy clashed with the traditional Chinese preference for boys. Confucianism views the failure to have a son as a capital negligence in family responsibility. Yet, the reality was that many families could not have a son under the new rule. The preference for sons resulted in selective abortions. On average, 118 boys are born in China for every 100 girls. The shortage of girls has created a large imbalance in the marriage market.[37]

Moreover, the decline in the number of children has undermined the traditional system of elderly care provided within families.[38] In China, sons are expected to take responsibility for their elderly parents, while daughters contribute to the care of their husband's parents. Under the one-child policy, many families found themselves deprived of old age support. The issue continues to be a pressing one in rural areas, while in cities the culture has progressively adapted to the new reality. Today, most parents in Beijing and Shanghai report not to have any preferences between boys and girls, nor to desire to have more children than the one-child policy permits. The low reported desire for children lines up with the observation that in Taiwan, Hong Kong, and Singapore family size is unrestricted by policy, yet total fertility rates are among the lowest in the world (around 1.2). These observations confirm the central role of economic forces: in all these regions, as in Beijing and Shanghai, the high costs of housing and child-rearing are more persuasive forces than cultural tradition.

Another consequence of the one-child policy is the so-called "Little Emperor" effect. Under the one-child policy, each child commands the full and undivided attention of two parents and four grandparents. This was in part an intended outcome and is what economic theory of fertility predicts. According to Gary Becker's quantity-quality theory discussed previously, a law that limits fertility should induce families to concentrate their time, money, and effort on the single child. In a recent survey, more than half of parents report that they regard good school achievements of their only children as the happiest moments for their families. At the same time, they are prepared to punish their child if she or he fails an exam. The study also reports that the parents of only children devote significantly more time to work with their children on their studies than parents with multiple children.[39]

In our earlier discussion, we attributed the intensive parenting style of Chinese parents to the high level of inequality and to the importance of education for economic success. Here, we see that a specific institution, the one-child policy, also interacts with choice of parenting style.

The "Little Emperor" effect adds another facet to the overall explanation for intensive parenting in China.

A recent study by the economists Taha Choukhmane, Nicolas Coeurdacier, and Keyu Jin aims to quantify the impact of the one-child policy on investment in children. To do this, the study compares the behavior of parents of only children to that of parents who happened to give birth to twins. They find that only children attract significantly more attention and resources than twins do. The consequence is that twins accumulate less human capital. For instance, twins are 40 percent less likely to pursue higher education than only children, and significantly less likely to attend an academic high school. These large effects suggest that in spite of the social and psychological costs it caused, the one-child policy may have contributed to the recent rapid growth in the Chinese economy.[40] The results also confirm our general claim that incentives matter for parenting: even though presumably the parents of twins love their children just as much as the parents of only children do, the tighter constraints in families with multiple children lead to very different outcomes in terms of human capital investment.

IN SUMMARY

Whether to have children and, if so, how many are among the most important and consequential decisions that people face in their lifetime. In other words, the stakes are high, which makes the economic approach to human behavior, namely the view that decisions are driven by incentives, particularly powerful when it comes to fertility decisions.

In this chapter, we have seen that the economic approach can explain why fertility rates fell rapidly once rising returns to human capital induced parents to invest more in their children's education and to rely less on child labor. The economic approach can also explain the close connection between women's decisions to work and fertility choices in our time.

Decisions on child-bearing are consequential not just from the individual but also from the national perspective. In some of the poorest developing countries, reducing population growth is still a central policy goal, whereas some of the more advanced economies deal with the opposite problems of population aging and ultra-low fertility rates. The economic approach to fertility choice can be used to map out the policy options that can help deal with both of these challenges in the future.

CHAPTER EIGHT

Parenting and Class

Aristocratic versus Middle-Class Values

Most of the parents we encountered in the first few chapters of this book would probably agree that doing well in school and having a fulfilling and successful career are desirable outcomes for one's children. For these parents, the choice of parenting style is about how to best achieve these objectives and how to weigh them relative to, say, a happy and relaxed family life. The emphasis on education and career success is an element of middle-class values, and in today's economy, which runs on human capital, middle-class values have become culturally dominant.

Taking a broader perspective, parents may differ not just in their methods of parenting but also in their ideas of what children should learn. In past centuries, divisions across social classes were much sharper than they are today, and parents who lived very different lives had widely varying aspirations for their children. Some of the middle-class values of education, hard work, and thrift were rejected by members of other social classes, from both the bottom and the top rungs of society. As the name of their class suggests, members of the working class certainly valued hard-working children, but unlike most modern parents, they had little use for education. At the other end of the spectrum, to members of the European aristocracy (familiar to all of us from Jane Austen novels, the *Downton Abbey* television series, etc.), the very idea that their children should be taught to work hard would have been abhorrent. Indeed, they encouraged the opposite in their children, namely, an appreciation of leisure and the "finer things" in life and a disdain for labor.

In our view, such class differences in the fundamental values that underlie parenting choices can be understood in the same way as the differences in parenting styles across countries or socioeconomic groups in modern times.[1] We maintain that regardless of social class, parents care about their children and strive to equip them as best as they can for the lives they can expect to live. We argue that it is sharp differences in economic incentives across social classes that can explain not just the intensity of parents' attempts to instill values in their children but also which specific values the parents will choose to stress.

We apply this analysis to the contrast in basic values emphasized by parents from different social classes at the time of the Industrial Revolution. We rely on the case of England, the cradle of industrialization, as the main example, but many of the ideas apply equally to other European societies at the time.

PARENTING IN A CLASS-BASED SOCIETY

Historians conceive of English society before the Industrial Revolution as divided into three broad social classes.[2] At the top was the English aristocracy, familiar from literature, movies, and television. Apart from noble status and aristocratic privilege, a central characteristic of this upper class in economic terms was that its principal source of income was land (i.e., rents and other income derived from aristocratic estates). Indeed, the upper class of this period generally coincided with the land-owning class and were often referred to as the "landed gentry."

At the bottom of society was the working class, which at the time comprised the large majority of the population. The defining economic characteristic of the working class was not just that it relied on labor instead of land for most of its income but also that this labor was mostly unskilled: Members of the working class generally had little or no schooling, almost all were illiterate, and there was also little practical education or training. Members of the working class could be found in different sectors of the economy, from day laborers in agriculture to factory workers in the industrializing towns. What they all had in common was that they relied on wages from unskilled labor.

In between the aristocracy and the working class was a third group, which mostly consisted of artisans, craftspeople, and merchants, and which we may call the preindustrial middle class. This group can be found in most sectors of the economy, but generally was more likely to live in towns and cities rather than in the countryside. Like the working class, this group relied mostly on labor for income. However, in contrast to the working class, education and skills played an important role for the middle class. To some extent, these were "modern" skills such as literacy and numeracy. Such skills were important, for example, for merchants who had to deal with contracts, finance, and correspondence. But even the least literate artisans generally needed a lot of education, albeit of a more practical kind. For the skilled urban classes, the route to success consisted of a long apprenticeship (generally seven years in England) to acquire the tacit knowledge required in the chosen profession, often followed by a period as a journeyman. Many professions were regulated by guilds, in which young artisans could ultimately qualify as masters in their chosen profession. This step held the promise of a relatively comfortable and prestigious position for the time, but usually one could become a master only in one's thirties or forties.

In addition to economic class divisions, substantial barriers to social mobility, both formal and informal, were in place that made it difficult or impossible for families to rise on the social ladder, even across generations. The formal barriers were strongest at the top. Entry into the titled aristocracy was most restricted and limited to inheritance, marriage, and the granting of titles by the sovereign. Barriers to mobility between the working class and the middle class were less impenetrable, but still substantial enough to reinforce the concept of separated social classes. Sometimes these barriers were formal, as in the case of guilds who established monopolies and successfully controlled entry into their field. Even in more open professions, entering apprenticeships usually required an up-front fee paid from parent to master, which effectively excluded children from working-class families without sufficient resources.[3]

Turning back to parenting, just like modern parents, parents in preindustrial society faced a choice in the values and attitudes they should encourage their children to develop. The economic approach to human behavior assumes that people from different social backgrounds and historical time periods are fundamentally similar in their motivations. Hence, we argue that all parents aimed to equip their children with values that would prove useful in their adult lives. What distinguishes parents from different walks of life is their views on which specific attitudes and skills the success of their children was dependent on. In the preindustrial society, the distinct economic lives of the social classes implied that the values that put children on the path to success also varied across classes. Hence, sharp economic class distinctions led to equally sharp differences in parents' incentives.

THE WORKING CLASS

For working-class parents, the economic and social conditions of the day dictated that they had an incentive to emphasize a strong work ethic and discourage the enjoyment of leisure. As the name "working class" implies, work was a precondition of existence for a member of this class. Of course, it is still true today that most people rely on work to make a living, and hence many parents continue to encourage a work ethic in their children. But the strength of the parents' incentives for instilling a work ethic depends on the size of the stakes, and there can be no doubt that the stakes were much higher for working-class parents in the preindustrial era compared to most parents today.

Consider what would happen if parents fail to instill a work ethic, and a child grows up to be a lazy and work-shy adult. Today, such a child probably would not have a tremendously successful career and may well end up at the lower end of the income distribution. Still, there are many jobs today where the required hours and effort are low, and even if the child ends up not working at all, in today's welfare states, survival usually is not at stake.

In the preindustrial working class, in contrast, there was simply no place for someone who wished to avoid work. Given that income levels were generally low and near subsistence levels for poorer individuals, there was little scope for slacking off. As in some developing countries today, families relied on contributions from everyone (adults and children alike) just to get by and could not tolerate freeloading family members to rely on the efforts of others. Even worse, once on his or her own, an unmotivated person (or "slacker" in today's vernacular) without a sufficient income would have trouble getting enough food, and malnutrition would increase the probability of succumbing to one of the many infectious diseases that were untreatable at the time.

What is more, without an income, marriage and hence having legitimate children would be out of the question. Bluntly put, a working-class parent who did not make sure that their children developed a work ethic would have every reason to worry about the child's and ultimately the entire family's long-term survival.

The historical evidence strongly supports the notion that a solid work ethic was a central cultural value for the working class. The members of this class worked hard, and enjoying leisure activities was frowned upon and strongly discouraged. Moreover, given that the stakes were high, economic incentives also explain why parents so forcefully impressed their views of the "proper" life upon their children. As discussed in chapter 5, parents would routinely resort to corporal punishment to make sure that children "behaved."

Whereas the emphasis on work ethic is shared between preindustrial parents from the working class and many of today's parents, there is a contrast in terms of the value of education. Today, most parents regardless of background want their children to do well in school. In contrast, working-class parents in the past did not push their children toward academic achievement. Rather, even after public financing made formal schools more affordable, many working-class parents continued to actively discourage their children from extending their education beyond the bare minimum. Once again, this behavior can be explained with the incentives provided by the economic environment of the day.

Unlike today, formal education (which at the time primarily meant literacy and basic arithmetic) was not required for most workers, and certainly not for the kind of work that the members of the working class could get. In the cities, there was some need for formal skills among merchants, artisans, and craftsmen. But in the countryside, where the majority of the population lived, reading was an important skill only for members of the clergy. As mentioned in the previous chapter, before the nineteenth century, most schools were Sunday schools organized by the church, which taught literacy primarily to be able to read the Bible. Thus, schooling was associated either with religion or with the upper class's leisurely pursuits or social refinement, but it did not have productive value for most of the population. Neither did literacy bring a high likelihood of being able to join the clergy, as such positions generally went to children from families better situated in society. Hence, promoting formal education would not get parents any closer to ensuring a successful future for their children.

On the contrary, parents had reason to worry that too much education could even hurt their children. An awakened interest in religion could result in a desire to engage in prolonged reflection and contemplation, which might inhibit putting hard effort into physical work. Literate children might also develop an interest in reading novels and other literature, which is not a productive activity. A preindustrial, working-class parent would have every reason to view too much reading by children as a problem, just as modern parents disapprove when kids watch TV or play video games all day. Given the economic incentives at the time, it should be no surprise that the value system of working-class parents was fundamentally different from what is the norm today.

An appreciation of hard work was not the only value emphasized by working-class parents. There was also an emphasis on moral values, such as a strong taboo on premarital sex, which was enforced in ways that may seem draconian today. To a modern observer, the attitudes of parents in earlier times toward sexuality and morality may seem, at best, old-fashioned and backward. Yet, as we already touched on in a previous chapter, even these seemingly noneconomic values can be understood if we take parents' incentives into account. When it comes to sexual morality, what should be on parents' minds are the consequences for children engaging in premarital sex. To be sure, even today some parents would prefer their adolescent children to remain abstinent. Yet there is a massive difference in the stakes—that is, the consequences—for children who deviate from the norm.

Nowadays, adolescents have access to various forms of birth control that massively reduce the risk of pregnancy and of getting sexually transmitted diseases. Hence, engaging in premarital sex is unlikely to have severe consequences. In earlier times, the risks were incomparably greater. Not only were those defying the social norm of the day more likely to end up pregnant or diseased, but they also faced much more severe consequences. Many bacterial sexually transmitted diseases that are easily curable in today's era of antibiotics, in the past, led to severe disability or even death.

Even today, many parents would consider getting pregnant out of wedlock or during the teenage years as problematic and possibly leading to challenges in terms of future education or career prospects. Still, even if there were an "accident," abortion is a legal option in most countries, and having a child out of wedlock would not be such an existential threat. In earlier times, by contrast, apart from the risk of social ostracism, unmarried mothers and their children faced dire prospects. At a time where income levels were barely above subsistence and infant mortality could reach 30 to 40 percent, having a child without the support of a husband could literally be a question of life and death. Considering these prospects, it is not an accident that caring parents had every incentive to enforce a strict moral code with all the means they had at their disposal.

PARENTING AND ARISTOCRATIC VALUES

Now consider parents at the other end of the social spectrum, namely, members of the aristocracy. The economic environment experienced by the aristocracy was the exact opposite of that of the working class. In economic terms, aristocrats were primarily landowners. Aristocratic titles were tied to ownership of estates, and the income of aristocratic families consisted of the agricultural income and rental income generated by these estates. As a consequence, hard physical work had little relation to the economic status of the upper class, and most aristocratic families left the management of their estates to employees.

Given that working hard would provide no major advantage in later life, aristocratic parents had little incentive to instill a work ethic in their children. On the contrary, there were returns to doing the opposite, namely, instilling an appreciation of refined leisure activities like hunting for boys or music for girls. Such leisurely skills could later be useful for social advancement and matchmaking. It is not by chance that the upper class also used to be known as the *leisure class*. Not having to work for a living was a defining characteristic of this social group and an opportunity to emphasize the social divide between themselves and the rest of society. In his famous book *The Theory of the Leisure Class*, Thorstein Veblen pointed out the use of "conspicuous consumption" and "conspicuous leisure" for accentuating class distinctions. He remarked, "Abstention from labour is the conventional evidence of wealth and is therefore the conventional mark of social standing; and this insistence on the meritoriousness of wealth leads to a more strenuous insistence on leisure."[4]

Hence, leisure was not just an end in itself. The specific skills associated with leisure activities could also be a means of advancement. For daughters, success was measured primarily by advantageous marriage, and skills in socially valued areas such as music and dancing could help advance this goal. Even for boys, opportunities for further advancement relied more on social skills rather than work. In England, aristocratic titles were passed on to the first sons, meaning that younger sons had to find other ways to make a living. Rather than work in some kind of business, however, almost all younger sons ended up in coveted positions that were only available to those with the right social connections.

Table 8.1 displays the professional choices of Cambridge graduates in the years 1752–1899.[5] In the eighteenth and nineteenth centuries, Cambridge was not so much a university in the modern sense but rather a finishing school for the upper class. Indeed, relatively few practical

TABLE 8.1. Professional choices of Cambridge graduates

	1752–1799	1800–1849	1850–1899
Church	60%	62%	38%
Land-Owning	14%	14%	7%
Teaching	9%	9%	12%
Law	6%	9%	14%
Administration	3%	1%	6%
Medicine	1%	2%	7%
Banking	0%	0%	2%
Business	0%	0%	5%
Other	7%	3%	9%

skills were taught, and instead a university education served to support the cohesion of the aristocracy and help social advancement. The professional careers of Cambridge graduates provide a good impression of where the boys from aristocratic families ended up (Cambridge was all-male until the late nineteenth century, and women could not become full members of the university until 1948).[6] The first sons were the ones who became landowners, who made up 14 percent of the graduates from 1752 until 1849. Of the younger sons, the vast majority took up positions in the Church of England, which was controlled by the upper class and provided a safe and steady income. A few others entered select professions such as law or medicine. What is notable is that before 1849, there is not a single graduate who ended up either in business (essentially any profit-oriented enterprise) or banking. The young men of the upper class had no reason to earn their money in such a nonprestigious way, given that their social connections provided them with access to less strenuous and more lucrative opportunities.

Another interesting observation is that members of the aristocracy actually did very little parenting themselves. Infants were routinely handed off to wet nurses, governesses were in charge of young children, and boys would often be packed off to boarding school once they reached ten or eleven years of age.[7] The standard was for parents to see their children for one hour a day, nicely dressed and prepared by their nannies. Again, this is not surprising given the aristocracy's immense wealth. Employing others to watch the children was easily affordable for parents from the upper class. Given that not all of childcare is pleasant and entertaining, it made perfect sense to outsource the dreary parts to others and focus only on the occasional enjoyment of the children's company.

Indeed, even today we observe that the very rich often rely on the services of nannies, and boarding schools continue to be primarily the domain of the rich. However, one factor that works against charging others with childcare today is that the modern economy is driven by human capital, and parents may fear that hired help will be less able to equip their youngsters with the skills needed for success than the parents themselves. Such concerns were absent in the preindustrial upper class, which built its wealth on land, and whose necessary skills were of a kind that could easily be taught by others.

Overall, then, we see that parents from both the top and the bottom of the social scale were motivated by the same thing, namely, to prepare their children as best as possible for future success. It so happens that the social and economic environment of the day implied opposite strategies in terms of what children should actually be taught—hard work and self-denial on the part of the working class, and refined leisurely tastes on the part of the aristocracy.

THE PREINDUSTRIAL ROOTS OF MIDDLE-CLASS VALUES

The third important group in preindustrial society was a middle class that consisted of artisans, craftsmen, and merchants. Like the working class, this class relied on labor, so a strong work ethic was appreciated. In addition, however, a key characteristic of this class is the importance of education and the acquisition of professional skills. Of course, education took a different form from what we are familiar with today. Formal schooling essentially did not exist for this group, and while some learned to read and write, those were not the skills their careers were built on. Rather, it was practical skills in their chosen professions that were essential to the success of people from the middle class. The primary mode of acquiring such skills was through working with experienced elders, often known as "masters." In many trades and professions, this learning took place through formal systems of apprenticeship, which were the norm for artisans and craftsmen. For other occupations, such as various types of merchants, the acquisition of skills was less regulated, but it remained true that learning on the job from skilled tradesmen was an essential ingredient for a successful career.

Even though the nature of their human capital was different from that of the educated classes in our times, the values required for success were similar. First and foremost, the road to acquiring top-end human capital is long and requires a long-term perspective and patience. In modern times, the most education-intensive occupations require close to thirty years of human capital accumulation and training. American doctors, for example, generally spend twelve years in school, four years in college, and four years in medical school, followed by residency and fellowships, which can take another five to eight years or more. Individuals who seek instant gratification and who would like to earn money as soon as possible are unlikely to choose such a path and succeed in it, which is why parents who would like their children to prosper in a field such as medicine start emphasizing the importance of patience and long-term thinking early on.[8,9]

Now consider the training that a future master craftsman had to go through in preindustrial society. The early years would be spent with their own family, their parents and siblings. If the father was a craftsman too, this would probably involve a fair amount of work helping in the father's business and the acquisition of some skills through learning by doing. The first phase of formal education would consist of an apprenticeship. In England, apprenticeships generally lasted seven years, and many boys would start at around thirteen years of age. The life of an apprentice was not an easy one. There was no salary; on the contrary, in many cases the apprentice's family had to pay the master for teaching him. Apprentices would often sleep on a bench in the kitchen and work long hours. Many apprentices did not finish their term; it took a fair amount of dedication to finish training under such circumstances.

Once the apprenticeship was completed, a young craftsman could start to work for other masters, but would still be far from becoming a master in his own right. Becoming a master required additional training and experience, which in many fields involved a period of journeymanship, that is, traveling from town to town to work for different masters and learn a variety of techniques. Becoming a master required not only skill but also considerable savings. A young master would need to have the resources to buy all the tools and equipment required in his profession, and where guilds were influential, there could be other requirements, such as having to pay for a banquet for the older masters in the guild. Thus, if he wanted to succeed, a craftsman would have to save most of his meager income, all with the aim of ultimately joining the ranks of the masters.

Only a few of those who started as apprentices would make it all the way to master. If they did succeed, they would be admitted as masters in their thirties (a similar age to that of doctors or scientists entering the work force today). At that point, life was good for the standards of the day. The young master would probably marry and start a family, begin to accumulate wealth, and might even be involved in city government or the management of the local guild.

Clearly, among the characteristics required of future masters, patience was a very important one. The economic incentives faced by the parents of the day therefore suggest that the middle class was also the patient class: only parents who instilled a sufficient long-term outlook in their children could expect them to succeed. In this regard, the preindustrial middle class is similar to the modern upper-middle class, where education is paramount and a long-run perspective is required to thrive in professions requiring postgraduate education like law, business, medicine, or academia.

No such requirement of patience applied to the members of the working class and the upper class. In the working class, accumulation of skill played a relatively minor role, as the income of workers was mostly based on their physical labor. The reliance on physical labor implied that wages were related to strength and stamina, and thus

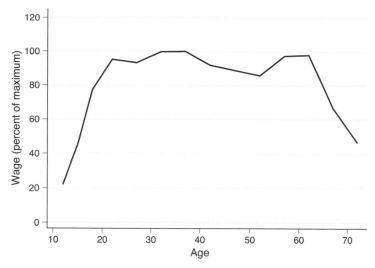

FIGURE 8.1. Lifetime income profile of agricultural workers in England in the early nineteenth century

peaked relatively early in life. Figure 8.1 shows the average wage for agricultural workers of different ages in England during the early nineteenth century.[10] During the teenage years, wages would increase steeply year by year, as physical strength increased and basic experience was acquired. However, workers were close to peak earnings already in their early twenties, and subsequently wages were essentially flat until strength begins to wane after a worker reached the age of sixty.

The figure shows that manual workers had little to look forward to in terms of higher earnings after their early twenties. Neither did the acquisition of specialized skills or similar forward-looking investments play an important role in their economic lives. As a result, a long-run perspective was not of particular importance for this class.

In the upper class, while at least a minimum amount of patience and foresight certainly would have been desirable, it was not at all essential for a successful life. Given that income was derived from land and most noblemen did not work, accumulation of productive skills did not play an important economic role for this class. Instead, the aristocratic value system emphasized the value of preservation. The mark of a life well lived for an upper-class man was to be able to pass on the inherited estate in undiminished form to one's own first-born son, perhaps with a few improvements included. Indeed, the legal concept of "entail" was designed to encourage preservation, by restricting the ability to sell property and ensuring that entire estates would be passed on to a single heir. While the idea of preservation suggests at least some patience, there is a large gap between wishing one's child to continue the family tradition in a secure position, on the one hand, and the quintessential middle-class value of wishing for one's children to be much better off than their parents, on the other.

To summarize, economic incentives predict that the working class would emphasize a strong work ethic, whereas the upper class would push their children toward a greater appreciation for leisure. In neither of these classes was there a strong incentive to instill patience and future-orientation in children. This was the case, however, in the skilled middle class of artisans and merchants, who had incentives to push their children both toward a strong work ethic and toward patience and an understanding of the benefits of delayed gratification.

This basic classification rhymes well with contemporary descriptions of the different social classes, not just in literature but also in scientific works such as Weber's famous book *The Protestant Ethic and the Spirit of Capitalism*.[11] In his book, Weber considers religion to be the driving force of class-based differences in values. While the view of religion as a causal factor has found only limited support in later studies, we view religious values as part of the mechanism through which values and attitudes in different social classes are regulated. Whatever the mechanism, the values among the skilled middle class that Weber describes line up nicely with what our analysis of economic incentives predicts.

THE IMPACT OF PARENTING VALUES ON THE CLASS-BASED SOCIETY

The class-specific parenting values that were driven by economic incentives also had major consequences for the fate of different social classes after the onset of industrialization. Industrialization implied that accumulation of physical capital, rather than land, became a key driver of wealth. Accumulating capital, however, requires delayed gratification, so only sufficiently patient individuals or families would be expected to be able to do so. Keeping in mind our analysis of social classes, this implies that the patient middle class should benefit disproportionately from the new opportunities and rise over the existing elite.

That is, of course, exactly what happened. The vast majority of industrialists had middle-class origins. The economic historian Francois Crouzet examined the social origins of the founders of the main industrial enterprises in the first century of the Industrial Revolution, between 1750 and 1850. Crouzet finds that neither the upper class nor the lower (working) class accounted for a significant fraction of the founders' generation. Instead, a full 85 percent came from the middle class, including the lower end of the middle class such as "shopkeepers, self-employed craftsmen and artisans, cultivators of various kinds."[12] The upper class, consisting of peerage and gentry, contributed only 2.3 percent. Of course, the upper class made up a small fraction of the population to begin with, but even relative to population shares, the middle class is overrepresented and the upper class is underrepresented.[13]

A good example of the typical origins of industrial founders is James Watt, inventor and producer of the steam engines that powered the Industrial Revolution. His father was a "craftsman and trader—shipwright, carpenter, house-builder, ship-chandler, [and] eventually merchant."[14] After leaving school, Watt began to work in his father's workshop and lived in considerable poverty for some time while training to be an instrument maker in London. He then worked as an instrument maker in Glasgow before turning to steam engines.[15]

Perhaps the best-known proponent of the view that starting out rich can be a hindrance to future success is Andrew Carnegie, a leading industrialist in the US steel industry in the nineteenth century. Carnegie grew up in poverty in Scotland as the son of a weaver. The Carnegie family immigrated to the United States to escape the depressed economic conditions in Scotland. Andrew started working in a cotton factory at age thirteen and ultimately worked his way up to become one of the richest men of his time.[16] Carnegie credited his success in part to having had to work from a young age: "The eldest son of parents who were themselves poor, I had, fortunately, to begin to perform some useful work in the world while still very young in order to earn an honest livelihood and was thus shown even in early boyhood that my duty was to assist my parents and, like them, become, as soon as possible, a bread-winner in the family."[17] Later on, Carnegie became an outspoken proponent of the view that parents should not bequeath their wealth to their children, but rather follow his example and devote their fortunes to philanthropy. Part of his argument was that inheriting wealth would not do any good for the children. In his *Gospel of Wealth*, Carnegie writes: "That the parent who leaves his son enormous wealth generally deadens the talents and energies of the son, and tempts him to lead a less useful and less worthy life than he otherwise would, seems to be capable of proof which cannot be gainsaid."[18] Carnegie's views line up well with the observation that the upper class played little role in the Industrial Revolution.

The economic and social consequences of the work-hostile parenting style of the aristocratic elite were far-reaching. The exclusion of the upper class from the industrial sector was limited not just to active participation in terms of founding enterprises but even extended to more passive methods of participation, such as financing investments. Given the high appreciation of leisure in the upper class and the view that working for money was beneath one's dignity, it is not too surprising that the lords, earls, and counts preferred not to get their hands dirty in early industrial enterprises. But they still would have been able to participate as financiers, and given the enormous concentration of wealth in the upper class at the time, they would have been in a perfect position to do so. Yet, the upper class chose to stay on the sidelines. Instead, early industrialists were predominantly self-financed, and to the extent that equity investment was used in later stages, middle-class merchants from the cities were much more enthusiastic participants compared to the upper class.

The upper class's lack of interest in financing industrial investment can be related to a family upbringing that not only included an appreciation for leisure but also a lack of emphasis on patience and thrift.

The lack of patience in the upper class became an increasing financial burden once financial instruments were developed that allowed aristocrats to borrow against the value of their estates. It was convenient to finance expenditures such as allowances for other family members and the construction of beautiful estates through debt rather than going through a phase of limiting one's extravagant lifestyle. The result was that throughout the nineteenth century, rather than growing rich from industrial investment, the old aristocracy became increasingly indebted, exactly what we would expect from a class lacking in patience.

The burden of debt was sustainable as long as the estates generated sufficient earnings, but rising debt levels increasingly exposed the upper class to economic shocks. For most families, the accumulation of debt combined with a fall in agricultural prices (on which income from estates was based) ultimately led to economic decline and the dispersal of vast estates.

While patience and hard work did not feature prominently in the aristocratic ranking of parenting values, an appropriate marriage choice would have been among the most important factors. In the British television series *Downton Abbey*, Lord Grantham manages to prevent the downfall of the Crawley family by marrying Cora, an American heiress whose money saves the estate. While fictional, this was a fairly common real-life option to escape debt. Between the 1870s and the 1920s, a few hundred American so-called "dollar princesses" married into British aristocratic families.[19] A real-life example is Winston Churchill's mother, Jeanette, who was the daughter of a New York financier.[20] However, the relief provided by American money was usually only temporary. The aristocracy never regained its previous significance. In our view, the class-based preferences that were rooted in economic incentives had a key role to play in the aristocracy's downfall.

While aristocratic families gradually lost their wealth, the dynasties started by the industrial founders, who often started with little or no wealth, became increasingly rich throughout the nineteenth century. By the turn of the twentieth century, industrial dynasties that once started from humble origins became dominant among the wealthy elite in England.

We can get a fairly accurate impression of the economic elite in Britain by considering estate records, that is, the assets left by wealthy individuals at their death. In the first half of the nineteenth century, the truly rich were still almost entirely from the upper class. The economic historian William Rubinstein studied individuals who died owning wealth exceeding one million pounds, which was a true fortune at the time (equivalent to about 100 million US dollars today).[21] Between 1809 and 1858, the upper class, consisting of wealthy landowners, still accounts for 95 percent of this wealthy elite. Throughout the century, the wealth of the leading industrialists first approached and then surpassed that of most members of the aristocracy. Between 1900 and 1939, the landed elite accounted for a mere 7 percent of the largest estates. Instead, the vast majority of large fortunes were now those of the owners of large industrial enterprises, with a smaller contribution from rich merchants and financiers.

ARE WE HEADED TOWARD A NEW CLASS-BASED SOCIETY?

The meaning and significance of the concept of social class has changed substantially during the transformation of societies triggered by industrialization and modern economic growth. In the preindustrial world, social class was a primary attribute of an individual and held more importance than, say, occupation or even nationality. Part of the significance of social class stemmed from the fact that barriers existed that lowered mobility between social classes. A second factor, highlighted by the economic analysis of parenting in a class-based society, is that in a society with high barriers to social mobility, we should also observe divergent attitudes and values in the different parts of societies. In other words, class was not just an arbitrary label or a signifier of social position but was linked to substantial differences in the value systems that people held.

Even today, distinctions between social classes can be identified, but these are much milder in nature compared to preindustrial society. The middle-class values of patience, appreciation of education, and social advancement have been adopted by a large fraction of the population, including the upper reaches of society, whereas a separate leisure class has largely disappeared.

What is less clear is whether the trend toward a diminished role of social class distinctions will continue into the future. The economic analysis of parenting identifies social mobility as a key determinant of class distinctions. If social mobility is high, parents from different backgrounds will have similar expectations and aspirations for their children, resulting in similar parenting choices. In contrast, if those from the lower rungs of society have little hope of their children rising to the top, they will not see the point in endowing them with the skills and aspirations that would only pay off if they chose a path in which they are unlikely to succeed.

We have already touched on divergent trends in family life across the social spectrum in chapter 4, such as the retreat from marriage and a corresponding rise in single parenting among lower-income households, and a trend toward more time-intensive and engaged parenting that is particularly pronounced among the well off and well educated. If these trends lead to an increasing isolation of different social classes similar to what was the norm in preindustrial times, we may enter a new phase of sharpened social class distinctions. These distinctions would concern not just, say, the intensity of parenting effort, but the entire value system adopted by different social classes.

Such a new divergence of values and attitudes across social classes would be a worrying trend and present new challenges for democratic societies based in part on the ideals of equal opportunity, social mobility, and broad political participation. However, democratic countries are not powerless in the face of such challenges. As we argue in this chapter, social-class distinctions reflect and respond to the economic environment, but at the same time, economic forces are not the sole determinant of the makeup of society: political forces also have an important role to play.

In preindustrial times, political decision-making was usually dominated by an aristocratic elite, and policies (including taxation, access to public office, access to education, and political representation) were chosen in large part with the objective of preserving the existing social order. Likewise, in our own times, political choices regarding the education system, taxation and transfers, social insurance, and career choice also help determine social mobility and the incentives faced by parents from the different rungs of the social ladder. In times when economic forces move to accentuate inequality and lower mobility, a democratic society can push back against these trends through policy choices that promote equal opportunity.

PART THREE

How Policy Affects the Way We Raise Our Kids

CHAPTER NINE

The Organization of the School System

Throughout this book, we have emphasized that parents' decisions respond not just to economic forces such as the degree of inequality and the state of technology, but also to the institutions and public policies of the society in which they live. For parenting, a key part of this environment is made up of the school system. In this chapter, we describe how the organization of the school system varies across countries and how this feeds back into parenting decisions.

Schools affect children from a variety of directions. First, educators have a direct effect on children via the knowledge they teach and the values they convey. The state's desire to imbue children with a shared set of values and convictions has been a key driving force throughout the history of public education. Rather than just as vehicles for teaching useful knowledge, public schools were also established with the objectives of fostering social cohesion, strengthening the stability of the state, and, not least, bolstering the acceptance of the military draft. Second, children socialize with peers at school, and these interactions also help form their preferences and values. Peer effects can sometimes reinforce and complement, and at other times counteract, the efforts of teachers and parents. Third, the organization of the school system affects parents' behavior. Parents adjust their parenting style, and possibly their fertility decisions, in response to the incentives provided by the school system.

Schools and families may be more or less in tune with each other. Fabrizio recalls trying to teach preschool-aged Nora to read and write when they were living in Sweden. In Italy, teachers would approve of doing this and view it as a sign of good and responsible parenting. In Sweden, Fabrizio got a different response. To his surprise, the (excellent) educators at Nora's nursery frowned on his initiatives rather than praising them. In their view, small children should learn by playing, whereas formal teaching methods would be counterproductive at an early age. This cultural clash exposed little Nora to confusing contradictory messages at home and in school.[1]

The organization of the school system also shapes incentives for extracurricular activities. When we were children, it was rare for kids to have scheduled activities outside school, except perhaps soccer. Today, it is common for children to have a full after-school schedule starting in elementary school. Yet, parents' motives for signing up their kids for these activities may vary from country to country. In continental Europe, most parents view extracurricular activities merely as a way for children to have fun while helping their personal development. In contrast, in the United States and the United Kingdom, many parents think of extracurriculars as an essential part of their children's résumé, which will later on help them gain admission to top colleges and universities.

Incentives provided through the education system's organization explain these different approaches. In Scandinavia, there is little quality variation across schools, little or no tracking, and broad access to high-quality higher education. Most children attend local public schools, and, conditional on graduating from high school, access to public universities is not competitive. Therefore, when parents take their little ones to various activities, they are simply trying to make them happy, or, at the most, they are thinking about enhancing their independence and maturity. The idea that extracurricular activities are gate openers to "good schools" is foreign to them.

In Germany, as in Scandinavia, most families rely on public schools, but in some states, students are tracked after grade four or six into schools leading either to university qualification (*Gymnasium*) or to vocational training (*Realschule* or *Hauptschule*). From the perspective of an "ambitious" parent, getting a child into Gymnasium is an important objective, but extracurricular activities play no role in the admission process. Later on, a diploma from any Gymnasium or other university-qualifying school provides free and open access to most public universities, which are of relatively uniform quality.

In the United States, parents face decidedly different circumstances. There, the higher education system is highly differentiated, with a limited number of slots at a small number of selective, elite universities. If anything, the admission process to these schools is becoming increasingly competitive over time. For the class of 2021, the admission rate of Ivy League universities such as Harvard and Yale (as well as for top STEM-oriented schools like the Massachusetts Institute of Technology and Stanford) was below 7 percent. Admission figures underestimate the extent of competition, since only the very best students are advised to apply. Gaining access to such universities requires not just near-perfect grades in high school and top scores in college entrance exams like the SAT but also a portfolio of extracurricular activities that make the candidate stand out from the crowd.

These features alone already imply that American parents have much sharper incentives to push their children hard during the teenage years.[2] In fact, the competitive pressure trickles down to earlier stages of education. The quality of high schools is also highly variable, with the best high schools providing a much higher likelihood of gaining admission to a top university. The goal of gaining access to top schools leads to "competitive parenting" even for very young children. In places like New York and Los Angeles, many parents are anxious about their children's performance almost from birth because entering a top preschool (a highly competitive process relying, among other things, on evaluations of both parents and the child) makes gaining access to a top elementary school later on much more likely. In turn, that opens the gate to top high schools, and eventually to elite universities.

In other countries, parenting incentives are steep due to high-stakes university entrance exams. In China, France, South Korea, and Turkey, exams administered before finishing high school are crucial determinants of a student's chance of being admitted to an elite university. Gaining admission to one of these schools, in turn, can be the ticket to a successful career in business, government, or academia. Given these stakes, many parents push their kids to study hard every day, often with the help of external tutors. The role of high-stakes exams may help explain why some low-inequality countries such as France or South Korea are, nevertheless, characterized by intensive parenting.

Finally, there are countries such as Italy where the best schools are public, and there are no formal entry barriers in high schools. Yet, high schools are differentiated and specialized. Some of them (*Licei*) emphasize more academic knowledge, while others have a more vocational character (*Istituti Tecnici*). While students from both Licei and Istituti Tecnici can go to university, the Licei provide better academic preparation. Moreover, while admission to different high schools is unrestricted (and tuition-free), grade repetition and failure are common, so that many students end up struggling and are forced to abandon the school in which they had initially enrolled (often, to move to a less demanding track). Thus, in spite of the absence of formal barriers, academic success hinges, to some extent, on students' commitment and self-discipline. Overall, the Italian system provides some incentives for families and pupils to work hard to succeed, without being characterized by an exacerbated competition for the best schools or top grades.[3]

SCHOOLING PRACTICES THROUGHOUT HISTORY

Schooling practices and pedagogic fashions have also changed a lot over time. In the past, authoritarian practices prevailed not only in the family but also at school. Corporal punishment was commonplace, and parents generally approved of its use. Interestingly, opposition to physical punishment in schools preceded its demise in the family. Arguably, people felt that the option of beating children should be restricted to parents, rather than emotionally detached educators who might exercise punishment in arbitrary and abusive forms.

The history of corporal punishment in schools is diverse across countries. Poland outlawed corporal punishment at school as early as 1783, although the ban turned out to be short-lived because the country disappeared from the map of Europe in 1795. Most continental European countries outlawed physical punishment in school in the first half of the twentieth century, but in Germany, a comprehensive nationwide ban was passed only in 1983.

In English-speaking countries, corporal punishment in schools has proven more resilient. The common law doctrine of *in loco parentis* argues that educational institutions can act with the same rights over children as their parents. The British Parliament outlawed corporal punishment in school only in 1987, five years later than Ireland. The British ban originally applied only to state schools, so that caning continued to be practiced in some private schools until a comprehensive ban passed in England in 1998. In the United States, the Supreme Court ruled in 1977 that corporal punishment in school does not violate constitutional rights. As of today, it continues to be legal in nineteen states. A study published by the Society for Adolescent Medicine in 2003 estimated that two to three million episodes of corporal punishment occur every year in US schools, including 10,000 to 20,000 cases where students request subsequent medical treatment.[4]

Corporal punishment in school is also legal in Australia, Egypt, India (only in some states), Malaysia, Mexico, Nigeria, and Singapore.[5] In China, corporal punishment has officially been outlawed since 1986, but in reality, it continues to be dispensed in many schools, especially in rural areas.[6] Even when there is no officially sanctioned corporal punishment, Chinese children continue to be subject to the tradition of "hitting-and-cursing education" (*dama jiaoyu*) both at home and in school. The situation is similar in Japan and South Korea, where corporal punishment is officially illegal, but tolerated.[7] In a survey of 481 Korean students run by Dong-eui University in 2012, 95 percent of the respondents said they had experienced corporal punishment in school, including being spanked, hit in the face, or even punched.[8] In contrast, any form of physical correction practiced by teachers in many European countries is now a serious matter that leads to judicial prosecution and dismissal.

The presence or absence of corporal punishment in school feeds back into parents' behavior. Loving parents are likely to refrain from encouraging their children to question the authority of their teacher if doing so might lead to them being beaten or humiliated. Conversely, if corporal punishment is stigmatized in school, parents will be less likely to beat their children at home. Fabrizio recalls the case of a schoolmate whose mother insisted that the teacher should feel entitled to slap her ill-behaved boy. The school not only ignored this request but also pressured the mother to refrain from using such harsh methods even at home, although spanking one's own child was not illegal in Italy at the time. Fabrizio's father, on the other hand, described with horror the physical punishment inflicted by a particular teacher when a child spoke the local dialect in school, which was the only language spoken by many rural families. In those days, children who were beaten in school would certainly not look for consolation from their parents: complaining about being targeted by the teacher might trigger a second dose of punishment at home.

The history of corporal punishment is only one example of the decline of authoritarian practices in schools. Teaching practices changed dramatically over time, especially in the second half of the twentieth century. Until the 1950s, with few exceptions, schools in the industrialized countries were dominated by "vertical" authoritarian teaching models. Primary education used to be delivered in silence. Children were expected to listen carefully to the teacher, and teaching success was measured by the pupils' ability to repeat what teachers had said. Then, a revolution of teaching methods started in the 1960s. The new doctrine shifted the emphasis toward teamwork, open discussion, and children's welfare, which progressively became the core of the teaching mission. In 1972, a study conducted in England asked primary school teachers how they would measure the success of their teaching strategy by the time their pupils finished primary school.[9] The three most frequent answers were that children should be happy, cheerful, and well-balanced; that they should enjoy school work and find satisfaction in their achievements; and that individuals should be encouraged to develop in their own ways.

Two factors were central to the popularity of the liberal (or permissive) education model. One was the growing intellectual influence of Freudian ideas on repressiveness, namely, "the idea that harsh discipline or undue restraint imposed on the young was not conducive to healthy emotional development, but was likely to have undesirable repercussions."[10] The other factor, in our view more important, was the economic conditions of the time. Unemployment and inequality were at historical lows. Parents could feel secure that when their children left school, they would be able to get good jobs without much difficulty.

Schooling methods and parenting practices complement each other. Children growing up in antiauthoritarian school environments are more likely to resist authoritarian methods at home. Conversely, when school success hinges on children's ability to reason and argue independently, parents feel encouraged to nurture independent thinking at home. Causation runs in both directions. Permissive parents may reject the use of authoritarian methods in schools and exercise pressure for institutional change.

Recent trends in schooling practices track the evolution of parenting styles. In the United Kingdom, after the permissive trend of the 1960s and 1970s and with the advent of Thatcherism, the same word "permissive" acquired a negative connotation, often associated with children's underachievement. Lenient schools were increasingly blamed for failing to prepare new generations of children for new labor market challenges. A revisionist wave in education policy triggered a new shift of emphasis, this time toward subject specialization and strong academic results.[11] The culture of evaluation grew pervasive, with an increasing insistence on tests and cross-school competition in academic achievement.

While the overall trends described so far are shared by most advanced economies, there continue to be major differences in education institutions across countries. To map out what specific institutions imply for how parents behave, we now focus on a few individual countries that present polar cases in their design of the education system. We believe that understanding the role of institutions is especially important because these, at least in principle, can be reformed to respond to changing needs in a society. In this book, we have linked a pervasive rise in intensive parenting to the push of global economic forces toward higher inequality. The following examples show how specific institutional choices can either reinforce or counteract these trends.

CHINA: COMPETITION AND HIGH-STAKES EXAMS

If there is a country where the organization of the school system revolves around evaluations and high-stakes exams, that country is China.
The tradition of competitive exams stretches back to the imperial exam
system (*keju*) instituted under the Sui dynasty (581–618). Under the
Ming dynasty (1368–1644), keju became the standardized procedure
for selecting the imperial bureaucracy.[12] The exam was very challenging
and stakes were high, since a position in the upper level of the administration guaranteed generous earnings and an elevated social status: in
traditional Confucian culture, civil service was the most noble among
all professions. The imperial exam was abolished in 1905 during the
late years of the Qing dynasty. However, the communist government
restored competitive school admission examinations in 1952. This system was again abolished in 1966, when the Cultural Revolution vowed
to break the link between school performance and careers, and to elimi-
nate the gap between students from different backgrounds.[13] A nationwide university entrance examination was eventually reintroduced in
1977, one year after the death of Mao Zedong. Since so much time had
passed since the earlier exams, candidates of ages thirteen to thirty-
seven were allowed to take the exam.[14]

Today, the entire education system revolves around exams. The time
children spend in the classroom is dominated by mock tests meant to
prepare them for true tests. The race for good grades starts at a young
age. In nursery schools, educators push children hard to learn English
and to study multiplication tables. Wealthy parents aim to secure a head
start for their children by sending them to elite kindergartens. Hong
Kong has a different education system from mainland China, but shares
similarly competitive principles in its organization. One of Fabrizio's
friends living there relates the stressful experience for the whole family
of preparing his two-year-old daughter for an admission interview at a
selective nursery school. The daughter ended up being admitted, to
everyone's great relief.

At age fifteen, after nine years of compulsory education, Chinese
students wishing to continue their formal education must pass the se-

nior high school entrance examination (*zhongkao*). Based on the test results, students are then assigned to either regular or vocational high school. To obtain a high school diploma, students must meet certain credit requirements and pass either the general examination for high school students (*huikao*) or, alternatively, the so-called academic proficiency test.

While *huikao* is a mere formality for most students, it is the prelude to the make-or-break event: the National College Entrance Examination, or *gaokao*, a prerequisite to enter college.[15] In 2017, 9.4 million students took the exam. In most provinces, the gaokao lasts for two days in early June, during which the whole of China holds its breath. On the first day of the exam, most newspapers cover gaokao on their front page. Construction work near the examination halls is halted and traffic is diverted to avoid disturbing students. At subway stations, travelers are requested to allow gaokao students to cut in line. Ambulances stand ready outside of the examination halls to assist children and parents who might experience nervous breakdowns. Draconian measures are in place to prevent cheating: students face up to a seven-year prison sentence if caught red-handed.[16] The monitoring of exams is intense: surveillance drones and metal detectors are used to detect illegal equipment, and students are fingerprinted to make sure they are who they claim to be.

The stakes are huge. Gaokao determines not only whether students can continue their studies but also which universities they can attend. Indeed, the gaokao ranking gives the best students priority in choosing their place of study. In China, the quality of universities is highly variable, and graduating from a top school has far-reaching benefits. High grades open the gates of prestigious campuses like the Peking and Tsinghua universities in Beijing, the Fudan and Jiao Tong universities in Shanghai, and Zhejiang University in Hangzhou. The gaokao score is also crucial for admission to the best universities in Hong Kong. These academic institutions score high in international rankings and offer a cosmopolitan atmosphere with frequent international visitors (Fabrizio holds a regular visiting position at Tsinghua University). Students attending the top schools turn into the future elite, including top government officials and executives at major firms and banks. Lower-ranked universities offer no comparable opportunities. About a quarter of the gaokao examinees fail and cannot get into any university. Success in this exam is a blessing for life; failure is an indelible curse. It is then no surprise that loving parents are obsessed with pushing their children to work hard to succeed. A strong score on the gaokao may well be worth sacrificing other things one might in principle appreciate, such as imagination and independence.

The subjects children study in school are also telling. The gaokao tests students in few core subjects, and there has been a trend toward reducing the range of subjects even more. All students are examined in Mandarin, mathematics, and a foreign language (usually English). In addition, students must choose between tracks that include different disciplines, such as social sciences or natural sciences.[17] Art, music, and physical education are not part of the gaokao and hence have progressively lost importance in high school curricula. There is little incentive for parents to nurture their children's artistic spirit and drive for creativity. Membership to the "Dead Poets Society" may be a costly distraction.

The organization of the Chinese school system places immense psychological pressure on parents, teachers, and pupils. Its effectiveness is a contentious issue. On the one hand, many Chinese parents question whether so much stress is productive. On the other hand, it is also true that high-powered incentives succeed in pushing Chinese students toward excellence. The math test scores of Chinese students are especially impressive. More than one in four students in the Chinese regions that take part in PISA (Beijing, Shanghai, Jiangsu, and Guangdong) are top performers in mathematics in PISA 2015. According to PISA experts, these students can handle tasks that require the ability to formulate complex situations mathematically, using symbolic representations. No Western country comes even close to the Chinese standards. The other top-performing participants are Hong Kong, Macao, Singapore, and Taiwan, all countries and regions with an ethnic Chinese majority and a school organization that shares similarities with that of mainland China.[18]

The advocates of the current system argue that, together with promoting hard work and proficiency, the gaokao is an instrument to equalize opportunities. In principle, the gaokao allows children from any socioeconomic background to gain admission to elite universities no matter which high school they attended, whether they are rural or urban residents, or whether their parents are wealthy or from humble origins. However, it would be an exaggeration to say that gaokao provides a level playing field in terms of opportunities. Take differences between cities and rural areas, for instance. While, on average, around half of Chinese students attend the academic track of the upper secondary school, in an affluent city like Shanghai, this share is as high as 97 percent. The quality of courses offered by urban schools is typically higher compared to rural schools. The average class size is twice as large in rural schools—this, in a country where the national average is fifty students per class. Families also play an important role. Middle-class urban families often send their children to expensive "cram" schools. Well-educated parents can also follow their children's academic progress more closely and are better able to help them in their studies. The result is a substantial socioeconomic gap in gaokao outcomes. For instance, only 10 percent of the students admitted at Peking University come from a rural background. Segregation is increasing over time: the share was 30 percent as recently as the 1990s.[19]

The opportunity gap is aggravated by the fact that Chinese people cannot simply move from rural areas to cities in order to offer their children a better education. Migration is regulated by a peculiar residence system (*hukou*) whose roots stretch back to 1958, when the communist government introduced a rigid system of residence permits and internal passports to control migration between urban and rural areas. Today, even though people can move from rural areas to cities, the majority of rural migrants cannot register as urban residents. Non-resident workers do not have access to the social services offered to residents, including health insurance and the local public schools. Since elite private schools are typically unaffordable for poor migrants, they resort to enrolling their children in inexpensive schools that cater specifically to the nonresident population. These schools offer lower academic standards than regular public schools, leaving the children of migrants less well prepared for gaokao.

Inequality is also exacerbated by differences in university admission quotas for different regions. Aside from gaokao results, local residents have preferential access to local universities. Since the best universities are concentrated in first-tier cities like Shanghai and Beijing, applicants residing in these cities have an advantage. In 2016, a group of Henan residents issued an open letter to the State Council of China protesting against discrimination. According to the letter, in 2013, 758,000 students from the Henan province competed for eighty-five spots at Peking University, while 73,000 students from Beijing competed for 226 positions.[20]

Such disparities notwithstanding, the prospect of upward mobility that the gaokao system provides is an important factor underlying parents' incentives in China. Success in the gaokao hinges on working hard. The door is open for gifted but poor children to do well, and access to top opportunities is not guaranteed even for the children of wealthy and well-educated parents.[21]

Yet, there are important side effects. Critics blame the organization of the school system for suffocating students' creativity. They argue that preparing for the gaokao involves obsessive rote learning, where memorizing and repeating codified information comes at the expense of developing an independent critical mind. In addition, the critics blame dismal learning methods for causing unhappy childhoods and long-lasting trauma. Many adult Chinese report having recurring nightmares about gaokao. In PISA 2015, Chinese students score among the lowest in the world in terms of self-reported life satisfaction. Stress and dissatisfaction can sometimes lead to tragic consequences. According to the 2014 edition of the *Annual Report on China's Education*, a high share of teenagers who committed suicide were pushed to the brink by the heavy pressure of tests and exams.[22] The report describes the cases of a middle school student from Inner Mongolia who jumped from a building after receiving a low score in a test; a thirteen-year-old boy from Nanjing who took his life after failing to complete his homework; and

FIGURE 9.1. Chinese students taking a school examination (photo provided by *China Daily*)

a girl from Sichuan who killed herself after a disappointing performance in the gaokao.[23] A study that examined a set of teenage suicide cases in 2013 concluded that 93 percent of them are related to pressure and anxiety associated with exam preparation. Moreover, 63 percent of the suicides occurred during the time of the year when students take major exams.

In 2012, a scandal followed the online publication of photographs showing middle school students from the province of Hubei being administered intravenous drips in the classroom while preparing for the gaokao. According to the school, the students were merely offered an injection of amino acids for replacing energy. The school arranged injections locally so that students could avoid wasting time traveling between a clinic and their classrooms.[24] This episode is certainly not representative of what happens in regular Chinese schools, but the attention it received in the media is an indicator of how strongly people feel about this debate.

The debate on the repercussions of the gaokao system has led to pressure toward reforming the educational system. The reformers argue for mitigating the competitive excesses and for promoting a more student-oriented engagement. Another impetus for reform comes from the notion that independence and creativity, values that are not strongly promoted by the current system, may become increasingly important for students if China's economic model switches from imitation and production of existing technology toward more innovation.[25]

Some reforms are already being carried out at a local level. Since 2001, Shanghai has used its own higher education entrance examination instead of the national college entrance examination. Relative to the standard exam, Shanghai's system is geared toward testing pupils' raw intelligence by including essay questions about multiple disciplines rather than focusing on hard knowledge that students can memorize. The city of Shanghai also legislated a maximum amount of homework and set a minimum of one hour of physical activity a day.[26] However, these rules are not always enforced. According to the OECD, fifteen-year-old pupils from Shanghai spend on average 13.8 hours per week doing homework, and many attend "cram" schools on top of that.[27] These schools offer afternoon sessions, which start after the end of regular classes and continue late into the evening. To draw a comparison, children in Northern Europe spend barely three hours a week doing homework. There, some parents complain about the inhumane workload and advocate getting rid of homework altogether. British and American high school students spend, respectively, five and six hours on homework each week.

The Chinese school system is an extreme example of high-powered incentives embedded in a high-stakes exam. Children's future success hinges on passing a single test, the preparation for which requires heavy effort, rote learning, and focused attention to a few core subjects. We saw in chapter 3 that 90 percent of Chinese parents believe that hard work is a key virtue in child-rearing, whereas only 23 percent emphasize imagination. There, we argued that high levels of inequality can help to explain the attitude of Chinese parents. Here, we see that the organization of the education system drives the stakes even higher and adds a further incentive for Chinese parents to adopt an intensive parenting style.

JAPAN: HIGH STAKES MEET INDEPENDENCE

Once again, Japan provides an interesting contrast to China. Unlike China, Japan's society has a low level of income inequality. However, as in China, the school system is characterized by high-stakes exams and high pressure on children to perform. Japanese parents respond by pushing their children to succeed in school, even if not quite to the same extent as Chinese parents do.

The race for success starts early in Japan. An article in the *Japan Times* titled "Prepping for University Straight from the Crib" describes the phenomenon of "escalator schools."[28] The distinctive feature of these elite schools is that they offer education from kindergarten to university, typically without requiring students to pass tests to advance from grade to grade. Many of the pupils who follow this elite track obtain admission to top universities such as University of Tokyo or Kyoto University.

The selective admission process for escalator schools puts a great strain on families. The *Japan Times* article portrays a five-year-old child preparing for her *juken*, the exam that will determine whether she can gain admission to the desired school. "She has already identified photographs of fruit and will soon be told a story about a panda, after which she'll have to draw a picture and offer an ending. How she does with these activities could determine where she attends university, and nobody is more nervous than her parents being interviewed next door." Children start preparing for this high-stakes exam when they are just three years old. The admission process is very competitive. Around 8 percent of the five-year-old kids in Tokyo attend escalator schools, but many more would like to. The selection process works through interviews of both parents and children. Children are ranked based on their ability to quickly follow precise instructions, as well as on their mental acuity and responsiveness. The test also assesses family dynamics, manners, and discipline.

Later on, the Japanese education system features a number of additional hurdles. A high school entrance examination determines admission into secondary schools, which vary in quality and ambition. After finishing the upper secondary school, students seek admission to universities. Admission to Japan's national and public universities (which include the best academic institutions) requires taking two steps. First, students must pass the National Center Test for University Admissions, which covers all subjects, including sciences and the liberal arts. Next, they must take a university-specific exam.[29] There is strong competition for slots in the top universities, so this second step represents the biggest challenge. Some students try repeatedly over the years to gain admission to their desired course of study. These students are nicknamed *ronin*, which is the traditional term for a samurai without lord or master.

Given the importance of the university entrance tests, like Chinese students, many Japanese students attend cram schools to prepare. This adds to an already heavy schoolwork burden: Japanese students spend 240 days a year at school, sixty days more than Americans. Cram schools and long school days explain why Japanese students report spending a mere 3.8 hours per week on regular homework. In the end, even though the sun rises early in Japan, the day still lasts only twenty-four hours!

Cram schools are an important social barrier. Attendance is expensive. Children from rich families who fail to gain admission to good universities have the option of enrolling in a full-year cram school to prepare for their second chance to pass the test. Less wealthy families cannot afford to do the same.

As in China, high-stakes exams encourage families to emphasize discipline and hard work. Parents, especially mothers, play an important role in pushing children toward success and imbuing them with the right values.[30] Still, parenting values differ substantially between China and Japan. In the WVS data, only 34 percent of the Japanese parents emphasize hard work, far below the Chinese figure of 90 percent. We believe that the primary reason for the difference is that Japan, as already noted, is a much less unequal society than China. While high-stakes exams may induce parents to push kids to work hard, they also see a relatively low return to school performance, which provides an offsetting force. This observation is in line with our main thesis that economic factors are important.

Another interesting observation is that independence is held in high regard by the Japanese (this is also true in China). Part of the reason may be that independence has a different meaning in the East Asian culture compared to Western countries. Japanese parents foster their children's independence not so much by letting children do what they like, but rather by entrusting them with adult-like chores. For instance, children are required to clean their school, they are allowed to walk to school alone, and they are expected to take responsibility for their uni-cycle (riding unicycles is a popular recreational activity for Japanese children in elementary school). Lunchtime is an important educational moment. Children fetch their food from the kitchen, serve themselves, and eat together with their teachers in their classroom. After lunch, they are required to clean up. Students sometimes grow and harvest some of the food they eat. The emphasis on independence means that children must learn quickly to act responsibly and to be self-reliant. In terms of parenting style, these examples suggest that in Japan independence is more closely associated with authoritative rather than permissive parenting.

FINLAND: LOW PRESSURE AND ACADEMIC ACHIEVEMENT

If China's school system is all about competition and high stakes, schools in the Nordic countries (Denmark, Finland, Norway, and Sweden) emphasize teamwork and a laid-back approach to education. Competitive evaluations do not play a major role. Among the Nordic countries, Finland is regarded as a compelling success story and a role model for reforms elsewhere. The main reason is that Finnish students have achieved consistently high scores in various editions of the PISA studies of student performance without the motivation of high-stakes exams.

The characteristic traits of the Finnish system are low competition and low pressure. Children start primary school rather late, at age

FIGURE 9.2. An informal and relaxed school environment in Saunalahti School, Espoo (Photo by Andreas Meichsner/Verstas)

seven. Before reaching school age, all children are entitled to attend nursery schools and kindergarten. Attendance rates are close to 100 percent; the service, whether public or private, is (almost) tuition-free. Learning through play, as opposed to formal teaching, is the institutional creed. Neither nursery schools nor kindergartens work on preparing children for reading, writing, or math. Selecting children into elite nursery schools based on interviews would sound bizarre to Finnish parents.

The vast majority of Finnish children attend public schools. The few existing private schools cannot charge tuition, but do receive state subsidies. Schools cannot select pupils, and most parents enroll their children in the local school in their neighborhood. In addition to free tuition, pupils receive free learning materials, free meals, health checks, dental care, and transportation to and from school. The atmosphere in the classroom is informal: students do not wear uniforms and call the teachers by their first names.

There are no official school rankings. All schools share the same national teaching goals and draw from a common pool of university-trained educators, although districts and schools enjoy some autonomy in adjusting their own school curricula. The result is that Finnish children from rural villages receive an education that is very similar, in both content and quality, to that of children living in university towns or cities. Although the reputations of schools may vary, most differences hinge on the managerial skills of school principals, and the differences across schools are never large. The same is true at the university level.

For most of their studies, Finnish students face no high-stakes examinations. Teachers do perform periodical evaluations, but the assessment system is geared toward improving instruction by providing teachers with feedback about the students' progress, rather than toward ranking students or pushing them to work harder. In its guidance, the Finnish National Board of Education recommends that assessments be supportive and help students form a realistic understanding of their development. In line with these guidelines, when primary school teachers run an evaluation, they never present it as an individual test of proficiency. Feedback comes in the form of tests marked on a scale ranging from "very good" to "needs practice"; numerical grading is not used at all. Often, neither the children nor the parents learn about the results, which are instead used by the teacher as feedback and for planning purposes.

The share of Finnish students dropping out of education is very low.[31] This reflects both the intrinsic success of schools that do not leave students behind, and the general preference for supporting weaker students rather than incentivizing the more gifted ones to work hard. The practice of grade repetition, which is still common in Germany and Southern Europe, is very rare and widely regarded as obsolete.

There are two consequential exams in the Finnish curriculum. The first takes place at age sixteen, when students leave basic education. This exam allows students who have earned better grades to select schools with a better reputation, although, as mentioned previously, quality differences across high schools are limited. The second takes place at the end of secondary school, when students take the so-called Matriculation Examination, which serves as a criterion for college admission. Passing the exam entitles the candidate to continue his or her studies at a university. It provides a measure of students' general maturity, including their readiness to continue studies in higher education. Students must not only answer standard academic questions but also must show their ability to cope with real-world issues, such as losing a job or dieting, and to discuss issues such as politics, ethics in sports, sex, drugs, and popular music. This is quite different from the emphasis on core subjects that is characteristic of the Chinese system.

Finnish educators are proud of their system. According to Pasi Sahlberg, a former school teacher, government advisor, and author of an award-winning book on the Finnish education system, the absence of standardized tests is a point of strength in the system.[32] In his view, preparing children for national exams would simply distract teachers from their focus on improving children's learning and understanding. He argues that the release of data from standardized tests and the ensuing school rankings are a source of "toxic competition," which prevents collaboration and cooperation from flourishing.[33] Somewhat paradoxically given Mr. Sahlberg's views, Finland owes the international popularity of its schools to the success of Finnish pupils in the standardized PISA test.

What explains the Finnish success story? As Mr. Sahlberg argues, there may be an upside to the lack of competitive exams. However, another distinct feature of the education system in Finland is a strong emphasis on the qualifications of its teachers. The Finnish National Agency for Education insists on high educational requirements for teachers of all levels, all of whom are required to hold a master's degree. In addition, even primary school teachers with a major in education need to specialize in at least two additional areas by taking courses in other departments. Despite these strict requirements and teacher salaries that are broadly in line with international averages, training to become a teacher is among the most popular choices of Finnish university students. Many students apply for teacher training, and universities are able to select the most qualified among them in each cohort.

How does Finland manage to have highly qualified teachers without paying them huge salaries? We turn to the notion of "compensating wage differentials" coined by the economist Sherwin Rosen for the explanation.[34] His theory stipulates that competition in labor markets equates the net advantages of different jobs requiring equal qualifications. An example is academic jobs. Professors of economics typically earn less than people with a PhD in economics who work in the private sector. The explanation is not that we care less about money. Rather, we think that doing research and not having a boss makes academic jobs more fun. As a result, private sector firms must offer people holding a doctoral degree in economics a salary premium. Compensating wage differentials can also explain premia attached to locations. For instance, Norwegian engineers working in offshore oil extraction earn significantly more than those working in Oslo. The pay difference is set to counter the inconvenience of spending days and nights on remote oil platforms in the rough sea rather than having dinner with the family or friends in the capital at the end of the workday.

One reason why well-educated and capable Finnish people become teachers in spite of the unremarkable salaries is that in Finland, being a teacher commands a high social status. The demanding education requirements, which ensure that only the best-qualified students can become teachers, contribute to their position of respect. An indicator of the popularity of teaching is that a mere 10 to 15 percent of teachers abandon their profession.[35] The intrinsic satisfaction of Finnish teachers is a gift to taxpayers who receive great value for their money. To attract equally qualified and well-educated people in countries where the teaching profession is less popular would force the government to pay high salaries. Finland's ability to create attractive working conditions that generate high satisfaction among teachers explains a good deal of their success story.

SWEDEN: ALMOST FINLAND BUT NOT QUITE THE SAME

The case of Finland is especially popular with the adversaries of competitive school systems and of high-stakes exams. The low-stress approach that emphasizes cooperation and children's intrinsic motivation, they argue, is the real cause of Finnish success. Sweden poses a challenge to this interpretation, offering instead an argument that learning requires some pressure on children and appropriate incentives.

The organization of Sweden's school system is broadly similar to that of Finland. It emphasizes low competition, low stress, and team cooperation. The Swedish curriculum is also broadly similar to the Finnish one. All children are entitled to nursery schools and kindergarten, and most attend public institutions, where the emphasis is on learning through playing. Primary school starts at age seven, as in Finland. Private schools cannot charge fees.

The education system is geared toward curbing inequality. Dropout rates are low. There is no formal tracking system, although it has become common practice in recent years to group students by ability within comprehensive compulsory schools. Yet, the Swedish National Agency for Education stipulates that groupings should only be temporary and with specific academic purposes. Children do not receive grades in school until grade six. Thereafter, students start to receive term grades in the various subjects, and a final grade is assigned at the end of the ninth grade. This final grade forms the basis for applications to high school.

Like in Finland, there are no major high-stakes exams. After ninth grade, students take a national standardized test on core subjects (English, Swedish, and mathematics) that is supposed to make sure that students' learning standards are comparable throughout the country. Almost all students continue on to high school, which lasts for three years. Admission to a university is based on the grades received in high school.

The homework load is low. According to PISA 2015, Swedish students spend only 3.8 hours a week doing homework. Even so, parents often complain about an excess of homework. In 2014, members of the Left Party in the city council of Hallstahammar put forward a proposal to ban homework altogether.[36] Although the initiative was not successful in the end, it is indicative of the views of many parents.

Overall, the school systems of Finland and Sweden share many similarities. Both systems emphasize equality of opportunity in a supportive environment where children can learn without being subject to much competitive pressure. However, if we believe in the validity of international test scores, there is an important difference between the two countries. Between 2000 and 2012, Sweden recorded the sharpest deterioration in scores among the thirty-two countries with available data. These poor results temporarily pushed Sweden into the bottom group of OECD countries before a significant rebound occurred in 2015. Perceptions line up with the data. If our Finnish friends are generally proud of their education system, Swedes are more often critical of and dissatisfied with their own.

A possible reason is that the school systems of Finland and Sweden are, in reality, more different than a first impression might suggest.[37] One difference is that the teaching profession in Sweden does not appear to have the same high social status as in Finland. Swedish teachers report low levels of job satisfaction. In a survey carried out by the Swedish teaching union, almost nine out of ten primary school teachers reported that their workload is too high and administrative tasks eat up too much valuable teaching time.[38] One in three teachers in Sweden report that they "probably" or "definitely" will not continue working in schools until they retire. The low status and low satisfaction of teachers also translates into difficulties in recruiting them.[39]

Another difference is that in the 1990s Sweden introduced a reform that appears to have yielded dismal results. The reform granted parents vouchers that could be spent either in public or in private schools. Private schools continued to be subject to government regulation even after the reform. Like state schools, they cannot select their students, nor can they charge fees on top of the vouchers. In case of oversubscription, the selection of children should follow general nondiscriminatory criteria approved by the Swedish Schools Inspectorate (although, in practice, exceptions are common).

In spite of these limitations, this was an important change. When the government introduced the reform, there were hardly any private schools in Sweden. Today, there are eight hundred "independent" schools across Sweden, many of them run by profit-seeking companies. Twelve percent of compulsory school students and 24 percent of senior high school students attend independent schools. The idea was popular, especially among upper-middle-class parents anxious to separate their children from the "ordinary" children attending state schools. Some parents saw it as a vehicle of emancipation from the allegedly social-democratic values of state schools.

As economists we have sympathy with the argument that competition from private schools can provide incentives for public schools to deliver better results. Yet, this did not happen in Sweden. A number of studies document rather clearly that the voucher system has had a negative impact on student achievement.[40]

What went wrong? We conjecture that there might have been a clash between the dominant parenting culture and the spirit of the reform. Swedish families are imbued with permissive principles, which, in turn, stem from a low-inequality economy that provides only weak economic incentives for individualistic success. In response to this environment, the market mechanism appears to have pushed independent schools to cater to the demand for fun and games, rather than to compete as an institution of academic excellence. One symptom is that competition appears to have translated into grade inflation in both public and independent schools.

Some independent schools take a radically permissive approach. For example, an independent school in Kista, a suburb of Stockholm, offers pupils the possibility of a personalized approach to learning, which allows them to negotiate their own timetable each week and to attend as many, or as few, classes as they wish. Students also set their own personalized academic goals, which they can revise.[41] To be clear, we do not mean to judge this particular school nor to imply that its results are good or bad. Rather, we take it as an example that supports the claim that competition between private and public schools appears to have resulted in a lower emphasis on academic intensity, which certainly was not among the stated goals of the reform.

The comparison of Finland and Sweden suggests that exporting a successful model of school organization to another country might be more complicated that one would expect. Small differences in local circumstances can lead to large differences in outcomes, even when two countries share many characteristics and adopt broadly similar education systems. Exporting the Finnish model to China or the United States would probably be even harder than making Swedish parents and children embrace more achievement-oriented values.

Another lesson is that parenting values and school systems are complementary. Nordic parents value imagination and independence more than hard work and obedience; the same values are reflected in the school systems' organization in these countries. Parents support institutions that emphasize low competitive pressure, low stress, and cooperation among students. However, causation runs in both directions: the organization of the school system, together with low economic inequality, reinforces parents' permissive orientation. This is not meant to say that Swedish and Finnish children turn into unproductive adults. While Scandinavians work shorter hours than American and Chinese workers do, Finland and Sweden score near the top among countries in terms of innovativeness. This might be an unexpected economic dividend of a relaxed education system.

FRANCE: VERTICAL TEACHING PRACTICES

High-stakes exams are not the only aspect of the school system organization that interacts with parenting styles. In a recent study, the economists Yann Algan, Pierre Cahuc, and Andrei Shleifer document that the methods used to teach children differ substantially across countries.[42] Some countries are dominated by "vertical" teaching practices, that is, a hierarchical system where the teacher-student relationship is the core element of the classroom interaction. Teachers lecture and students take notes or read textbooks. The students are evaluated on their ability to reproduce the material covered by the teachers. In other countries, schools promote "horizontal" teaching practices, that is, a less hierarchical system where the teacher-student relationships are complemented by interactions among students. In a horizontal environment, students work in groups, do projects together, and are invited to ask questions and even challenge the teachers.

By looking at a variety of measures, the study documents that horizontal teaching practices are most common in Scandinavian countries, the Netherlands, and Switzerland, but also in the United Kingdom and the United States. Vertical teaching practices are instead popular in France, Japan, Belgium, Turkey, Russia, and Eastern Europe. Countries that are classified as intermediate cases include Italy, Germany, Spain, Australia, and (somewhat surprisingly to us) Finland.

Algan, Cahuc, and Shleifer show that teaching practices affect the extent to which people trust and are willing to cooperate with each other in adulthood. People who were exposed in youth to vertical teaching practices are less trustful and cooperative, while teamwork and open discussion in the classroom forge more collaborative individuals.

Different teaching practices are also correlated with our measures of parenting styles. Figure 9.3 plots the vertical teaching measure presented by Algan and his coauthors (horizontal axis) against the share of parents who adopt each of the three parenting styles.[43] In countries with more vertical teaching practices, parents tend to be less permissive and more authoritative. Somewhat surprisingly, there is no significant correlation with the authoritarian parenting style. This is mostly due to two countries, Germany and Japan, where teaching methods are fairly (Germany) or very (Japan) vertical, but parents do not single out obedience as an important virtue. Among the other countries, the correlation between vertical teaching and the authoritarian parenting style is high and statistically significant.

France is a particularly interesting case. In chapter 3, we noted that given the low level of inequality, France has a surprisingly large share of parents who praise hard work, whereas the share emphasizing imagination and independence is low. French parents also emphasize obedience more than parents in any other continental European country, and as shown in figure 9.3, French schools adopt vertical teaching practices more than those anywhere else in the sample. This suggests that the organization of the school system influences the values that French parents emphasize in rearing their children.

The classification of French teaching methods as highly vertical lines up with the nation's conventional wisdom. A book on French culture

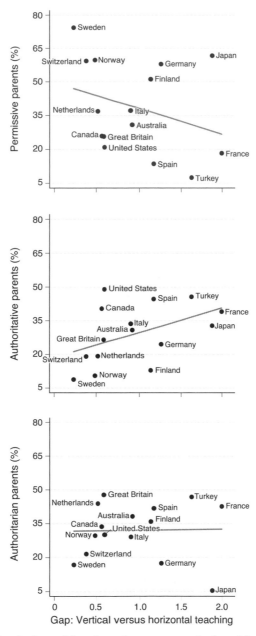

FIGURE 9.3. Vertical teaching (gap between vertical and horizontal teaching practices) versus percentage of parents adopting a permissive (upper panel), authoritative (center panel), and authoritarian (lower panel) parenting style across OECD countries.

by the Canadian journalists Jean-Benoit Nadeau and Julie Barlow describes French schools as pitiless and authoritarian: "An outstanding feature of French education is the authority of teachers. The French don't regard childhood as an age of innocence but see it as an age of ignorance. Children must be set straight and corrected."[44] While this description may be hyperbolic, it is consistent with the widespread impression that French schools emphasize a forceful transmission of formal knowledge from teacher to pupils over the notion of positive reinforcement, namely, supportive teachers encouraging children's learning instinct.

The evaluation system is strict, some might say harsh. Unlike in Scandinavian schools, grade repetition is a common fate for children who have learning difficulties. More than a quarter of French children are forced to repeat at least one grade, more than double the international average according to the OECD. A system in which schools do not support weak students but rather leave them behind provides incentives for parents to take additional measures to avoid failure. Thus, parents emphasize the virtues of obedience and hard work.

Other features of the French schooling system also encourage a strict parenting style. First, as many as 20 percent of French children attend private schools in France, far more than in the United Kingdom or the United States. Most of these private schools are Catholic schools, where religious instruction is part of the curriculum. Catholic private schools are inexpensive and are attended by children of various socioeconomic backgrounds. Strict discipline is a typical trait of religious schools, which, in turn, means that school success hinges more on discipline and hard work than on independence and imagination.

An even more important factor in explaining French parents' focus on obedience and hard work is inequality across schools and universities. By continental European standards, inequality across high schools is already significant. Although in theory all public high schools (*lycées*) offer the same curriculum in the framework of the national education system, in practice there is a common perception that some schools are much better than others. A few lycées command a high level of prestige, like the Lycée Louis-le-Grand and the Lycée Henri-IV in Paris, or the Lycée Fermat in Toulouse. Until recently, the best schools were state schools. In recent years, an increasing number of private lycées have climbed the ladder in rankings. An example is the Collège Stanislas in Paris, a large Catholic private lycée.

At the university level, there is pronounced inequality at the top of the distribution. Admission works through high-stakes exams. Already the regular final exam for high school graduates, the so-called *Baccalauréat* or *Bac*, is important in determining students' access to university studies. Even more important is that France has a dual system for higher education. There are regular universities, and there are *Grandes Écoles*. The Grandes Écoles are a set of elite institutions that are separate from the rest of the university system and provide a highly ambitious education for the national elite in the French government, administration, and private sector. Less than 5 percent of students attend Grandes Écoles. To gain admission, students first apply after high school for admission to a *classe préparatoire*. In these classes, students are expected to work relentlessly (forty hours of courses each week, frequent tests, a lot of homework). Two or three years down the road, the students take a highly competitive test to gain admission to one of the elite Grandes Écoles in the system.

Admission to a Grande École is not only based on raw intelligence; it hinges very much on the effort and perseverance of the candidates. Some claim that gaining entry is the main hurdle and that after a successful admission process students can actually relax. Admission into a prestigious Grande École is a key marker of success in France. While only a limited fraction of French parents contemplate access to this elite system for their children (children of former Grande École graduates are overrepresented among the students), the fiercely competitive selection process provides powerful incentives for ambitious parents to emphasize the value of endurance and resilience. Therefore, it contributes to the explanation of why hard work is such a popular child-rearing value among French parents, about as much as it is in the United States, which is a much more unequal society.

TAKING STOCK

In this chapter, we have argued that a school system's organization is a powerful determinant in the choice of parenting styles across countries. In some cases, the educational institutions reinforce the effect of economic fundamentals on parenting. For instance, China and the United States are economies with high income inequality, a high return to education, and weak social safety nets. We have argued that these characteristics push mothers and fathers toward an intensive parenting style, with authoritative characteristics in the United States and an authoritarian flavor in China. In both countries, the organization of the school system magnifies the incentives to adopt an intensive parenting style. In the United States, this works through competition for admission slots at top schools and universities, which are allotted based not just on grades and test scores but also on a student's résumé of extracurricular activities. In China, the biggest impact of the education system on parenting works through high-stakes exams, especially the gaokao. In other countries, such as Finland and Sweden, we observe a combination of highly egalitarian societies with schools that put low pressure on students and that emphasize teamwork and horizontal teaching methods. Here, the economic environment and the school system combine to provide strong incentives for parents to adopt a permissive parenting style.

The most interesting cases are countries where the two factors, economic fundamentals and the organization of the school system, shape incentives in opposite directions. We discussed two such cases: France and Japan. In France, institutions such as high-stakes exams and vertical teaching methods sharpen the incentives for parents to be pushy. This can explain why French parents are more authoritative and authoritarian than the moderate economic inequality of France would predict. Japan has also low inequality and relatively high stakes in its school system. Japanese parents promote children's independence, but are altogether less pushy than Chinese parents and, specifically, put less emphasis on hard work and obedience. However, the phenomenon of "education mothers" and "monster parents," which are often discussed in the Japanese media, show that the Japanese parenting culture has some elements of intensive child-rearing that are unusual for low-inequality countries. These cases show that both economic inequality and the organization of the school system matter and interact with each other.

CHAPTER TEN

The Future of Parenting

In this book, we have investigated the forces that shape parenting in the modern world, using the toolkit of economics. Why was parenting a seemingly relaxed affair just a generation ago, whereas today frantic parents drive their children from activity to activity and push them to succeed? Why do parenting styles differ across countries and socioeconomic groups? Why has corporal punishment, almost universally practiced in the past, been shunned in recent decades? We have argued that understanding the economic incentives of parents can go a long way in answering these questions.

Our view is that most parents, at any time and in any place, have the same objective, namely, for their kids to be happy and do well in life. Clearly, there are exceptions to this rule. Some parents neglect or even abuse their children. While these are important social issues, thankfully, they concern a minority. Most mothers and fathers love their children and wish the best for them. Such well-meaning parents, who are the object of our analysis, attempt to do what it takes to get their children to succeed, given the economic conditions in play.

WHICH ECONOMIC CONDITIONS MATTER MOST

Income inequality and educational stakes are key. When only children who excel both in education and extracurricular activities have a guaranteed path to success, parents will push them hard to get there. In contrast, when economic inequality is low or when there are plentiful opportunities for children doing "just fine" to enjoy a comfortable middle-class life, the stakes in parenting are also lower, and parents can afford to be more relaxed. In our exploration of parenting, we have sought to explain the origins and effects of different parenting styles and the driving forces behind historical changes in parenting by taking a tour of child-rearing practices around the world and considering how the organization of schools and educational systems feed back into parents' choices.

Over the past two hundred years, economic life has been radically transformed by industrialization, technological progress, urbanization, and the gradual shift of production from a predominance of agriculture to industry, and later, to services. These economic transformations have led to equally drastic changes in decisions within the family. The rising demand for human capital and the establishment of public schools incentivized parents to provide their children with an education, rather than sending them to work at an early age. The same changes increased the cost of children, thereby explaining the steady decline in fertility rates in the process of modern development.

Economic inequality fell sharply in the West after World War II, especially throughout the 1960s and 1970s. These changes accelerated the demise of authoritarian parenting and its by-products (e.g., corporal punishment of children), paving the way to more liberal parenting and pedagogical practices designed to foster children's independence and imagination. Thereafter, the tide turned again. Since the 1980s, rising economic inequality and higher returns to education have increased the importance for children to work hard and succeed in school. Parents have responded by pushing their kids harder, leading to the modern phenomenon of "helicopter parenting." We have documented that parents did indeed shift into a higher gear when the economic return to education started growing in the 1980s, after two decades in which the child-rearing culture had been permissive and the return to education had been low.

We have also documented large differences in parenting styles across a set of industrialized countries. Over recent decades, tiger moms and helicopter parents have gained significant ground in countries where inequality has grown fast, like the United States. In contrast, the appeal of these parenting styles remains limited in countries where economic inequality is low, like the Nordic countries and (to a lesser extent) Germany, Switzerland, and the Netherlands.

While in principle one might have expected high economic stakes to make parents both more authoritarian and more authoritative, the main shift has been in the direction of the latter. The authoritarian parenting style has continued its decline. We believe the main reason to be that in modern societies children are ultimately responsible for the make-or-break decisions that determine their success. In an economy increasingly driven by knowledge, and where most human capital accumulation takes place through formal education that extends well into adult life, parents cannot simply monitor their children and tell them what to do. Hence, authoritarian methods are bound to fail. Instead, parents' only option is to motivate their children and to instill the right attitudes in them. These are the defining features of the authoritative parenting style.

WHY WE DID NOT WRITE A PARENTING GUIDE

We have refrained from making recommendations for what good parents should do. We do not believe that one parenting style is inherently better than another. Rather, as economists we take the perspective that all parenting styles involve trade-offs. For instance, an authoritarian parenting style might work well in a society characterized by low social mobility, where success requires strict conformity to traditional roles, and where an anticonformist attitude could become a source of trouble as children grow up. Recent research in developmental psychology points to negative emotional and behavioral consequences on children of a very strict upbringing. We do not dispute those findings, but believe that, at least in part, these negative effects are specific to modern societies where authoritarian parents are the exception rather than the rule. We do not recall our parents blaming their own parents for being strict. At the time, it was the common fare. An occasional slapping or spanking was not perceived as humiliation or abuse. In traditional societies, most parents loved their children, and most children loved their parents, just as they do today.

An invasive authoritative parenting style can strengthen the drive to individual success, but at the same time, it may suffocate the child's independent initiative and imagination. Moreover, while authoritative parents may succeed in enhancing their children's school grades, this may not always benefit society. In Scandinavian countries, where most parents are permissive, children are less competitive and arguably less willing to exert relentless effort, but they become excellent team players.

As to helicopter parents, which we view as the coddling version of authoritative parents, their protective efforts may succeed in shaping their children's preferences and attitudes, and in keeping them out of trouble. Yet, this comes at the cost of delaying their natural transition into adulthood, as stories about "mama's boys" living at home with their parents into their thirties indicate.

Nor do we view liberal parenting as a panacea. Permissive parenting may be good at fostering children's imagination and independence. Yet, in certain environments, children left to their own devices may be tempted to experiment with alcohol, drugs, or other risky activities. A lack of parental guidance may also cater to some children's drive to seize the day without regard for the future consequences. Some children may fail to work hard enough to earn a good education. The consequences of slacking off are more severe in competitive environments, for instance, where grades matter for admission to good universities.

While we focused primarily on economic incentives, the choice of parenting style is also influenced by broader cultural factors. These are not independent of economic forces but rather interact with them, sometimes reinforcing and sometimes offsetting the economic incentives. We discussed religiosity and documented that strictly religious parents are more prone to value obedience and adherence to tradition. Thus, it is not surprising that religiosity is associated with a more authoritarian approach to parenting. Strictly religious parents believe in transmitting absolute values and hold in low regard letting children work out their own version of the world. Interestingly, as societies grow

more dynamic and mobile, some faiths adopt more flexible inter-
pretations of religious precepts. The decline of the traditional model of
religiosity goes hand in hand with the wider economic changes and
transformations of society that lead to the decline of authoritarian
parenting.

GIRLS AND BOYS

Another dimension of parenting that at first sight may appear to have
a strong cultural connotation concerns the different child-rearing strategies parents adopt for girls and boys. The feminist movement has long
considered parenting as a source of traditional role models that perpetu-
ate discrimination in society. Reflecting this perspective, a widely held
view today is that parents should treat boys and girls equally and avoid
gender stereotypes in their upbringing. In this view of the origin of
gender roles, parenting is shaped by cultural forces, and the role models
emphasized by parents, in turn, affect what girls and boys do when they
grow up. Our approach points out a reverse channel, which runs from
economic conditions to gender roles in parenting.

Consider a society where fertility rates are high and where taking
care of the household is demanding in terms of time, say, because of
the lack of modern household appliances. In such an economic environment, more specialized roles for women and men are likely to arise
compared to an advanced economy where men and women compete on
equal terms in the labor market and where a market for childcare services exists. In a society where the economic and social roles for women
and men are vastly different, parents will tend to raise girls and boys
differently. From this perspective, the trend we observe in many societies toward more equal treatment of girls and boys by parents is not an
independent cultural force but in part reflects changed economic
circumstances.

Over time, economic changes and cultural dynamics can mutually
affect and reinforce each other. If cultural values are persistent, they
can initially slow down the spread of new role models. However, once

cultural views adjust, they can speed up the economic change. For example, if parents raise their children with the expectation that girls and boys should have the same labor market opportunities, they might also support antidiscrimination regulation in the workplace, which helps make this vision a reality and reinforces the underlying trend.

Conversely, social and economic discrimination reinforces gender-biased parenting. If women face discrimination in labor markets, parents will have weaker incentives to invest in their daughters' human capital, since the return to such investment is low. This type of vicious circle is relevant in some developing countries where women's participation in labor markets is low. Going back to personal experience, a friend of Fabrizio became the temporary foster mother of a girl from Western Sahara while she was offered some medical treatment in Spain. Since she proved to be a brilliant student, Fabrizio's friend offered to pay for her full education in Spain. The girl's family thanked her but declined the offer, saying that this would be useless for a girl, while they could have agreed to the plan in the case of a boy.

In summary, in this book we have argued that parenting decisions are in large part driven by economic factors. An economic theory of parenting style can explain the main trends and fashions in child-rearing culture over time, it can account for the differences in the popularity of various parenting styles across countries, and it can also explain how economic and cultural forces interact in shaping parenting decisions.

WHAT CAN THE ECONOMIC APPROACH SAY ABOUT THE FUTURE?

We believe that future parenting practices will continue to be influenced by economic changes. While the future is uncertain, the experience of two hundred years of economic growth and transformation allows us to make educated guesses about the future of parenting. We have identified increasing returns to education and greater returns to independence as two key factors that have driven changes in parenting since the onset of industrialization. In particular, the trend toward smaller families with a higher investment in children's education, the decline of authoritarian parenting, and the rise of authoritative parenting can all be traced back to these long-run trends.

When we consider the future of parenting in developing countries, we see no compelling reason why the trends that shaped the transformation in parenting in the industrialized world should not work in the same way there. Technological progress tends to replace low-skilled labor and complement high-skilled labor. Moreover, low returns to independence are in part the result of artificial barriers to mobility and of financial constraints, which should continue to lose significance in a modern globalized economy.

Hence, the model of a typical middle-class family with a small number of children and a strong emphasis on education is likely to spread further to countries that today are still at an earlier stage of their development process. The changes in parenting will be especially pronounced in countries where fertility rates are still high but are now falling rapidly. The demographic transition is a universal feature of economic development: every single country that has developed a successful, knowledge-based economy has undergone a transition to low fertility rates. In most developing countries, the demographic transition is already proceeding rapidly today, and we have every reason to believe that the trend toward lower fertility will continue.

The economics of parenting developed in this book predicts that this decline in the number of children in each family will have a profound effect on child-rearing practices. The smaller number of children will lead to more investment in human capital and to the further spread of the time-intensive parenting practices that we already observe in industrialized countries. Think of China: the one-child policy introduced in 1979 mandated that most Chinese families could only have one child. This has shaped parenting practices in China, inducing each couple to spend an unprecedented effort in boosting its only child's human capital, which we refer to as the "Little Emperor" effect. What has happened in China because of draconian legislation is likely to repeat itself in other developing countries even without policy interventions that restrict fertility. In many countries, lower fertility will also increase female participation in the labor market, and ultimately change the role models that parents present to girls and boys. Over time, phenomena such as helicopter parenting will be common around the world instead of being confined to the most developed economies.

THE HOLLOWING OF THE MIDDLE CLASS

The future of parenting in industrialized countries will continue to be shaped by economic inequality. The long-run trend in industrialized societies has been toward less inequality. In the 1960s and 1970s, the income distribution in rich societies was more equal than at any time during the previous two hundred years. Yet over the past thirty to forty years these trends have reverted. Some economists such as Thomas Piketty conjecture that this trend will continue, leading to a repetition of the sharp contrasts between the poor and the rich observed in the Victorian era in Britain and the "Gilded Age" in the United States.[1] If this proves true, we expect the same sharpening contrasts to show up in parenting as well, with an increasingly anxious upper and upper-middle class redoubling their efforts to further the advancement of their children.

Parenting choices are affected not only by inequality but also by social mobility.[2] In a society where the ranks of society are predetermined and do not depend on effort in school (as in the class-based, preindustrial society in Europe), one should observe weak incentives for intensive parenting. The economist Miles Corak conjectures that in the United States intergenerational earnings mobility will decline in the coming years, unless there are changes in public policy that foster the human capital of disadvantaged children.[3] Nevertheless, we do not expect that future societies will be characterized by rigid class divisions like in the preindustrial world. Rather, what this and other studies capture is the risk that some groups of the population remain excluded from the American Dream, for the reasons we discuss in chapter 4. The children of more affluent families tend to be successful in part because their parents push them to succeed. Instead, less wealthy families may be increasingly discouraged from taking part in a rat race in which the odds are stacked against them. In the end, one might observe a decline in social mobility, especially between the lowest and the highest echelons of society. Still, we expect that competition for success among upper-middle-class families will continue.

A recent, widely debated phenomenon is the so-called "hollowing of the middle class."[4] New technologies and machines are progressively replacing mid-skill jobs such as bank clerks, white-collar factory workers, and public sector employees. Changes in the organization of firms are slashing lower-lever managerial jobs, while granting top managers more autonomy and power (and higher pay).[5] In all OECD countries, mid-skill occupations are shrinking relative to high- and low-skill ones. This polarization of society is a source of concern, since many economists and political scientists regard middle-class consensus as the glue that holds a functioning democracy together. A collapse of the middle class might undermine social cohesion, inducing, on the one hand, the growing resentment of those on the lower rungs of the social ladder, and on the other hand, the reluctance of the elite to invest in public goods for the majority. As to parenting, this technological trend may accentuate competition for the educational opportunities that can guarantee children the possibility of moving upward in society.

Will it then be just "more of the same," that is, more and more intensive parenting in the years to come? Not necessarily. Future generations of parents in advanced countries will face new issues. Robotization will not remain confined to mid-skill jobs and will soon invade and make obsolete some of today's most prestigious professions. In a column in the *New York Times*, Alex Williams discusses how parents will have to "robot-proof" their children's future.[6] The demand for labor services is predicted to fall in high-skill medical professions such as radiology and surgery where machines are already replacing many tasks. The same is true for lawyers, airline pilots, and jobs in the financial sector.

Yet, concerns that this transformation will lead to mass unemployment and widespread poverty is unwarranted. There will be a major reshuffling of demand for skills, with large changes in the wages paid by different professions. Medical doctors will need more and more sophisticated knowledge of machines. The demand for programmers, applied mathematicians, engineers, and physicists will continue to grow. Top lawyers will continue to thrive, but likely only a few of them, while the total number of chargeable hours at law firms will fall as machines take over routine tasks. Top universities, especially liberal arts colleges, will have to adjust their supply of education services.

If this scenario materializes, some authoritative parents might be dismayed when they realize that years of relentless effort did not pay off and that their children's professional future is less brilliant than they had expected even with a degree from an elite school. Majoring in the right subject will become increasingly more important than entering the right school.

PARENTING GAPS AND RESIDENTIAL SEGREGATION

As emphasized by Robert Putnam, the rise of intensive parenting in the United States has been accompanied by a growing gap between the environments in which children from different socioeconomic backgrounds grow up.[7] We have argued that a parenting gap can turn into a parenting trap. Poor families do not have the means to give their children access to good educational opportunities, especially in a country where public schools are locally funded, leading to underfunded schools in less affluent areas. This generates even more residential segregation, with middle-class families progressively moving out of poor neighborhoods. For poor children, increased segregation means less hope of making it to the high ranks of society. To make the disadvantages of the poor worse, family ties appear to be weakening among the less wealthy. A manifestation of this phenomenon is the retreat from marriage; that is, a growing number of people never form a stable family.

In other areas, such as Southern Europe, family institutions are more resilient. Yet, discouragement takes different forms. Since the onset of the Great Recession of 2008–9, there has been a sharp rise in the phenomenon of NEET ("youth not in employment, education, or training"), also known by the Spanish shorthand phrase, "Ni-Ni." In Italy,

25 percent of the male population in the age group fifteen to twenty-nine was neither working nor in education in 2016.[8] The share of NEETs also exceeded 20 percent in Greece, Bulgaria, Romania, and Spain. NEETs come typically from low-income and low-education households that continue to share the limited family resources with their grown-up children who have given up the hope of succeeding on their own.

In Italy, like in many other countries, there has been a decrease in the share of married adults. What is specific to Italy is that the main reason for the decline is not divorce, but the phenomenon that grown-up children (especially, young men) continue to live with their parents. Some of them turn into "mama's boys" who neither work nor study. (Italy also has one of the lowest shares of college graduates in Europe.). Weak labor market conditions, precarious jobs, a poor quality of education, and high housing costs in a large part of the country make the family shelter especially attractive. However, the NEET boom also reflects the fact that many families feel powerless given the challenges of our time and so resort to helping their children with persistent financial aid and comforting warm meals. These families love their children, too, but see no point in fighting the adverse situation.

The negative spiral operates through successive generations. Discouraged poor families become less involved with their children's education. The impoverished children, in turn, do not provide opportunities to their own children. In contrast, well-heeled parents devote a growing amount of time and resources to their children's advancement. The hollowing of the middle class can accentuate this contrast.

THE ALLOCATION OF TIME AND KEYNES'S PROPHECY

When we consider the resources that families can draw upon to help their children, money is only part of the story. The other crucial input in raising children is time. For many families, the time cost of raising children (measured as the forgone earnings from time spent on childcare) is a more binding constraint than monetary expenses. When we consider the future of parenting, it is therefore also essential to consider how the allocation of time will change over time, including, most importantly, how much time future parents will need to spend at work.

In the course of economic development, the overall trend has been for work hours to fall. Earlier generations could only dream of a life of eight-hour workdays, free weekends, vacation time, and years of retirement to look forward to, all of which we take for granted today. If these trends continue, we might expect that work time will continue to fall, freeing up more time for other uses, such as parenting.

As far back as 1930, John Maynard Keynes made this exact prediction.[9] He argued that, within a century, growth and technological change would allow humankind to solve its economic problem: working time would be drastically cut, to perhaps fifteen hours a week. He also expected the new era to bring about "great changes in the code of morals," such that the new society will "honour those who can teach (us) how to pluck the hour and the day virtuously and well, the delightful people who are capable of taking direct enjoyment in things."[10]

To what extent have his predictions proven accurate? People today indeed spend a smaller fraction of their lives working. However, there are large differences in both standards of living and attitudes toward work across countries and individuals.[11] And one might expect that the main change in work habits is still to come. Machines have already changed our family life, for instance, by replacing household chores with the services of household appliances. This earlier stage of the technological revolution has stimulated rather than reduced the time spent working in the market by contributing to the growth of women's labor force participation. In our day, in contrast, robots and other machines are taking the place of labor services in the workplace. If routine tasks are performed more productively by machines, we will have access to cheaper goods to satisfy our material needs. This automation process will also keep increasing skill requirements in the labor market.

In times of growing automation, we expect people to adjust their use of time in two dimensions: they will spend more time on human capital investment (including parenting time for the benefit of their children), and they will have more free time for fun and leisure activities. Both would be in line with Keynes's prophecy. However, among these two uses of time, the increasing trend in leisure is, so far, less pronounced than the one in parenting.

Keynes may have been overly optimistic, not so much about the power of technical progress to make labor redundant, but rather about the ability of societies to share the benefits of technical progress among its members. If societies are unable to do so, they may be trapped in a hypercompetitive world where people spend a lot of time and effort trying to climb up the social ladder. The stakes may rise so high that we end up wasting the potential gains from technical progress by trying to outdo one another. Economists call this mechanism "yardstick competition."[12] An example of such a competition is the joke in which two campers are confronted by an aggressive-looking bear who runs toward them. One of the campers rushes to tie up his sneakers. The other says: "What are you doing? You can't outrun a bear!" The first one replies: "I don't have to outrun the bear—I just have to outrun you!" Increasingly intensive parenting may be part of such a socially inefficient scheme.

POLICIES TO CURB INEQUALITY AND PARENTING GAPS

Summing up, there are good reasons to fear that the broad economic trends over the near future will exacerbate the parenting gap between children from different backgrounds, thereby reinforcing social inequality and further restricting social mobility. However, these outcomes are not inevitable. As we have emphasized throughout the book, while the economic conditions in a society are one key determinant of what parents do, government policy also matters. Indeed, we have described large differences in parenting across rich countries such as the United States, Germany, and Sweden that are subject to similar forces of economic and technological change, but differ in their institutions and social and educational policies.

From this perspective, we can view trends toward higher inequality and lower social mobility as a challenge for policy makers to update institutions and policies to meet the challenges posed by a changing economy. To be clear, as economists, we do not believe that fighting inequality is an end unto itself. Some inequality is beneficial because it provides incentives for entrepreneurs and innovators, and in a society that values individual freedom, some differences in outcomes across individuals should be accepted. Still, when it comes to inequality in parenting, there are good reasons to think that laissez faire is not the best state of affairs, and that some government intervention is called for.

The first reason to support policy interventions is philosophical in nature. While individual freedom is a cornerstone of modern liberal democracies, equality of opportunity is also important. Children do not choose which family or social class they are born into. If the ability of families from different backgrounds to provide opportunities to their children grows apart, intervention is called for to level the playing field. Indeed, many programs and policies today are already justified on this basis, from public education to children's health insurance.

A second reason for intervention mirrors economists' arguments for interventions in other areas, namely, the possibility of externalities. A common example of an externality in the business world is pollution. If a factory's pollution has a negative impact on the health and well-being of its neighbors, laissez faire is not the best solution; instead, better outcomes can be achieved either by regulation or by creating a market where pollution permits are traded, so that the factory is forced to take the full cost of its activities into account. Externalities can also arise from a *commons problem*, such as when many fishing boats fish in the same seas, each one contributes to a depletion of fish stocks and thereby imposes a negative spillover on the others.

Similarly, negative externalities can arise in parenting if there are artificial bottlenecks that restrict opportunities only to a limited number of children. This goes back to the discussion of yardstick competition. If access to the most lucrative and influential positions in society requires graduating from a small set of elite universities, and access to these universities is limited through a test, parents will have an incentive to push their children hard to study for the test, so they can beat out their competitors. However, no matter how hard parents push and children study, the number of available slots will not go up. As a result, even though going through all the work makes perfect sense from the perspective of an individual, from the perspective of society it can be a wasted effort. In this scenario, policy intervention can be justified, for instance, in the form of expanding the number of institutions providing high-quality education and facilitating the access to them.

We have described examples of countries where a rat race of this type is almost all consuming for middle-class families, leaving parents and children exhausted and less able to enjoy their time together. In the United States, parents with high aspirations for their children need to worry not just about grades and tests but also about the extracurricular accomplishments (such as volunteer work, entrepreneurship, and musical or athletic accomplishments) that can pave the way to admission into one of America's elite colleges.

These examples of externalities across families ultimately arise from institutional features, such as the design of the education system and of admission policies, which policy makers can control. Public policy can also shape inequality, for example, through the progressivity of the tax code and the redistribution built into the transfer and old-age pension system.

As we have argued throughout this book, parenting choices are among the most important decisions people make in their lifetimes and are a major determinant of the evolution of social inequality in a society. Hence, we believe that future policy debates in the areas of taxation, redistribution, and education should give considerable attention to how such decisions affect parenting. Many of the potentially worrying ongoing trends concerning inequality and social mobility can be offset or even reversed by well-chosen policies.

A central policy area is education. An education system that is highly stratified and predetermines children's economic future at an early age can trigger a "parenting war" between families who all want to give their children the best shot at success. In contrast, an education system that emphasizes equal access and downplays competition until early adulthood will give more leeway to parents and children to relax. In our comparison of parenting across rich countries with different education systems, we have already seen that differences in education systems correspond to different parenting styles and different levels of social inequality. If economic forces push toward increasing inequality, policy makers can react by tweaking education systems such that they place less emphasis on competition between students for limited opportunities of advancement.

Other dimensions of family policy are also important. Lack of financial resources and shortage of time (e.g., for single working parents) are constraints that can make it difficult for poorer families to provide their children with the same opportunities that more affluent parents can offer. Recent economic research pioneered by the Nobel laureate James Heckman has established that what is particularly important is investment in the early years, from birth to about four years of age. Here policies such as provision of high-quality day care, parental leave, and early childhood interventions can make a large difference and lessen the impact of income inequality across households on the prospects of children. The research of Heckman and his collaborators shows that early childhood interventions in favor of disadvantaged children can counteract future achievement gaps, improve health, reduce crime, and boost earnings in a cost-efficient way.[13]

IN CONCLUSION

The many policy options that are available to counteract potentially concerning trends toward higher inequality allow us to conclude on an optimistic note. Clearly, there are substantial challenges on the horizon, but there are also good reasons to believe that it will be possible to meet these challenges. Part of our confidence stems from the observation that in the grand course of economic development, changes in parenting have generally been toward the better. This may not hold for every single time and in every single place, and without doubt there is something to the perception of many parents in countries such as the United States that parenting is more intense and stressful than a few decades ago. But even in our lifetimes, there are other trends that we see in a positive light. Certainly, children should appreciate that authoritarian parenting and corporal punishment are giving way to parenting styles that grant more independence to them. For parents, being more closely involved with their children may sometimes be a source of stress, but can also be a reward.

For fathers like us, the trend toward a more even distribution of childcare duties across genders has allowed us to have much closer relationships with our children than what was the norm for our own fathers and grandfathers. Being a parent has been the greatest joy in our lives. If given the choice, we would much prefer the "intensive" experience of fatherhood in our time over the ways of earlier eras. If societies make policy choices that keep up with economic trends, informed by the economic basis of parenting as outlined in this book, we can be optimistic that future parents will feel just as lucky as we do.

Notes

PREFACE

1. Matthias Doepke and Fabrizio Zilibotti, "Parenting with Style: Altruism and Paternalism in Intergenerational Preference Transmission," *Econometrica* 85, no. 5 (2017): 1331–71.

INTRODUCTION

1. Robert D. Putnam, *Making Democracy Work: Civic Traditions in Modern Italy* (Princeton, NJ: Princeton University Press, 1993).
2. Kendall King and Alison Mackey, *The Bilingual Edge* (New York: HarperCollins, 2007), 233.
3. In the German language, the polite form *Sie* is used to address strangers and acquaintances, while the informal *du* is reserved for close friends. Adults use the *du* when addressing children, while children are supposed to use the *Sie* when speaking to adults to emphasize their respect. Similar distinctions exist in other European languages (French, Italian, Spanish, etc.). In the Swedish language, like in English, people use the second-person singular pronoun *du* as a universal form of address. Interestingly, this has not always been the case and is the result of a reform that abolished the use of various polite forms a half a century ago. The reform was explicitly meant to be a step in a more egalitarian direction through the abolishment of barriers and distinction between people of different age and rank in society.
4. We do not rule out, of course, that there may be cognitive limitations preventing them from discerning the appropriate solution to every problem. Likewise, some parents truly lack altruism and do not have their children's best interests in mind. Thankfully, parents who abuse or consciously harm their children are the exception rather than the rule. We do not dwell on them in this book.

CHAPTER ONE: THE ECONOMICS OF PARENTING STYLE

1. People sometimes refer to this extensive use of our method as *economic imperialism*. The term was coined by Ralph William Souter, who refers to an "enlight-

ened and democratic 'economic imperialism', which invades the territories of its neighbors, not to enslave them or to swallow them up, but to aid and enrich them and promote their autonomous growth in the very process of aiding and enriching itself." See Ralph William Souter, *Prolegomena to Relativity Economics: An Elementary Study in the Mechanics and Organics of an Expanding Economic Universe* (New York: Columbia University Press, 1933), 94. Much of Gary Becker's work on the family is summarized in his book *A Treatise on the Family: Enlarged Edition* (Cambridge, MA: Harvard University Press, 1993). For a more recent summary of the main findings in family economics, see Shelly Lundberg and Robert A. Pollak, "The American Family and Family Economics," *Journal of Economic Perspectives* 21, no. 2 (2007): 3–26. A broader overview of the current state of family economics is provided in Martin Browning, Pierre-André Chiappori, and Yoram Weiss, *Economics of the Family* (Cambridge: Cambridge University Press, 2014).

2. We do not mean here that parents of working children do not love their children and pursue purely individualistic objectives. Yet, in many cases, it is useful to think of children in part as the object of affection and in part as an economic resource for the family. See Matthias Doepke and Fabrizio Zilibotti, "The Macroeconomics of Child Labor Regulation," *American Economic Review* 95, no. 5 (2005): 1492–1524.

3. James Duesenberry, "Comment on 'An Economic Analysis of Fertility' by Gary Becker," in *Demographic and Economic Change in Developed Countries*, ed. NBER (Princeton, NJ: Princeton University Press, 1960), 231–34.

4. Diana Baumrind, "Effects of Authoritative Parental Control on Child Behavior," *Child Development* 37, no. 4 (1966): 887–907; Baumrind, "Child Care Practices Anteceding Three Patterns of Preschool," *Genetic Psychology Monographs* 75, no. 1 (1967): 43–88.

5. Baumrind, "Effects of Authoritative Parental Control on Child Behavior," 890.

6. *Fanny and Alexander*, directed by Ingmar Bergman (1982; Sweden: Sandrew Film & Teater, 1983), DVD.

7. Andre Agassi, *Open: An Autobiography* (London: HarperCollins, 2010), 57.

8. Baumrind, "Effects of Authoritative Parental Control on Child Behavior," 889.

9. In common parlance, the adjective permissive tends to have a negative normative connotation, being associated with an *excessive* freedom of behavior. The terminology is borrowed from the tradition of the development psychology literature and should be regarded as neutral.

10. E. E. Maccoby and J. A. Martin, "Socialization in the Context of the Family: Parent-Child Interaction," in *Handbook of Child Psychology: Vol 4. Socialization, Personality, and Social Development*, ed. P. H. Mussen and E. M. Hetherington (New York: Wiley, 1983), 1–101.

11. Bruce Zeines, "The Opposite of Tiger Mom," in *The Free School Apparent*, January 29, 2011, https://bzeines.wordpress.com/2011/01/29/opposite-of-tiger-mom/.

12. Baumrind, "Effects of Authoritative Parental Control on Child Behavior," 891.

13. Sanford M. Dornbusch, Philip L. Ritter, P. Herbert Leiderman, Donald F. Roberts, and Michael J. Fraleigh, "The Relation of Parenting Style to Adolescent School Performance," *Child Development* 58, no. 5 (1987): 1244–57. In this study, the parenting styles are classified according to students' responses to a battery of questions concerning family behavior. For instance, the extent to which a child is exposed to an authoritative parenting style is measured by the agreement with the following nine statements: "In their family communication, parents tell the youth to look at both sides of issues, they admit that the youth sometimes knows more, they talk about politics within the family, and they emphasize that everyone should help with decisions in the family; as a response to good grades, parents praise the student, and give more freedom to make decisions; as a response to poor grades, they take away freedom, encourage the student to try harder, and offer to help."

14. Susie D. Lamborn, Nina S. Mounts, Laurence Steinberg, and Sanford M. Dornbusch, "Patterns of Competence and Adjustment among Adolescents from Authoritative, Authoritarian, Indulgent, and Neglectful Families," *Child Development* 62, no. 5 (1991): 1049–65; Laurence Steinberg, Nina S. Mounts, Susie D. Lamborn, and Sanford M. Dornbusch, "Authoritative Parenting and Adolescent Adjustment across Varied Ecological Niches," *Journal of Research on Adolescence* 1, no. 1 (1991): 19–36.

15. Tak Wing Chan and Anita Koo, "Parenting Style and Youth Outcomes in the UK," *European Sociological Review* 27, no. 3 (2010): 385–99.

16. Kaisa Aunola, Hakan Stattin, and Jari-Erik Nurmi, "Parenting Styles and Adolescents' Achievement Strategies," *Journal of Adolescence* 23, no. 2 (2000): 205–22.

17. Laurence Steinberg, Susie D. Lamborn, Sanford M. Dornbusch, and Nancy Darling, "Impact of Parenting Practices on Adolescent Achievement: Authoritative Parenting, School Involvement, and Encouragement to Succeed," *Child Development* 63, no. 5 (1992): 1266–81.

18. Ruth K. Chao, "Beyond Parental Control and Authoritarian Parenting Style: Understanding Chinese Parenting through the Cultural Notion of Training," *Child Development* 65, no. 4 (1994): 1111–19.

19. Steinberg et al. "Impact of Parenting Practices on Adolescent Achievement" document similar findings. However, their interpretation is different. In their view, among Asian American students, peer support for academic excellence neutralizes the negative consequences of authoritarian parenting.

20. Our approach is consistent with what the economist Flavio Cunha labels subjective rationality, namely, "Investment in children and parenting style choices can be explained by a model of optimization under constraints." See Flavio Cunha "Subjective Rationality, Parenting Styles, and Investments in Children," in *Families in an Era of Increasing Inequality: Diverging Destinies*, ed. Paul R. Amato, Alan Booth, Susan M. McHale, and Jennifer Van Hook (New York: Springer, 2015), 83–94.

21. See Doepke and Zilibotti, "Parenting with Style: Altruism and Paternalism in

Intergenerational Preference Transmission," *Econometrica* 85, no. 5 (2017): 1331–71. In this article, we provide a mathematical formulation of parents' preferences and formally define altruism and paternalism.

22. Becker, *The Economic Approach to Human Behavior* (Chicago: University of Chicago Press, 1976). In economics, discounted utility is the well-being associated with some future event as perceived at the present time instead of the time of its occurrence.

23. The mathematical argument underlying this claim is provided in Doepke and Zilibotti, "Parenting with Style." There, we postulate that parents and children make choices to maximize utility functions, a standard tool in economic theory. When parents are purely *altruistic* (and not at all *paternalistic*), the choices children make maximize both the parents' and the children's utility functions. Therefore, parents rationally choose not to interfere, that is, they adopt a permissive parenting style.

24. A qualification is in order here. Altruistic parents may actually want to affect their children's behavior when there are opportunities for strategic behavior, namely, when children try consciously to exploit their parents' altruism. For instance, the child of well-off parents may consciously decide to be lazy in school, expecting that if life turns sour, her altruistic parents will bail her out (at their own or at her siblings' expense). We will not emphasize this type of strategic behavior, known in the economic literature as the Samaritan's Dilemma. See Neil Bruce and Michael Waldman, "The Rotten-Kid Theorem Meets the Samaritan's Dilemma," *Quarterly Journal of Economics* 105, no. 1 (1990): 155–65.

25. Our notion of paternalism is related to the recent economic literature on imperfect empathy. See, for example, Alberto Bisin and Thierry Verdier, "The Economics of Cultural Transmission and the Dynamics of Preferences," *Journal of Economic Theory* 97, no. 2 (2001): 298–319; Esther Hauk and María Sáez Martí, "On the Cultural Transmission of Corruption," *Journal of Economic Theory* 107, no. 2 (2002): 311–35. For broader perspectives on the economic literature on cultural transmission and its connection with other social sciences, see María Sáez Martí and Fabrizio Zilibotti, "Preferences as Human Capital: Rational Choice Theories of Endogenous Preferences and Socioeconomic Changes," *Finnish Economic Papers* 21, no. 2 (2008): 81–94; Bisin and Verdier, "The Economics of Cultural Transmission and Socialization," in *Handbook of Social Economics*, vol. 1A, ed. Jess Benhabib, Alberto Bisin, and Matthew O. Jackson (Amsterdam: North Holland, 2011), 339–416.

26. The influence of neighborhoods on parenting styles has been discussed by the development psychology literature. For a review, see Jessica Cuellar, Deborah J. Jones, and Emma Sterrett, "Examining Parenting in the Neighborhood Context: A Review," *Journal of Child and Family Studies* 24, no. 1 (2015): 195–219.

27. Doepke and Zilibotti, "Parenting with Style" provides a mathematical formula-

tion for this argument. When parents are not purely *altruistic* (and are, thus, to some extent *paternalistic*), the choices children would make on their own do not maximize the parents' utility function. Therefore, parents rationally choose to interfere, either by forbidding certain actions (authoritarian parenting) or by molding their children's preferences and persuading them to act in a way that parents like better than if they followed their natural inclinations (authoritative parenting). The more paternalistic parents are, the more they interfere, that is, the less permissive they are.

28. An alternative (or complementary) view of what parents do when they adopt different parenting styles is that parents are altruistic (as opposed to paternalistic) but possess superior information about the consequences of certain actions. Parents can then intervene to protect children from the consequences of ill-informed choices. Different parenting strategies hinge on whether parents aim to shelter their children from the consequences of their actions or instead wish to maximize learning opportunities. See Alessandro Lizzeri and Marciano Siniscalchi, "Parental Guidance and Supervised Learning," *Quarterly Journal of Economics* 123, no. 3 (2008): 1161–95.

29. María and Fabrizio's daughter, Nora, experienced the conflict between two different parenting styles. Accustomed as she was to a parenting style where any demand or rule was carefully motivated, and where her viewpoint would be given thorough consideration, she would get deeply frustrated every time her loving grandmother would address her objections with a smile and barely take any notice of them.

30. Joseph Nye, *Soft Power: The Means to Success in World Politics* (New York: Public Affairs, 2004).

31. The link between parenting style and occupational choice is quite stark within the families of María's siblings. Two of her sisters adopted a permissive parenting style. Of their four children altogether, three have undertaken an artistically oriented career (though one is doing a PhD in physics). Another sister is a more conservative type, who adopted a more intensive parenting style with both authoritative and authoritarian elements. Both of her children have moved from Spain to Germany to study engineering in college. The single child of a brother who adopted a similar parenting style graduated in economics.

32. Steven Pinker, *The Blank Slate: The Modern Denial of Human Nature* (New York: Viking, 2002); Judith Rich Harris, *The Nurture Assumption: Why Children Turn Out the Way They Do* (New York: The Free Press, 1998). In economics, the idea that parents can shape children's preferences and that nurture is important was proposed by Gary Becker. See Gary Becker, Kevin M. Murphy, and Joerg L. Spenkuch, "The Manipulation of Children's Preferences, Old Age Support, and Investment in Children's Human Capital," *Journal of Labor Economics* 34, no. S2 (2016): S3–S30. Gary Becker and Casey Mulligan, "The Endogenous Determination of Time Preference," *Quarterly Journal of Economics* 112, no. 3

(1997): 729–58, discuss the possibility that people can even affect their own preferences.

33. Luigi Luca Cavalli-Sforza and Marcus W. Feldman, *Cultural Transmission and Evolution: A Quantitative Approach* (Princeton, NJ: Princeton University Press, 1981); Samuel Bowles and Herbert Gintis, "The Inheritance of Inequality," *Journal of Economic Perspectives* 16, no. 3 (2002): 3–30; Peter J. Richerson and Robert Boyd, *Not by Genes Alone* (Chicago: University of Chicago Press, 2004).

34. Anders Björklund, Mikael Lindahl, and Erik Plug, "The Origins of Intergenerational Associations: Lessons from Swedish Adoption Data," *Quarterly Journal of Economics* 121, no. 3 (2006): 999–1028.

35. Cognitive skills include the ability to perform math or logic, or process complex information. Noncognitive skills are softer, more socially oriented skills.

36. James J. Heckman, "Policies to Foster Human Capital," *Research in Economics* 54, no. 1 (2000): 3–56; Pedro Carneiro and James J. Heckman, "Human Capital Policy," in *Inequality in America: What Role for Human Capital Policies?* ed. James J. Heckman, Alan B. Krueger, and Benjamin M. Friedman (Cambridge, MA: MIT Press, 2003), 77–240. Similar conclusions are reached by the following studies in child development psychology: Jack P. Shonkoff and Deborah A. Phillips, eds., *From Neurons to Neighborhoods* (Washington, DC: National Academy Press, 2000); Jeanette Taylor, William G. Iacono, and Matt McGue, "Evidence for a Genetic Etiology of Early-Onset Delinquency," *Journal of Abnormal Psychology* 109, no. 4 (2000): 634–43.

37. James J. Heckman, Jora Stixrud, and Sergio Urzua, "The Effects of Cognitive and Noncognitive Abilities on Labor Market Outcomes and Social Behavior," *Journal of Labor Economics* 24, no. 3 (2006): 411–82.

38. Thomas Dohmen, Armin Falk, David Huffman, and Uwe Sunde, "The Intergenerational Transmission of Risk and Trust Attitudes," *Review of Economic Studies* 79, no. 2 (2012): 645–77.

39. Orazio P. Attanasio, "The Determinants of Human Capital Formation during the Early Years of Life: Theory, Measurement, and Polices," *Journal of the European Economic Association* 13, no. 6 (2015): 949–97. See also Orazio Attanasio, Sarah Cattan, Emla Fitzsimons, Costas Meghir, and Marta Rubio-Codina, "Estimating the Production Function for Human Capital: Results from a Randomized Control Trial in Colombia," (NBER Working Paper 20965, 2015).

40. Bruce A. Weinberg, "An Incentive Model of the Effect of Parental Income on Children," *Journal of Political Economy* 109, no. 2 (2001): 266–80.

CHAPTER TWO: THE RISE OF HELICOPTER PARENTS

1. Haim G. Ginott, *Between Parent and Teenager* (New York: Macmillan, 1969).

2. Wendy Wisner, "15 Ways You Know You Were the Child of Hippie Parents," *Scary Mommy*, http://www.scarymommy.com/15-ways-you-know-you-were-the-child-of-hippie-parents/.

3. "Tom Brokaw: 1960s Radicals Have Become the 'Helicopter Parents,' Shopping at Whole Foods . . . ," https://www.yelp.com/topic/san-francisco-tom-brokaw -1960s-radicals-have-become-the-helicopter-parents-shopping-at-whole-foods.

4. Amy Chua, *Battle Hymn of the Tiger Mother* (London: Bloomsbury Publishing, 2011), 62.

5. Chua, "Why Chinese Mothers are Superior," *Wall Street Journal*, January 8, 2011.

6. Ibid.

7. In her article "Why Chinese Mothers are Superior," Chua clarifies that she uses the term "Chinese mother" loosely and that her stereotypical portrayal applies to many mothers with non-Chinese immigrant background living in the United States. She also acknowledges that her preferred parenting style is popular among many Western parents.

8. Hara Estroff Marano, *A Nation of Wimps: The High Cost of Invasive Parenting* (New York: Broadway Books, 2008).

9. Marano, "Helicopter Parenting—It's Worse Than You Think," *Psychology Today*, January 21, 2014, https://www.psychologytoday.com/blog/nation-wimps/201 401/helicopter-parenting-its-worse-you-think.

10. Tanith Carey, *Taming the Tiger Parent: How to Put Your Child's Well-Being First in a Competitive World* (London: Hachette, 2014).

11. Julie Lythcott-Haims, *How to Raise an Adult: Break Free of the Overparenting Trap and Prepare Your Kid for Success* (New York: Henry Holt & Company, 2015).

12. For an analysis of the effect of overparenting, see also Chris Segrin, Michelle Givertz, Paulina Swiatkowski, and Neil Montgomery, "Overparenting Is Associated with Child Problems and a Critical Family Environment," *Journal of Child and Family Studies* 24, no. 2 (2015): 470–79.

13. Our analysis of parents' time diaries builds on the important contribution of the economists Garey and Valerie Ramey from University of California at San Diego. See Garey Ramey and Valerie A. Ramey, "The Rug Rat Race," *Brookings Papers on Economic Activity* (Spring 2010): 129–76. Their analysis focuses on Canada and the United States.

14. A detailed description of this project can be found in Daniel S. Hamermesh, Harley Frazis, and Jay Stewart, "Data Watch: The American Time Use Survey," *Journal of Economic Perspectives* 19, no. 1 (2005): 221–32.

15. See, for example, the Multinational Time Use Study (MTUS, http://www.time use.org/mtus), which collects this data for a number of countries.

16. Judith Burns, "Parents' Mobile Use Harms Family Life, Say Secondary Pupils," *BBC News*, April 23, 2017, http://www.bbc.com/news/education-39666863.

17. We use version 9 of the MTUS, where the data for Italy in 2009 are not included. We add them to the dataset, following the code used to prepare the 1989 data.

18. See US Department of Education, "Statistics about Nonpublic Education in the United States," https://www2.ed.gov/about/offices/list/oii/nonpublic/statistics .html.

19. Nancy Gibbs, "The Growing Backlash against Overparenting," *Time*, November 30, 2009.

20. For example, consider two hypothetical employees, a member of a profession and a blue-collar worker, earning salaries of 200,000 and 100,000 lire per month, respectively, in 1970. Imagine a 20 percent annual inflation rate, and suppose the allowance was 20 percent of the average of the two wages. Five years later, in 1975, the salary of the two workers would be 423,000 and 323,000 lire, respectively. The professional's salary, which used to be twice as high as that of the blue-collar worker in 1970, was only 31 percent higher in 1975.

21. Thomas Piketty and Emmanuel Saez, "Income Inequality in the United States, 1913–1998," *Quarterly Journal of Economics* 118, no. 1 (2003): 1–39; Thomas Piketty, *Capital in the Twenty-First Century* (Cambridge, MA: Harvard University Press, 2014). There is a large body of literature that started in the 1980s documenting the increasing inequality both across more- and less-educated workers and across equally educated workers. See, for instance, Peter Gottschalk, "Inequality, Income Growth, and Mobility: The Basic Facts," *Journal of Economic Perspectives* 11, no. 2 (1997): 21–40.

22. Margaret Thatcher, "No Such Thing as Society," interview by Douglas Keay, *Woman's Own*, September 23, 1987, https://www.margaretthatcher.org/document /106689.

23. OECD Income Distribution and Poverty database.

24. Daron Acemoglu and David Autor, "Skills, Tasks and Technologies: Implications for Employment and Earnings," in *Handbook of Labor Economics 4*, ed. Orley Ashenfelter and David E. Card (Amsterdam: North Holland, 2011), 1043–171.

25. Joanne Lindley and Stephen Machin, "Rising Wage Inequality and Postgraduate Education" (Centre for Economic Performance Discussion Paper, no. 1075, 2011).

26. Andrew Rendall and Michelle Rendall, "Math Matters: Education Choices and Wage Inequality" (mimeo, Monash University, 2016).

27. See Lawrence F. Katz and Kevin M. Murphy, "Changes in Relative Wages, 1963–1987: Supply and Demand Factors," *Quarterly Journal of Economics* 107, no. 1 (1992): 35–78; Daron Acemoglu, "Why Do New Technologies Complement Skills? Directed Technical Change and Wage Inequality," *Quarterly Journal of Economics* 113, no. 4 (1998): 1055–89.

28. Daron Acemoglu, Philippe Aghion, and Gianluca Violante, "Deunionization, Technical Change and Inequality," *Carnegie-Rochester Conference Series on Public Policy* 55, no. 1 (2001): 229–64.

29. John Hassler, Kjetil Storesletten, Jose-Vicente Rodriguez Mora, and Fabrizio Zilibotti, "The Survival of the Welfare State," *American Economic Review* 93, no. 1 (2003): 87–112.

30. Joseph Berger, "Born to Be Wild. Scratch That. Born to Be Mild," *New York Times*, December 4, 1994; Eric Pace, "Jerry Rubin, 56, Flashy 60's Radical, Dies;

'Yippies' Founder and Chicago 7 Defendant," *New York Times*, November 30, 1994.

31. Claudia Goldin and Lawrence F. Katz, "The Race between Education and Technology: The Evolution of U.S. Educational Wage Differential, 1890 to 2005" (NBER Working Paper no. 12984, 2007). See, in particular, table A8.1.

32. Note that we constructed the measure of intensive parenting by taking responses to questions that refer to the frequency of parent-child interaction rather than directly measuring parental support of children in their school activities. We chose that for two reasons. First, we aim to emphasize a parenting style that goes beyond the involvement of parents in schooling activities. Second, some parents may get involved precisely because their children need help. Since this is more common for weak-performing pupils, one might get the incorrect impression that parent help is counterproductive. For instance, we observe that the score of children whose parents help with homework is slightly weaker than those who are not helped by parents. This does not necessarily mean that helping children with homework is harmful. Parents of proficient pupils simply do not need to get involved with these activities. Yet, it may still be true that weak students benefit from the help they receive from parents in doing their homework.

33. Data from PISA 2012. The sample comprises 3,271 parents adopting an "intensive" parenting style and 1,662 parents adopting a "non-intensive" parenting style.

34. Multiple regression is a statistical technique used to predict the value of a variable (dependent variable) based on the influence of more than one variable (explanatory variables or regressors). For example, we can use multiple regression to study the extent to which a child's PISA test score can be predicted based on the parenting style she or he was subjected to, her or his gender, and the education of her or his parents. It can also inform us about the effect of explanatory variables while holding fixed the others at a common value. For instance, what is the effect of different parenting styles for two children of the same gender (e.g., a girl) whose parents have the same education level (e.g., college graduates).

35. More precisely, the answers to these questions were coded on a binary scale. If the youth answered "somewhat supportive" or "not very supportive" to the first question, it was coded as a 0, and otherwise, a 1. Similarly, for the second question, those who answered "permissive" were coded as a 0, and those who answered "strict/demanding" were coded as a 1. The parenting styles are then defined as follows: "Uninvolved parenting" corresponds to "not supportive, not strict"; "Permissive parenting" is defined as "supportive, not strict"; "Authoritarian parenting" is defined as "not supportive, strict"; and "Authoritative parenting" is defined as "supportive, strict." We restrict attention to residential parents (i.e., parents living in the same household as their children).

CHAPTER THREE: PARENTING STYLES
AROUND THE CONTEMPORARY WORLD

1. Emmanuel Saez, "Striking It Richer: The Evolution of Top Incomes in the United States" (mimeo, University of California, 2015).
2. The WVS collects nationally representative surveys conducted in different countries using a common questionnaire. These data are widely used for academic research by political scientists, sociologists, anthropologists, and economists interested in the nexus between cultural factors and economic development. To start with, we use the data from the fifth edition of the WVS (2005–9), which is the survey covering the largest set of countries among those available. Later in this chapter, we will extend the analysis to multiple editions.
3. We focus on countries that were either founding members of the OECD or acquired membership before 1994 (we use all countries for which data were available in the WVS). The data on Gini coefficients are from the OECD. We report the closest observation available to the year in which each country is surveyed. The countries that were OECD members before 1994 for which we have data are: Australia, Canada, Finland, France, Germany, Great Britain, Italy, Japan, Netherlands, New Zealand, Norway, Spain, Sweden, Switzerland, Turkey, and the United States. Similar findings are obtained if one adds the five countries that became members since 1994 (Chile, Korea, Mexico, Poland, and Slovenia). For comparison, we also added China and Russia to the figures.
4. WVS and OECD. We restrict attention to individuals mentioning at least one of the values we focus upon. This means that we dropped 12 percent of the individuals for which observations are available. Including these people does not change the results significantly.
5. The (Pearson's) correlation coefficient is a common measure of the extent to which two variables (e.g., inequality and a particular parenting style) are associated in the data. It is obtained by dividing the covariance of the two variables by the product of their standard deviations. The correlation coefficient ranges between -100 percent (perfect negative correlation) and $+100$ percent (perfect positive correlation) with 0 meaning there is no statistical pattern linking the two variables. For instance, a negative correlation between inequality and the percentage of parents praising imagination indicates that as one considers more unequal countries, a lower percentage of parents praise imagination.
6. Recent research suggests children's demand for autonomy and parents' decision to relinquish control are often intertwined. For instance, if a child demands more freedom, many parents evaluate, first, whether the child is capable of making a good decision, and second, which risks the environment presents in case of a wrong decision. See Jennifer L. Romich, Shelly Lundberg, and Kwok P. Tsang, "Independence Giving or Autonomy Taking? Childhood Predictors of Decision-Sharing Patterns between Young Adolescent and Parents," *Journal of Research on Adolescence* 19, no. 4 (2009): 587–600. While these are important consider-

ations, we find it appropriate to associate independence with a permissive parenting style, where we reassert that we attach no negative connotation to the word permissive.

7. UNICEF Office of Research, "Child Well-Being in Rich Countries: A Comparative Overview," *Innocenti Report Card* 11 (2013), https://www.unicef-irc.org/publi cations/pdf/rc11_eng.pdf.

8. Mihal Greener, "Are They the World's Most Relaxed Moms? What We Can All Learn from The Dutch," *Washington Post*, November 5, 2015.

9. E. Villamor, S. Hammer, and A. Martinez-Olaizola, "Barriers to Bicycle Helmet Use among Dutch Paediatricians," *Child: Care Health and Development* 34, no. 6 (2008): 743–47.

10. Sara Zaske, "How to Parent Like a German," *Time*, February 24, 2015.

11. Chantal Panozzo, "In Switzerland, Parents Observe. In the US, Hovering Is Required," *New York Times*, March 11, 2015.

12. Julian Schärer, "Parenting Style and Income Inequality in Switzerland," bachelor's thesis, University of Zurich, 2016.

13. Daniel Martin, "I Want Every Teacher to Be a Tiger Mum, Says Cameron. PM Praises 'Hard Work Ethos' and Demands End to 'All Must Win Prizes' Culture," *Daily Mail Online*, January 12, 2016.

14. Wendy Lee, "Have Helicopter Parents Landed in the UK?" *Guardian*, October 9, 2014.

15. In a recent study, the economists Cristina Borra and Almudena Sevilla conclude that increasing competition for admission to top universities can explain the different trends in time investments by parents with different educational attainments in the United Kingdom over the past three decades. Their results are in line with our arguments (see also the discussion on the effect of school admission systems in chapter 9 of this book). See Cristina Borra and Almudena Sevilla, "Parental Time Investments in Children: The Role of Competition for University Places in the UK," (IZA Discussion Paper 9168, 2015).

16. Amy Chua, *Battle Hymn of the Tiger Mother* (London: Bloomsbury Publishing, 2011), 5.

17. Li Yao, " 'Tiger Moms' Popular in China," *China Daily*, April 15, 2011.

18. Chua, *Battle Hymn of the Tiger Mother*, 53.

19. Selena Hoy, "Why Are Little Kids in Japan So Independent?" *Atlantic Citylab*, September 28, 2015.

20. Susan D. Holloway and Ayumi Nagase, "Child Rearing in Japan," in *Parenting Across Cultures: Childrearing, Motherhood and Fatherhood in Non-Western Cultures*, ed. Helaine Selin (Dordrecht: Springer Science + Business Media, 2014), 59–76.

21. Susan Holloway, Sawako Suzuki, and Yoko Yamamoto, "From Kyôiku Mama to Monster Parent: Changing Images of Japanese Mothers and Their Involvement in Children's Schooling," *Child Research Net* (2010), http://www.childresearch .net/papers/parenting/2010_04.html.

22. Roger Pulvers, "Monster Parents Make Matters Worse for Their Children and Teachers," *Japan Times*, August 19, 2012.

23. Kai-D. Bussmann, Claudia Erthal, and Andreas Schroth, "The Effects of Banning Corporal Punishment in Europe: A Five-Nation Comparison," in *Global Pathways to Abolishing Physical Punishment*, ed. Joan E. Durrant and Anne B. Smith (New York: Routledge, 2011), 299–322.

24. Gerhard E. Lenski, *The Religious Factor: A Sociological Study of Religion's Impact on Politics, Economics, and Family Life* (Garden City, NY: Doubleday, 1961).

25. WVS (our classification of parenting style) and OECD.

26. We continue to focus on the sample of early OECD members considered at the beginning of the chapter. For those countries, there were six waves between 1981 and 2013. In addition, we require the OECD data for income inequality to be available in correspondence for each survey year. This leaves us with the following list of country-waves (years in brackets): Australia (1995, 2005, 2012), Canada (2000, 2006), Finland (1996, 2005), France (2006), Germany (1997, 2006, 2013), Italy (2005), Japan (2000, 2005, 2010), Netherlands (2006, 2012), New Zealand (1998, 2004, 2011), Norway (1996, 2007), Spain (2007, 2011), Sweden (1996, 2006, 2011), Switzerland (1996, 2007), Turkey (2007, 2011), United Kingdom (2005), United States (1995, 1999, 2006, 2011).

27. Matthias Doepke and Fabrizio Zilibotti, "Parenting with Style: Altruism and Paternalism in Intergenerational Preference Transmission," *Econometrica* 85, no. 5 (2017): 1331–71.

28. The regressions control for individual characteristics include gender; age (linear and squared); education (high school dropouts, high school graduates, some college or more); countries' GDP; countries' fixed effects (in some regressions); and wave fixed effects. The results are robust to excluding respondents who are not parents, excluding waves with few countries and including additional controls for self-reported income.

29. For details, see Doepke and Zilibotti, "Parenting with Style."

30. In figure 3.3, three bars are associated with each parenting style. The first bar describes the situation for the current level of inequality in Sweden. The second and the third bar describe the probability for the individual to choose each of the three styles, once inequality is set at the level of the United States, corresponding to estimation with and without fixed effects. Note that the results are not very sensitive to which of the two specifications one uses.

31. The measure captures the marginal rate progression up to an income level equivalent to four times a country's GDP per capita. See "Andrew Young School World Tax Indicators," Georgia State University, https://aysps.gsu.edu/isp/wti.html.

32. OECD Social Expenditure Database.

33. Both the Turkey-vs.-Germany and the previous Sweden-vs.-United States exercise should be viewed as illustrations of the size of the correlation between inequality (and social policy) and parenting style. The effects cannot be regarded as causal and may reflect, in part, the effect of omitted variables.

34. Claudio E. Montenegro and Harry Anthony Patrinos, "Comparable Estimates of Returns to Schooling around the World" (World Bank Policy Research Working Paper 7020, 2014). Since this dataset contains only sparse information about how the returns to education vary over time within each country, we use only the parenting styles from the Wave 5 of the WVS (around year 2005) and plot the closest available observation for the return to schooling.

35. WVS (our classification of parenting style) and World Bank.

36. Transparency International, "Corruption Perceptions Index 2016," https://www .transparency.org/news/feature/corruption_perceptions_index_2016.

37. In figure 3.8, the data on parenting style refer to the Wave 5 of the WVS, and the indicators are measured in 2005 (the first year of Wave 5).

38. "The Global Innovation Index," https://www.globalinnovationindex.org/analysis -indicator.

CHAPTER FOUR: INEQUALITY, PARENTING STYLE, AND PARENTING TRAPS

1. See, for example, Melvin L. Kohn, *Class and Conformity: A Study in Values, with a Reassessment*, 2nd ed. (Chicago: University of Chicago Press, 1977); Murray A. Straus and Julie H. Stewart, "Corporal Punishment by American Parents: National Data on Prevalence, Chronicity, Severity, and Duration, in Relation to Child and Family Characteristics," *Clinical Child and Family Psychology Review* 2, no. 2 (1999): 55–70.

2. Joel Kotkin, "Where Inequality Is Worst in the United States," *Forbes*, March 20, 2014.

3. George Galster, Jackie Cutsinger, and Jason C. Booza, "Where Did They Go? The Decline of Middle-Income Neighborhoods in Metropolitan America," *Brookings Metropolitan Policy Program* (2006).

4. Robert D. Putnam, *Our Kids: The American Dream in Crisis* (New York: Simon & Schuster, 2015).

5. See Annette Lareau, *Unequal Childhoods: Class, Race, and Family Life* (Berkeley and Los Angeles: University of California Press, 2003).

6. Jonathan Guryan, Erik Hurst, and Melissa Kearney, "Parental Education and Parental Time with Children," *Journal of Economic Perspectives* 22, no. 3 (2008): 23–46.

7. We already noted in chapter 2 that the classification of permissive/authoritative parents provided by the NLSY97 is different from that in the WVS. In the NLSY97, parents are classified as authoritative when they are strict and supportive and as permissive if they are supportive but not strict. Many highly educated parents may be intensive parents (as shown by the evidence from the time diaries) and try to instill in their children the values of hard work and success without necessarily being strict. The WVS would probably define these parents as authoritative, while the NLSY97 labels them permissive. This issue is espe-

cially important for highly educated parents who possess the soft skills that can avoid the need to appear strict. This might explain why authoritative parents do not outperform permissive parents in the more-educated group.

8. Detailed regression results are available on request. One of the reasons why we cannot rule out that the results may be partially motivated by confounding factors driving both parenting style and upward social mobility is that we do not possess data for an exhaustive list of such factors. For instance, we cannot measure parents' soft skills.

9. These results hold in regressions that include the parenting style of both parents and control for the parents' education, race, and ethnicity, and the gender and age of the child.

10. The breakdown of NS-SEC social class categories is as follows: 1: Higher managerial, administrative, and professional occupations; 2: Lower managerial, administrative, and professional occupations; 3: Intermediate occupations; 4: Small employers and own account workers; 5: Lower supervisory and technical occupations; 6: Semi-routine occupations; 7: Routine occupations. The breakdown of academic qualification is as follows: 1: Higher degree; 2. First degree; 3. Diplomas in higher education; 4: A/AS/S levels; 5: O level/GCSE grades A–C; 6: GCSE grades D–G.

11. The Goldthorpe 7-group classification identifies the following seven social classes based on the parent's occupation: 1: "Higher Salariat," such as higher-grade professionals, administrators, and officials; and managers in large industrial establishments; 2: "Lower Salariat," such as lower-grade professionals, administrators, and officials; higher-grade technicians; managers in small industrial establishments; and supervisors of nonmanual employees; 3: Routine nonmanual occupations; 4: Self-employed; 5: Lower-grade technicians and supervisors of manual workers; 6: Skilled manual occupations; 7: Nonskilled manual occupations.

12. We use data for children who first entered the sample between 1994 and 2008 and combine data from the first interview (when parenting style is available and the parent's social class is available) to obtain outcomes for the children as adults in later surveys. The results are based on 827 pairs of parents and children matched in this way. The classification of parenting styles follows the work of Tak Wing Chan and Anita Koo, "Parenting Style and Youth Outcomes in the UK," *European Sociological Review* 27, no. 3 (2010): 385–99.

13. Results are based on the Goldthorpe-7 scale of social classes. Regressions include parenting style, social class of the parent, and age of the child. Detailed regression results are available on request.

14. Kids Count Data Center, "Children in Single-Parent Families by Race," *National Kids Count* (2017), http://datacenter.kidscount.org/data/tables/107-children-in -single-parent-families-by.

15. Alison Aughinbaugh, Omar Robles, and Hugette Sun, "Marriage and Divorce: Patterns by Gender, Race, and Educational Attainment," *Monthly Labor Review*, US Bureau of Labor Statistics, October 2013.

16. See Betsey Stevenson and Justin Wolfers, "Marriage and Divorce: Changes and Their Driving Forces," *Journal of Economic Perspectives* 21, no. 2 (2007): 27–52. Their study focuses on the cohort born in 1950–55.

17. See, for example, Jonathan Gruber, "Is Making Divorce Easier Bad for Children? The Long-Run Implications of Unilateral Divorce," *Journal of Labor Economics* 22, no. 4 (2004): 799–833.

18. Thomas Piketty, "The Impact of Divorce on School Performance: Evidence from France, 1968–2002" (CEPR Discussion Paper No. 4146, 2003).

19. Gretchen Livingston and Anna Brown, "Intermarriage in the U.S. 50 Years After Loving v. Virginia," *Pew Research Center*, 2017.

20. Lasse Eika, Magne Mogstad, and Basit Zafar, "Educational Assortative Mating and Household Income Inequality" (Federal Reserve Bank of New York Staff Report No. 682, 2014), table C.1.

21. Ibid., 13. Here, random mating refers to a hypothetical situation in which the probability of marrying does not depend on the educational level of the two partners.

22. US Census Bureau, "Income and Earnings Summary Measures by Selected Characteristics: 2014 and 2015," *Current Population Survey* (2016), http://www .census.gov/data/tables/2016/demo/income-poverty/p60–256.html.

23. Rakesh Kochhar and Richard Fry, "Wealth Inequality Has Widened Along Racial Ethnic Lines Since End of Great Recession," *Pew Research Center*, December 12, 2014, http://www.pewresearch.org/fact-tank/2014/12/12/racial-wealth-gaps -great-recession/.

24. US Census Bureau, "Percent of People 25 Years and Over Who Have Completed High School or College, by Race, Hispanic Origin and Sex: Selected Years 1940 to 2015," *CPS Historical Time Series Tables* (2016), http://www.census.gov/data /tables/time-series/demo/educational-attainment/cps-historical-time-series .html.

25. Sean F. Reardon, Demetra Kalogrides, and Kenneth Shores, "The Geography of Racial/Ethnic Test Score Gaps" (CEPA Stanford Working Paper nos. 16–10, 2017).

26. Evanston Township High School, *Annual School Statistical Report 2013–2014*, Office of Research, Evaluation, and Assessment (2014), https://www.eths.k12 .il.us/Page/757.

27. US Census Bureau, *American Community Survey* (2014).

28. Kids Count Data Center, "Children in Single-Parent Families by Race," *National Kids Count* (2017), http://datacenter.kidscount.org/data/tables/107-children-in -single-parent-families-by.

29. US Department of Justice, "Prison Inmates at Midyear 2009—Statistical Tables," *Bureau of Justice Statistics* (2010), http://www.bjs.gov/content/pub/pdf/pim 09st.pdf.

30. Derek Neal and Armin Rick, "The Prison Boom and the Lack of Progress after Smith and Welch" (NBER Working Paper 20283, 2014).

31. Mark Hugo Lopez and Ana Gonzalez-Barrera, "Women's College Enrollment Gains Leave Men Behind," *Pew Research Center*, March 6, 2014, http://www .pewresearch.org/fact-tank/2014/03/06/womens-college-enrollment-gains -leave-men-behind.

32. Northwestern University, *Fall 2015 Enrollment Statistics*, Office of the Registrar (2016), http://www.registrar.northwestern.edu/documents/records/enrollment -graduation-statistics/fall_2015_enrollment.pdf.

33. DePaul University, *Tuition Rates 2016–2017*, Student Financial Accounts (2017), http://offices.depaul.edu/student-financial-accounts/cost-of-attendance/tuition /Pages/2016–2017.aspx.

34. DePaul University, *Enrollment Summary 2015*, Division of Enrollment Management and Marketing (2016), offices.depaul.edu/enrollment-management-mar keting/enrollment-summary/Documents/EMMEnrollmentSummary2015 _FINAL.pdf.

35. Chicago State University, *2015–2016 Undergraduate Costs and Financial Aid*, Office of Student Financial Aid (2017), www.csu.edu/financialaid/costs.htm.

36. Chicago State University, *Enrollment, Retention & Graduation Fact Sheet*, Office of Institutional Effectiveness and Research (2012), www.csu.edu/enrollment management/enrollservices/pdf/CSUERGFactSheet_Fall2012.pdf.

37. A recent study argues that the marriage market return to education still plays an important role in the United States today; see Fatih Guvenen and Michelle Rendall, "Women's Emancipation through Education: A Macroeconomic Analysis," *Review of Economic Dynamics* 18, no. 4 (2015): 931–56.

38. Data is from the International Consortium for Political and Social Research, *General Social Survey*, Roper Center for Public Opinion Research (2013), https:// www.icpsr.umich.edu/icpsrweb/ICPSR/studies/34802; and from Sheldon G. Levy and Sandra Ball-Rokeach, "Study of Political Violence Attitudes, Personal Experiences with Violence, Emotional Reactions to Assassination and Violence in the Media, 1968" (International Consortium for Political and Social Research Study No. 7354, 2010). Data shows the fraction of adults who approve the use of corporal punishment in a given year, averaged over five-year intervals. The survey question in the 1968 survey is: "Are there any situations that you can imagine in which you would approve of a parent spanking his or her child assuming the child is healthy and over a year old?" The survey question in the GSS is: "Do you strongly agree, agree, disagree, or strongly disagree that it is sometimes necessary to discipline a child with a good, hard spanking?" Approval is defined as the sum of the fractions of parents who "strongly agree" or "agree."

39. Melvin L. Kohn and Carmi Schooler, "Class, Occupation, and Orientation," *American Sociological Review* 34, no. 5 (1969): 659–78.

40. The hypothesis that the choice of parenting style is constrained by parents' cognitive limitations, which restrict parents' ability to exert "the mental effort required to consistently pay attention to, engage with, monitor, and supervise their children" is tested empirically by Deborah Cobb-Clark, Nicolas Salamanca,

and Anna Zhu, "Parenting Style as an Investment in Human Development" (IZA Discussion Paper 9686, 2016). They find evidence that less-educated and disadvantaged parents are subject to more cognitive constraints when investing in child-rearing activities.

41. See María Sáez Martí and Anna Sjoegren, "Peers and Culture," *Scandinavian Journal of Economics* 110, no. 1 (2008): 73–92.

42. For the importance of role models, see the seminal contribution of sociologist Albert Bandura from Stanford University. See, in particular, Albert Bandura, *Social Learning Theory* (Englewood Cliffs: Prentice Hall, 1977). For a recent formal application of his theory to economics, see María Sáez Martí, "Observational Learning and Parental Influence" (mimeo, Yale University, 2017).

43. Along these lines, the economists Shelly Lundberg and Robert Pollak suggest that the marriage gap between more- and less-educated Americans is in large part due to the role of marriage as a commitment device for parents who plan to invest heavily into their children. See Shelly Lundberg and Robert A. Pollak, "Cohabitation and the Uneven Retreat from Marriage in the United States, 1950–2010," in *Human Capital in History: The American Record*, ed. L. Boustan, C. Frydman, and R. Margo, National Bureau of Economic Research Conference Report (Chicago: University of Chicago Press, 2014), 241–72. See also Shelly Lundberg, Robert A. Pollak, and Jenna E. Stearns, "Family Inequality: Diverging Patterns in Marriage, Cohabitation, and Childbearing," *Journal of Economic Perspectives* 30, no 2 (2016), 79–102.

44. See, for example, Flavio Cunha, James Heckman, and Susanne Schennach, "Estimating the Technology of Cognitive and Noncognitive Skill Formation," *Econometrica* 78, no. 3 (2010): 883–931.

45. See Orazio Attanasio, "The Determinants of Human Capital Formation during the Early Years of Life: Theory, Measurement, and Policies," *Journal of the European Economic Association* 13, no. 6 (2015): 949–97.

46. James Heckman, Rodrigo Pinto, and Peter Savelyev, "Understanding the Mechanisms through which an Influential Early Childhood Program Boosted Adult Outcomes," *American Economic Review* 103, no. 6 (2013): 2052–86.

47. Eliana Garces, Duncan Thomas, and Janet Currie, "Longer-Term Effects of Head Start," *American Economic Review* 92, no. 4 (2002): 999–1012. See also Janet Currie, "Early Childhood Education Programs," *Journal of Economic Perspectives* 15, no. 2 (2001): 213–38.

48. Similar conclusions are reached by studies in child development literature. See, for instance, Jack Shonkoff and Deborah Philips, eds., *From Neurons to Neighborhoods: The Science of Early Childhood Development* (Washington, DC: National Academy Press, 2000). The study emphasizes the importance of emotional, social, regulatory, and moral capacities, notions that are similar to that of noncognitive skills in the economics literature.

49. See, among others, Carmit Segal, "Misbehavior, Education, and Labor Market Outcomes," *Journal of the European Economic Association* 11, no. 4 (2013): 743–

79; James Heckman, Jora Stixrud, and Sergio Urzua, "The Effects of Cognitive and Noncognitive Abilities on Labor Market Outcomes and Social Behavior," *Journal of Labor Economics* 24, no. 3 (2006): 411–82; Robert Kaestner and Kevin Callison, "Adolescent Cognitive and Noncognitive Correlates of Adult Health," *Journal of Human Capital* 5, no. 1 (2011): 29–69.

50. Francesco Agostinelli and Giuseppe Sorrenti, "Money vs. Time: Family Income, Maternal Labor Supply, and Child Development" (HCEO Working Paper Series No. 2018–017, 2018, University of Chicago).

CHAPTER FIVE: FROM STICK TO CARROT

1. "10 Reasons Not to Hit Your Child," *Ask Dr. Sears*, http://www.askdrsears.com /topics/parenting/discipline-behavior/spanking/10-reasons-not-hit-your-child.
2. Proverbs 22:15.
3. Proverbs 20:30.
4. Hadith Collection, Abu Dawud Book 002, Hadith Number 0495, http://www .hadithcollection.com/abudawud. The Ahadith (literally, *narration*) is a set of reports describing the life of the Islamic Prophet Muhammad. Hadith are subordinate only to the Qur'an in the Islamic tradition and jurisprudence.
5. In the original Bangubangu language: "Atika mutosi ndaaluhega mwana." Bangubangu is a tribe from the eastern part of the Democratic Republic of the Congo, in the Kabambare Territory, who follows an African traditional religion. Elias Bushiri Elie, African Proverbs Working Group, Nairobi (Kenya), http:// quoterich.com/wp-content/uploads/2017/11/elias_bangubangu.pdf.
6. Plutarch, *De Liberis Educandis*, Section 12.
7. J. H. Plumb, "The New World of Children in Eighteenth-Century England," *Past and Present* 67, no. 1 (1975): 64–95.
8. Philippe Ariès, *Centuries of Childhood: A Social History of Family Life*, translated from the French by Robert Baldick (New York: Knopf, 1962).
9. Ibid., 38.
10. Ibid., 39 and 130.
11. Lloyd De Mause, *The Evolution of Parent-Child Relationships as a Factor in History* (London: Souvenir Press, 1976).
12. De Mause, *The History of Childhood* (New York: Psychohistory Press, 1974).
13. Hugh Cunningham, *Children and Childhood in Western Society since 1500* (New York: Longman, 1995).
14. Thomas Wiedemann, *Adults and Children in the Roman Empire* (New Haven: Yale University Press, 1989).
15. John Locke, *Some Thoughts Concerning Education* (Detroit: Gale Group, Eighteenth Century Collections Online; London: Printed for W. Baynes by Hemingway and Crook, Blackburn, 1800). Citations refer to the Eighteenth Century Collections Online edition.
16. Ibid., §40.

17. Ibid., §1.
18. Ibid., §40.
19. Jean-Jacques Rousseau, *Emile, or On Education*, translated by Allan Bloom (New York: Basic Books, 1979. 1st English ed., 1762).
20. "Zealous teachers, be simple, sensible, and reticent; be in no hurry to act unless to prevent the actions of others. Again and again I say, reject, if it may be, a good lesson for fear of giving a bad one. Beware of playing the tempter in this world, which nature intended as an earthly paradise for men, and do not attempt to give the innocent child the knowledge of good and evil; since you cannot prevent the child learning by what he sees outside himself, restrict your own efforts to impressing those examples on his mind in the form best suited for him." See Rousseau, *Emile*, 96.
21. Ibid., 102.
22. Maria Montessori, *The Absorbent Mind* (Adyar—Madras: The Theosophical Publishing House, 1949).
23. Ibid., 122.
24. Kai-D. Bussmann, Claudia Erthal, and Andreas Schroth, "The Effects of Banning Corporal Punishment in Europe: A Five-Nation Comparison," in *Global Pathways to Abolishing Physical Punishment*, ed. Joan E. Durrant and Anne B. Smith (New York: Routledge, 2011), 299–322.
25. Since 2007, Spain has prohibited corporal punishment, while it is still legal in France and Italy. The study mentioned previously came prior to a change in the Spanish legislation.
26. Save the Children Italia Onlus, "I metodi educativi e il ricorso a punizioni fisiche," *Ipsos Public Affairs* (2012), http://images.savethechildren.it/f/download/ri/ricercaipsosamaniferme.pdf.
27. The only exception in our sample is Turkey, where the share of parents believing in the value of obedience has remained high and stable since 1990.
28. Giovanni Verga, *The House by the Medlar Tree* (Berkeley: University of California Press, 1983). The book was originally published in Italian in 1881 under the title *I Malavoglia*.
29. Verga, *Fantasticheria*, in *Giovanni Verga. Tutte le novelle*, a cura di Carla Riccardi, 136 (Milano: Mondadori, 1979). Our translation from the original Italian text.
30. John Mainwaring, *Memoirs of the Life of the Late George Frederic Handel* (London: R. and J. Dodsley, 1760).
31. Oded Galor and Daniel Tsiddon, "Technological Progress, Mobility, and Economic Growth," *American Economic Review* 87, no. 3 (1997): 363–82; John Hassler and Jose V. Rodriguez Mora, "Intelligence, Social Mobility, and Growth," *American Economic Review* 90, no. 4 (2000): 888–908.
32. Linda Pollock, *Forgotten Children: Parent-Child Relations from 1500 to 1900* (Cambridge: Cambridge University Press, 1983).
33. Carl F. Kaestle and Maris A. Vinovskis, *Education and Social Change in Nineteenth-Century Massachusetts* (Cambridge: Cambridge University Press, 1980).

34. Antoine Prost, "Public and Private Spheres in France," in *The History of Private Life. Riddles of Identity in Modern Times*, ed. Antoine Prost and Gerard Vincent (Cambridge, MA: Harvard University Press, 1991), 1–144.

35. Chang-Tai Hsieh, Erik Hurst, Charles I. Jones, and Peter J. Klenow, "The Allocation of Talent and U.S. Economic Growth" (NBER Working Paper No. 18693, 2013).

36. See Ramon Marimon and Fabrizio Zilibotti, "Unemployment vs. Mismatch of Talents: Reconsidering Unemployment Benefits," *Economic Journal* 109, no. 455 (1999): 266–91; Gianluca Violante, "Technological Acceleration, Skill Transferability, and the Rise in Residual Inequality," *Quarterly Journal of Economics* 117, no. 1 (2002): 297–338.

37. The data for GDP per capita are in Purchasing Power Parities. See Penn World Tables 9.0. Note that the percentage of respondents mentioning obedience and independence in figure 5.1 and figure 5.2, respectively, is slightly different from figure 3.1 because here we report the proportion relative to the total number of respondents (see chapter 3 for the details of the construction of figure 3.1).

38. The correlation between the share of parents emphasizing obedience and GDP per capita is -55 percent, while that between independence and GDP per capita is $+40$ percent. Both correlations are statistically significant.

39. Christopher G. Ellison, John P. Bartkowski, and Michelle L. Segal, "Do Conservative Protestants Spank More Often? Further Evidence from the National Survey of Families and Households," *Social Science Quarterly* 77, no. 3 (1996): 663–73; Christopher G. Ellison, "Conservative Protestantism and the Corporal Punishment of Children: Clarifying the Issues," *Journal for the Scientific Study of Religion* 35, no. 1 (1996): 1–16.

40. A different channel from religion to parenting, not explored here, goes through education. For example, some religions emphasize the reading of ancient texts, which may provide incentives for parents to provide their children with literacy skills. See Maristella Botticini and Zvi Eckstein, *The Chosen Few: How Education Shaped Jewish History* (Princeton, NJ: Princeton University Press, 2012); and Sascha Becker and Ludger Woessmann, "Was Weber Wrong? A Human Capital Theory of Protestant Economic History," *Quarterly Journal of Economics* 124, no. 2 (2009): 531–96. For a more general exploration of the relationship between religious and economic attitudes, see Luigi Guiso, Paola Sapienza, and Luigi Zingales, "People's Opium? Religion and Economic Attitudes," *Journal of Monetary Economics* 50, no. 1 (2003): 225–82.

41. Kaestle and Vinovskis, *Education and Social Change in Nineteenth-Century Massachusetts*.

42. John P. Bartkowski and Christopher G. Ellison, "Divergent Models of Childrearing in Popular Manuals: Conservative Protestants vs. the Mainstream Experts," *Sociology of Religion* 56, no. 1 (1995): 21–34.

43. Ibid., 25.

44. Irwin A. Hyman, *The Case against Spanking: How to Discipline Your Child without Hitting* (San Francisco: Jossey–Bass, 1997), 6.

45. Our sample includes 14 percent nonreligious people, 23 percent Catholic, 31 percent Protestant, and 32 percent from other religions. The sample size is 5,674. "Other religions" is a residual category that also includes people who do not associate themselves with any particular denomination, but who regard religion as important.

46. The statistical analysis is based on a multinomial logistic model.

47. According to the estimates of our multinomial logistic model, the relative odds of being authoritative rather than permissive is 1.4 for Catholics and 1.6 for Protestants (relative to nonreligious people). The relative odds of being authoritarian rather than permissive are 2.2 for Catholics and 3.0 for Protestants.

48. According to the estimates of our multinomial logistic model, the relative odds of being authoritative rather than permissive are 1.2, and the relative odds of being authoritarian rather than permissive are 1.6 for nonreligious relative to religious people.

49. The result is not driven by Turkey (the only country with a Muslim majority), and in fact excluding Turkey strengthens the result.

50. As before, we control for country fixed effects. In other words, people are defined as right- or left-wing relative to the country average. Many voters for the Swedish conservative party (Moderaterna) are politically and socially more liberal than typical voters for the Democratic Party in the United States. This will not be an issue here, since we will be comparing Americans with Americans and Swedes with Swedes. As usual, we hold constant other characteristics such as age and gender.

51. The WVS asks each individual to state her/his own political orientation on a 10-point scale, where 1 is left and 10 is right. We classify as left-oriented those individuals with a level between 1 and 3, center-oriented those between 4 and 7, and right-oriented those between 8 and 10.

52. One might be tempted to interpret the observation that religiosity matters as evidence against the thesis that economic factors shape parenting styles. However, in our view this evidence is fully consistent with the broad thesis of the book. As we emphasize in chapter 1, we take the perspective that people act deliberately to achieve their objectives subject to constraints. There, we also discuss how these objectives may go beyond strictly economic factors. While we believe that economic factors play an important role for most people, our thesis does not rule out the possibility that other factors, such as religion or national identity, also matter. This argument is related to the thesis of the economists Alberto Bisin and Thierry Verdier, " 'Beyond the Melting Pot': Cultural Transmission, Marriage, and the Evolution of Ethnic and Religious Traits," *Quarterly Journal of Economics* 115, no. 3 (2000): 955–88). They argue that religious people, especially minorities, make investments in order to transmit their prin-

ciples to their children. This effort is responsible for the persistence of cultural and religious diversity in the population. Their results are consistent with the overall theme of this book as well as the more specific finding that religiosity matters for parenting.

53. Pew Research Center, "Changing Attitudes on Gay Marriage," June 26, 2017, http://www.pewforum.org/fact-sheet/changing-attitudes-on-gay-marriage/.

CHAPTER SIX: BOYS VERSUS GIRLS

1. We restrict our discussion here to girls and boys, and abstract from nonbinary gender, for example, transgender children. While it would be interesting to expand on this issue, the data sources we rely on make this infeasible at this time.
2. See, for example, Janis B. Kupersmidt, Donna Bryant, and Michael T. Willoughby, "Prevalence of Aggressive Behaviors among Preschoolers in Head Start and Community Child Care Programs," *Behavioral Disorders* 26, no. 1 (2000): 42–52.
3. For a popular statement of this view, see, for example, Richard Whitmire, *Why Boys Fail: Saving Our Sons from an Educational System That's Leaving Them Behind* (New York: AMACOM, 2010). For more formal evidence that bad schools are particularly bad for boys, see David H. Autor, David N. Figlio, Krzysztof Karbownik, Jeffrey Roth, and Melanie Wasserman, "School Quality and the Gender Gap in Educational Achievement," *American Economic Review: Papers & Proceedings* 106, no. 5 (2016): 289–95.
4. Ester Boserup, *Woman's Role in Economic Development* (London: George Allen & Unwin, 1970).
5. In recent work, a team of economists has argued that the history of plough use had a persistent impact on gender roles that can still be seen today. See Alberto Alesina, Paola Giuliano, and Nathan Nunn, "On the Origins of Gender Roles: Women and the Plough," *Quarterly Journal of Economics*, 128, no. 2 (2013): 469–530.
6. Loftur Guttormsson, "Parent-Child Relations," in *Family Life in the Long Nineteenth Century, 1789–1913*, ed. David I. Kertzer and Marzio Barbagli (London: Yale University Press, 2002), 251–81.
7. Joyce Burnette, "Women Workers in the British Industrial Revolution," EH.Net Encyclopedia, ed. Robert Whaples, March 26, 2008, http://eh.net/encyclopedia/women-workers-in-the-british-industrial-revolution/.
8. Joyce Burnette, *Gender, Work, and Wages in Industrial Revolution Britain* (Cambridge: Cambridge University Press, 2008).
9. Guttormsson, "Parent-Child Relations," 263.
10. Claudia Goldin, "Marriage Bars: Discrimination against Married Women Workers from the 1920s to the 1950s," in *Favorites of Fortune: Technology, Growth, and Economic Development since the Industrial Revolution*, ed. Henry Rosovsky, David

Landes, and Patrice Higonnet (Cambridge, MA: Harvard University Press, 1991), 511–36.

11. OECD, "Sex and Age Indicators," *OECD.Stat* (2017), https://stats.oecd.org /Index.aspx?DataSetCode=LFS_SEXAGE_I_R#; US Census Bureau, "Historical Statistics of the United States: Colonial Times to 1970," *US Department of Commerce* (2015), www2.census.gov/library/publications/1975/compendia/hist_stats _colonial-1970/hist_stats_colonial-1970p1-chA.pdf and www2.census.gov/library /publications/1975/compendia/hist_stats_colonial-1970/hist_stats_colonial -1970p1-chD.pdf: Table A119–134 and D29–41.

12. See Goldin, *Understanding the Gender Gap: An Economic History of American Women* (New York: Oxford University Press, 1990).

13. Michelle Rendall, "Brain versus Brawn: The Realization of Women's Comparative Advantage" (mimeo, Monash University, 2017). Rendall's argument does not rely on the presumption of any intellectual superiority of either gender. For instance, women would have a comparative advantage in brain-related activities if they were just as good as men in intellectual tasks, but less good than men at jobs requiring physical strength.

14. Jeremy Greenwood, Ananth Seshadri, and Mehmet Yorukoglu, "Engines of Liberation," *Review of Economic Studies* 72, no. 1 (2005): 109–33.

15. US Census Bureau, "Race and Hispanic Origin of People by Median Income and Sex: 1947 to 2015," *Current Population Survey* (2016), https://www2.census.gov /programs-surveys/cps/tables/time-series/historical-income-people/p02.xls; and Goldin, *Understanding the Gender Gap*, table 3.2 for the years 1890 and 1930.

16. Discrimination can discourage human capital investment in the discriminated group. In addition, parents may put less effort into pushing children to succeed if they expect that the children will be discriminated against in the labor market once they are adults. This argument applies to the discrimination of any group, such as gender or racial minorities. A formal economic theory capturing this feedback loop can be found in María Sáez Martí and Yves Zenou, "Cultural Transmission and Discrimination," *Journal of Urban Economics* 72, no. 2–3 (2012): 137–46.

17. Raquel Fernández, Alessandra Fogli, and Claudia Olivetti, "Mothers and Sons: Preference Formation and Female Labor Force Dynamics," *Quarterly Journal of Economics* 119, no. 4 (2004): 1249–99.

18. Raquel Fernández, "Cultural Change as Learning: The Evolution of Female Labor Force Participation over a Century," *American Economic Review* 103, no. 1 (2013): 472–500. For a related hypothesis, see also Alessandra Fogli and Laura Veldkamp, "Nature or Nurture? Learning and the Geography of Female Labor Force Participation," *Econometrica* 79, no. 4 (2011): 1103–38.

19. The data are from the American Time Use Survey, 2003–16. The definitions of core market and nonmarket hours and the method to control for compositional changes follow Mark Aguiar and Erik Hurst, "Measuring Trends in Leisure: The

Allocation of Time over Five Decades," *Quarterly Journal of Economics* 122, no. 3 (2007): 969–1006. In particular, core market work includes all time spent working on main jobs, second jobs, and overtime, including any time spent working at home, but it excludes time spent commuting or on breaks. Nonmarket work includes activities such as shopping, cleaning, and cooking, but excludes leisure and childcare.

20. US Census Bureau, "Percent of People 25 Years and over Who Have Completed High School or College, by Race, Hispanic Origin and Sex: Selected Years 1940 to 2015," *Current Population Survey* (2015), https://www2.census.gov/programs-surveys/demo/tables/educational-attainment/time-series/cps-historical-time-series/taba-2.xlsx.

21. One potential reason why more women than men now complete college is related to the marriage market implications of education. For a study making this point, see Pierre-André Chiappori, Murat Iyigun, and Yoram Weiss, "Investment in Schooling and the Marriage Market," *American Economic Review* 99, no. 5 (2009): 1689–1713.

22. For evidence on differences between the behavior of parents of daughters and sons in dimensions other than parenting style (such as marital stability and time use), see Shelly Lundberg, "Sons, Daughters, and Parental Behaviour," *Oxford Review of Economic Policy* 21, no. 3 (2005): 340–56.

23. As in the WVS, parents are asked a series of questions about which values they emphasize in child-rearing, ranked by priority. We classify parents as authoritarian if they list obedience among the top two values for children to learn from a list that contains "to obey," "to be well-liked or popular," "to think for himself or herself," "to work hard," and "to help others when they need help." The remaining parents are classified as authoritative if they mention "hard work" among the top two values, and otherwise they are classified as permissive.

24. This statement is based on a multinomial logit regression of parenting style, controlling for the answer to the question on separation of male and female work (distinguishing between strongly agree/agree and disagree/strongly disagree), family income, education, age and gender of the child, race, and region. The relative odds ratio of being authoritarian compared to permissive of those who agree or strongly agree is 1.86 relative to those who disagree or strongly disagree, with a standard error of 0.47.

25. Data from World Bank *International Comparison Program database*: https://data.worldbank.org/indicator/SL.TLF.CACT.FE.ZS, https://data.worldbank.org/indicator/NY.GDP.PCAP.PP.KD.

26. Ester Boserup, *Woman's Role in Economic Development* (London: George Allen & Unwin, 1970).

27. See, for example, Siwan Anderson, "The Economics of Dowry and Brideprice," *Journal of Economic Perspectives* 21, no. 4 (2007): 151–74.

28. Michèle Tertilt, "Polygyny, Fertility, and Savings," *Journal of Political Economy* 113, no. 6 (2005): 1341–71.

29. Data on polygyny from Demographic and Health Surveys (most recent survey). Data on GDP per capita from World Development Indicators.

30. Amartya Sen, "More Than 100 Million Women Are Missing," *New York Review of Books*, December 20, 1990.

31. Stephan Klasen and Claudia Wink, "Missing Women: Revisiting the Debate," *Feminist Economics* 9, no. 2–3 (2003): 263–99.

32. Seema Jayachandran and Ilyana Kuziemko, "Why Do Mothers Breastfeed Girls Less than Boys? Evidence and Implications for Child Health in India," *Quarterly Journal of Economics* 126, no. 3 (2011): 1458–538.

33. Jesus Fernández-Villaverde, Jeremy Greenwood, and Nezih Guner, "From Shame to Game in One Hundred Years: An Economic Model of the Rise in Premarital Sex and its De-Stigmatization," *Journal of the European Economic Association* 12, no. 1 (2014): 25–61.

34. Jeremy Greenwood and Nezih Guner, "Social Change: The Sexual Revolution," *International Economic Review* 51, no. 4 (2010): 893–923.

35. See Claudia Goldin and Lawrence Katz, "The Power of the Pill: Oral Contraceptives and Women's Career and Marriage Decisions," *Journal of Political Economy* 110, no. 4 (2002): 730–70.

36. Ebonya L. Washington, "Female Socialization: How Daughters Affect Their Legislator Fathers' Voting on Women's Issues," *American Economic Review* 98, no. 1 (2008): 311–32.

37. Matthias Doepke and Michèle Tertilt, "Women's Liberation: What's in It for Men?" *Quarterly Journal of Economics* 124, no, 4 (2009): 1541–91. See also Matthias Doepke, Michèle Tertilt, and Alessandra Voena, "The Economics and Politics of Women's Rights," *Annual Review of Economics* 4 (2012): 339–72; and Doepke and Tertilt, "Families in Macroeconomics," in *Handbook of Macroeconomics*, vol. 2B, ed. John B. Taylor and Harald Uhlig (Amsterdam: North Holland, 2016), 1789–891.

38. *London Times*, April 23, 1868.

39. *London Times*, March 27, 1869.

CHAPTER SEVEN: FERTILITY AND CHILD LABOR

1. Gallup News Service, "Desire to Have Children" (2013), www.gallup.com/file /poll/164630/Fertility_130925.pdf. Displayed is percentage of all respondents who stated a preference, including those who stated, "No opinion."

2. For a study of the causes of fertility decline in Europe as early as the fourteenth century, see Nico Voigtländer and Hans-Joachim Voth, "How the West 'Invented' Fertility Restriction," *American Economic Review* 103, no. 6 (2013): 2227–64.

3. Lant Pritchett, "Desired Fertility and the Impact of Population Policy," *Population and Development Review* 20, no. 1 (1994): 24–40. See also the discussion of this finding in David Weil, *Economic Growth*, 3rd ed. (New York: Routledge, 2016).

4. Source for England and Wales: Ron Lee and Roger Schofield, "British Population

in the Eighteenth Century," in *The Economic History of Britain since 1700*, vol. 1, ed. Roderick Floud and Deirdre McCloskey (Cambridge: Cambridge University Press, 1981) for the years 1800, 1820, and 1840; and Jean-Claude Chesnais, *The Demographic Transition: Stages, Patterns, and Economic Implications* (Oxford: Oxford University Press, 1992), tables A2.3 and A2.4 for all other years; and for the United States: Larry E. Jones and Michèle Tertilt, "An Economic History of the Relationship between Occupation and Fertility in the United States: 1826–1960," in *Frontiers of Family Economics*, vol. 1, ed. Peter Rupert (Bingley, UK: Emerald Group Publishing Limited, 2008), table 1A.

5. Data from World Bank *International Comparison Program database*: https://data.worldbank.org/indicator/SP.DYN.TFRT.IN, https://data.worldbank.org/indicator/NY.GDP.PCAP.PP.KD.

6. Thomas R. Malthus, *An Essay on the Principle of Population* (New York: Dover Publications, 2007).

7. Gary S. Becker's initial work on fertility choice is "An Economic Analysis of Fertility," in *Demographic and Economic Change in Developed Countries* (Princeton: Princeton University Press, 1960), 209–40. The concept of the quantity-quality trade-off was developed further in Gary S. Becker and H. Gregg Lewis, "On the Interaction between the Quantity and Quality of Children," *Journal of Political Economy* 81, no. 2 (1973): S279–S288; and Robert J. Barro and Gary S. Becker, "Fertility Choice in a Model of Economic Growth," *Econometrica* 57, no. 2 (1989): 481–501. A summary of Becker's contributions to the economics of fertility can be found in Matthias Doepke, "Gary Becker on the Quantity and Quality of Children," *Journal of Demographic Economics* 81, no. 1 (2015): 59–66.

8. The seminal paper developing a joint theory of industrialization and the demographic transition along the lines described here is Oded Galor and David N. Weil, "Population, Technology, and Growth: From Malthusian Stagnation to the Demographic Transition and Beyond," *American Economic Review* 90, no. 4 (2000): 806–28. See also Oded Galor and Oded Moav, "Natural Selection and the Origin of Economic Growth," *Quarterly Journal of Economics* 117, no. 4 (2002): 1133–91. Regarding the dynamics of fertility decline, see David de la Croix and Matthias Doepke, "Inequality and Growth: Why Differential Fertility Matters," *American Economic Review* 93, no. 4 (2003): 1091–113.

9. For an overview of child labor in the British industrialization period, see Jane Humphries, *Childhood and Child Labour in the British Industrial Revolution* (Cambridge: Cambridge University Press, 2010).

10. For example, Loftur Guttormsson writes: "Despite the well-known abuses of child labor, factory work was not as disruptive of family ties as one might have expected. In northern France it was not uncommon for one-third to one-quarter of factory children to be employed in the same mills as their fathers. In addition, many had older brothers or sisters on the shop floor. . . . This ensured a measure of protection for many factory children" ("Parent-Child Relations," in *Family Life*

in the Long Nineteenth Century, 1789–1913, ed. David I. Kertzer and Marzio Barbagli [London: Yale University Press, 2002], 271).

11. Michael Haines, *Fertility and Occupation: Population Patterns in Industrialization* (New York: Academic Press, 1979).

12. Fertility rate from Lee and Schofield, "British Population in the Eighteenth Century" for the years 1800, 1820, and 1840; and Chesnais, *The Demographic Transition*, tables A2.3 and A2.4 for all other years; and percent of children in school from Hugh Cunningham, "Combating Child Labour: The British Experience," in *Child Labour in Historical Perspective 1800–1985: Case Studies from Europe, Japan and Colombia*, ed. Hugh Cunningham and Viazzo Pier Paolo (Florence: UNICEF ICDC, 1996), 41–55.

13. The shift from child labor to education was further accelerated by the introduction of compulsory schooling and child labor laws; see Doepke, "Accounting for Fertility Decline during the Transition to Growth," *Journal of Economic Growth* 9, no. 3 (2004): 347–83.

14. The sources are the same as for table 7.4.

15. Data from OECD, "Gender Institutions and Development Database" and World Bank, "Education Statistics" (2016), https://data.worldbank.org/data-catalog/ed-stats.

16. Data from World Bank *International Comparison Program database*: https://data.worldbank.org/indicator/SP.DYN.TFRT.IN, https://data.worldbank.org/indicator/SL.TLF.0714.ZS.

17. Data from Chesnais, *The Demographic Transition* and the US Census Bureau.

18. See, for example, Yoram Ben-Porath, "Fertility Response to Child Mortality: Micro Data from Israel," *Journal of Political Economy* 84, no. 4 (1976): S163–78; and Michael R. Haine, "The Relationship between Infant and Child Mortality and Fertility: Some Historical and Contemporary Evidence for the United States," chapter 7 of *From Death to Birth: Mortality Decline and Reproductive Change*, ed. M. R. Montgomery and B. Cohen, (Washington DC: National Academy Press, 1998).

19. For a detailed discussion of the role of changes in mortality rates, see Matteo Cervellati and Uwe Sunde, "The Economic and Demographic Transition, Mortality, and Comparative Development," *American Economic Journal: Macroeconomics* 7, no. 3 (2015): 189–225.

20. For a more detailed elaboration of this argument, see Doepke, "Child Mortality and Fertility Decline: Does the Barro-Becker Model Fit the Facts?" *Journal of Population Economics* 18, no. 2 (2005): 337–66.

21. The common interest of the working class and capitalists in supporting public education is analyzed from an economic perspective in Oded Galor and Omer Moav, "Das Human-Kapital: A Theory of the Demise of the Class Structure," *Review of Economic Studies* 73, no. 1 (2006): 85–117.

22. See Matthias Doepke and Fabrizio Zilibotti, "The Macroeconomics of Child Labor Regulation," *American Economic Review* 95, no. 5 (2005): 1492–524.

23. See Doepke and Zilibotti, "Do International Labor Standards Contribute to the Persistence of the Child Labor Problem?" *Journal of Economic Growth* 15, no. 1, (2010): 1–37.

24. Data from Chesnais, *The Demographic Transition* and national statistical agencies.

25. Jeremy Greenwood, Ananth Seshadri, and Mehmet Yorukoglu, "Engines of Liberation," *Review of Economic Studies* 72, no.1 (2005): 109–33.

26. Greenwood, Seshadri, and Vandenbroucke, "The Baby Boom and Baby Bust," *American Economic Review* 95, no. 1 (2005): 183–207. Another aspect of improvement in technology that may have contributed to the baby boom is medical improvements that lowered women's risk of dying in childbirth and improved maternal health; see Stefania Albanesi and Claudia Olivetti, "Maternal Health and the Baby Boom," *Quantitative Economics* 5, no. 2 (2014): 225–69.

27. Matthias Doepke, Moshe Hazan, and Yishay Maoz, "The Baby Boom and World War II: A Macroeconomic Analysis," *Review of Economic Studies* 82, no. 3 (2015): 1031–73.

28. Data from US Census; see Doepke, Hazan, and Maoz, "The Baby Boom and World War II" for further details on how this data is constructed.

29. An early analysis of the impact of World War II on female labor market participation is provided in Claudia Goldin, "The Role of World War II in the Rise of Women's Employment," *American Economic Review* 81, no. 4 (1991): 741–56. For more recent work on this issue, see Claudia Goldin and Claudia Olivetti, "Shocking Labor Supply: A Reassessment of the Role of World War II on Women's Labor Supply," *American Economic Review* 103, no. 3 (2013): 257–62.

30. Data from Doepke, Hazan, and Maoz, "The Baby Boom and World War II."

31. Data from Chesnais, *The Demographic Transition* and national statistical agencies.

32. Data from World Bank, *World Development Indicators*.

33. Ibid. The positive relationship between female labor force participation and fertility rates across industrialized countries was first pointed out and analyzed by Luisa Fuster and José Da Rocha, "Why Are Fertility Rates and Female Employment Ratios Positively Correlated Across OECD Countries?" *International Economic Review* 47, no. 4 (2006): 1187–222.

34. James Feyrer, Bruce Sacerdote, and Ariel Stern, "Will the Stork Return to Europe and Japan? Understanding Fertility within Developed Nations," *Journal of Economic Perspectives* 22, no. 3 (2008): 3–22.

35. Matthias Doepke and Fabian Kindermann, "Bargaining over Babies: Theory, Evidence, and Policy Implications" (NBER Working Paper No. 22072, 2016).

36. See Kjetil Storesletten and Fabrizio Zilibotti, "China's Great Convergence and Beyond," *Annual Review of Economics* 6 (2014): 333–62; Zheng Song, Kjetil Storesletten, and Fabrizio Zilibotti, "Growing Like China" *American Economic Review* 101, no. 1 (2011): 196–233; Fabrizio Zilibotti, "Growing and Slowing Down Like China," *Journal of the European Economic Association* 15, no. 5 (2017): 943–88.

37. According to the thesis of economists Shang-Jin Wei and Xiaobo Zhang, the

policy is among the causes of the large increase in the saving rate experienced by China. See Shang-Jin Wei and Xiaobo Zhang, "The Competitive Saving Motive: Evidence from Rising Sex Ratios and Savings Rates in China," *Journal of Political Economy* 119, no. 3 (2011): 511–64.

38. See Zheng Song, Kjetil Storesletten, Yikai Wang, and Fabrizio Zilibotti, "Sharing High Growth Across Generations: Pensions and Demographic Transition in China," *American Economic Journal: Macroeconomics* 7, no. 2 (2015): 1–39.

39. Barbara H. Settles, Xuewen Sheng, Yuan Zang, and Jia Zhao, "The One-Child Policy and Its Impact on Chinese Families," in *International Handbook of Chinese Families*, ed. Chan Kwok-bun (New York: Springer, 2013), 627–46.

40. See Taha Choukhmane, Nicolas Coeurdacier, and Keyu Jin, "The One-Child Policy and Household Saving," (unpublished manuscript, Yale University, 2017). The study also shows that the one-child policy can explain a large proportion of the rise in aggregate saving rates in China. For a study of the overall growth implications of the one-child policy through the quantity-quality trade-off, see Pei-Ju Liao, "The One-Child Policy: A Macroeconomic Analysis," *Journal of Development Economics* 101 (2013): 49–62.

CHAPTER EIGHT: PARENTING AND CLASS

1. In this chapter we heavily draw on our earlier work on class differences in the Industrial Revolution; see Matthias Doepke and Fabrizio Zilibotti, "Occupational Choice and the Spirit of Capitalism," *Quarterly Journal of Economics* 123, no. 2 (2008): 747–93. See also Doepke and Zilibotti, "Culture, Entrepreneurship, and Growth," in *Handbook of Economic Growth*, vol. 2A, ed. Philippe Aghion and Steve Durlauf (Amsterdam: North Holland, 2013), 1–48; Doepke and Zilibotti, "Social Class and the Spirit of Capitalism," *Journal of the European Economic Association* 3, no. 2–3 (2005): 516–24.

2. See, for example, David Cannadine, *The Rise and Fall of Class in Britain* (New York: Columbia University Press, 1999). We leave out smaller groups such as the clergy and military officers, who generally combine characteristics of the upper and the middle class, but did not play a major role in terms of parenting.

3. For an overview of apprenticeship in the preindustrial era, see the discussion in David de la Croix, Matthias Doepke, and Joel Mokyr, "Clans, Guilds, and Markets: Apprenticeship Institutions and Growth in the Pre-Industrial Economy," *Quarterly Journal of Economics* 133, no. 1 (2017): 1–70.

4. Thorstein Veblen, *The Theory of the Leisure Class* (New York: Dover, 1994, first published in 1899), 26.

5. Hester Jenkins and D. Caradog Jones, "Social Class of Cambridge University Graduates of the 18th and 19th Centuries," *British Journal of Sociology* 1, no. 2 (1950): 93–116.

6. Suzanna Chambers, "At Last, a Degree of Honour for 900 Cambridge Women," *Independent*, May 30, 1998.

7. Valerie A. Fildes, *Breasts, Bottles, and Babies: A History of Infant Feeding* (Edinburgh: Edinburgh University Press, 1986).

8. The importance of patience for economic success has been documented by experimental studies conducted by anthropologists, economists, and psychologists. A classical longitudinal study conducted at Stanford University by a team of psychologists finds that individuals who were more patient as children were subsequently more likely to acquire formal education, to choose market-oriented occupations, and to earn higher income. See Walter Mischel, Yuichi Shoda, Monica L. Rodriguez, "Delay of Gratification in Children," in *Choice Over Time*, ed. George Loewenstein and Elster Jon (New York: Russell Sage Foundation, 1992). More recently, a study by experimental economists finds that measures of time preferences of young people aged ten to eighteen, elicited through experiments, predict saving behavior, smoking and alcohol abuse, body mass index (BMI), and conduct at school. See Matthias Sutter, Martin G. Kocher, Daniela Glaetze-Ruetzler, and Stefan T. Trautmann, "Impatience and Uncertainty: Experimental Decisions Predict Adolescents' Field Behavior," *American Economic Review* 103, no. 1 (2013): 510–31. Finally, a team of anthropologists studied the effect of patience on economic outcomes among the Tsimanes, an Amazonian tribal society that only recently transitioned from self-sufficiency to a market economy. They find that individuals who were already more patient in the pre-market environment acquired, on average, more education and engaged more often in entrepreneurial activity when the society introduced markets. See Victoria Reyes-Garcia, Ricardo Godoy, Tomas Huanca, William R. Leonard, Thomas McDade, Susan Tanner, and Vencent Vadez, "The Origin of Monetary Income Inequality: Patience, Human Capital, and the Division of Labor," *Evolution and Human Behavior* 28 (2007): 37–47.

9. Among nonexperimental studies, the importance of patience is emphasized as a value, among others, by David Figlio, Paola Giuliano, Umut Özek, and Paola Sapienza, "Long-Term Orientation and Educational Performance" (NBER Working Paper 22541, 2016).

10. Joyce Burnette, "How Skilled Were English Agricultural Labourers in the Early Nineteenth Century?" *Economic History Review* (new series) 59, no. 4 (2006): 688–716.

11. Max Weber, *The Protestant Ethic and the Spirit of Capitalism*, translation of the original 1905 edition by Talcott Parsons, with a foreword by R. H. Tawney (New York: Charles Scribner's Sons, 1958; republished by Dover, 2003).

12. François Crouzet, *The First Industrialists* (Cambridge: Cambridge University Press, 1985), 127.

13. At the beginning of the nineteenth century, peerage and gentry accounted for about 1.4 percent of the population in England and Wales, whereas the middle class made up about 30 percent.

14. Crouzet, *First Industrialists*, 112.

15. Jennifer Tann, "Watt, James (1736–1819)," *Oxford Dictionary of National Biography*, online ed. (Oxford University Press, 2004). doi:10.1093/ref:odnb/28880.

16. Geoffrey Tweedale, "Carnegie, Andrew (1835–1919)," *Oxford Dictionary of National Biography*, online ed. (Oxford University Press, 2004). doi:10.1093/ref: odnb/32296.

17. Andrew Carnegie, *The Gospel of Wealth and Other Timely Essays*, ed. Edward C. Kirkland (Cambridge, MA: Belknap Press of Harvard University Press, 1962), 3.

18. Ibid., 56.

19. Ruth Brandon, *The Dollar Princesses: Sagas of Upward Nobility, 1870–1914* (New York: Knopf, 1980).

20. Paul Addison, "Churchill, Sir Winston Leonard Spencer (1874–1965)," *Oxford Dictionary of National Biography*, online ed. (Oxford University Press, 2004). doi:10.1093/ref:odnb/32413.

21. William Rubinstein, *Men of Property: The Very Wealthy in Britain Since the Industrial Revolution* (London: Croom Helm, 1981).

CHAPTER NINE: THE ORGANIZATION OF THE SCHOOL SYSTEM

1. This situation seems to be common to the experience of immigrant children moving to countries with different learning cultures and institutions. Kushal, an Indian-American student at Yale who read a draft of this book and gave us many useful comments, reports a personal experience similar to Nora's. His parents, along with those of his Indian-American peers, taught him advanced math skills from a young age, whereas his peers who were not from immigrant communities did not receive any such instruction. He reports receiving the same kind of conflicted feedback that Nora recalls: "Learn math when you go home but don't talk about it with people outside your community, or you will feel like an outcast."

2. The economists Valerie and Garey Romer have argued that competition for admission to top universities is an important reason why time spent on parenting has gone up much more for well-educated parents in the United States compared to Canada; see Garey Ramey and Valerie A. Ramey, "The Rug Rat Race," *Brookings Papers on Economic Activity* (Spring 2010): 129–76.

3. To assess the power of incentives on Italian students and their parents, it is also useful to note that Italy has one of the lowest returns to education among the set of European countries. Only the Nordic countries have even lower returns to education. See table 4 in Mircea Badescu, Béatrice D'Hombres, and Ernesto Villalba: "Returns to Education in European Countries: Evidence from the European Community Statistics on Income and Living Conditions (EU-SILC)," JRC European Commission, 2011.

4. Donald Greynadus, Helen Pratt, Richard Spates, Anne Blake-Dreher, Marissa

Greynadus-Gearhart, and Dilip Patel, "Corporal Punishment in Schools," *Journal of Adolescent Health* 32, no. 5 (2003): 385–93.

5. Emily Cuddy and Richard V. Reeves, "Hitting Kids: American Parenting and Physical Punishment," *Brookings Social Mobility Papers*, November 6, 2014.

6. See, for example, Peony Lui, "School Incidents Highlight China's Corporal Punishment Debate," *South China Morning Post*, January 25, 2013.

7. "Corporal Punishment Rife in Schools in 2012: Survey," *The Japan Times*, June 3, 2013.

8. Nathan Schwartzman, "After Corporal Punishment Debate, Korean Students Still Being Hit," *Asian Correspondent*, July 18, 2012, https://asiancorrespondent .com/2012/07/after-corporal-punishment-debate-korean-students-still-being -hit/#1gYUIv4HlWUG1TCJ.992.

9. Patricia Ashton, Pat Kneen, Frances Davies, and B. J. Holley, *The Aims of Primary Education: A Study of Teachers' Opinions* (London: Macmillan, 1975); discussed by John Darling, *Child-Centred Education and Its Critics* (New York: SAGE Publications, 1994).

10. Darling, *Child-Centred Education and Its Critics*, 50.

11. Ibid.

12. See Ho Ping-ti, *The Ladder of Success in Imperial China: Aspects of Social Mobility, 1368–1911*. (New York and London: Columbia University Press, 1962); Ting Chen, James Kai-Sing Kung, and Chicheng Ma, "Long Live Keju! The Persistent Effects of China's Imperial Examination System" (mimeo, Hong Kong University of Science and Technology, 2017).

13. Guofang Wan, "The Educational Reforms in the Cultural Revolution in China: A Postmodern Critique," *Education*, 122, no. 1 (2001): 21–32.

14. David Lague, "1977 Exam Opened Escape Route into China's Elite," *The New York Times*, January 6, 2008.

15. For a recent appraisal of the importance of the gaokao for parenting and other aspects of Chinese culture, see Yanna Gong, *Gaokao: A Personal Journey Behind China's Examination Culture* (San Francisco: China Books, 2014).

16. Charlie Campbell, "Chinese Students Face Up to 7 Years in Prison for Cheating on College-Entrance Exams," *Time*, June 8, 2016.

17. The details of the exam vary across province. The text refers to the so-called "3 + X scheme," which is used today by the majority of provinces and cities. Here, the "3" refers to Mandarin, mathematics, and foreign language, and the "X" refers to a combination of subjects. For the social science track, "X" is a combination of political sciences, history, and geography; and for the natural science track, it is a combination of physics, chemistry, and biology. See "China: Gaokao UCAS Qualification Information Profiles" (https://qips.ucas.com/qip /china-gaokao).

18. See *PISA: Results in Focus* (OECD, 2015).

19. Helen Gao, "China's Education Gap," *The New York Times*, September 4, 2014.

20. Teddy Ng and Li Jing, "Chinese Protests over University Quotas Spread to Third Province," *South China Morning Post*, May 23, 2016.

21. See, for example, Zhuang Pinghui, "Gaokao: How One Exam Can Set the Course of a Student's Life in China," *South China Morning Post*, June 8, 2017.

22. Yang Dongping, *Annual Report on China's Education* (Beijing: Social Sciences Academic Press [China], 2014).

23. Zhao Xinying, "School Tests Blamed for Suicides," *China Daily*, May 14, 2014.

24. Fauna, "Chinese Students Get IV Drips While Studying for Gaokao Exam," *china-Smack*, May 7, 2012.

25. Fabrizio Zilibotti, "Growing and Slowing Down Like China," *Journal of the European Economic Association* 15, no. 5 (2017): 943–88.

26. John Sudworth, "China's Students Take on Tough Gaokao University Entrance Exam," *BBC News*, June 8, 2012.

27. OECD, "Education at a Glance 2014: OECD Indicators," *OECD Publishing* (2014).

28. Teru Clavel, "Prepping for University Straight from the Crib," *The Japan Times*, February 16, 2014, http://www.japantimes.co.jp/community/2014/02/16/issues/prepping-for-university-straight-from-the-crib/#.WQcPpNqGM2w.

29. "University Entrance Examinations," *Nippon.com*, April 11, 2015, http://www.nippon.com/en/features/jg00032/.

30. Anne Allison, *Precarious Japan* (Durham, NC: Duke University Press, 2013).

31. In 2016, 5 percent of students attending education at any level discontinued their studies. See Official Statistics of Finland (OSF), "Discontinuation of Education Decreased," *Statistics Finland* (2016).

32. Pasi Sahlberg, *Finnish Lessons: What Can the World Learn from Educational Change in Finland?* (New York: Teachers College Press, 2011).

33. Julie Nightingale, "Focus on Finnish Assessment," *Chartered Institute of Educational Assessors*, www.ciea.org.uk/focus-finnish-assessment/.

34. See Sherwin Rosen, "The Theory of Equalizing Differences," in *Handbook of Labor Economics 1*, ed. Orley Ashenfelter and Richard Layard (Amsterdam: North Holland, 1986), 641–92.

35. Harriet Alexander and Richard Orange, "OECD Education Report: Finland's No Inspections, No League Tables and Few Exams Approach," *The Telegraph*, December 3, 2013.

36. "Barnen i Hallstahammar kan få slippa läxor," *SVT Nyheter*, June 16, 2014, https://www.svt.se/nyheter/inrikes/har-kan-det-bli-laxfritt.

37. For an overview of research on factors that can account for differences in student achievement across countries, see Eric A. Hanushek and Ludger Woessmann, "The Economics of International Differences in Educational Achievement," in *Handbook of the Economics of Education*, vol. 3, ed. Eric A. Hanushek, Stephen Machin, and Ludger Woessmann (Amsterdam: North Holland, 2010), chapter 2.

38. See https://www.thelocal.se/20160525/why-swedens-teachers-have-no-time-for-their-students.

39. Anna Dorozynska, "Teacher Job Satisfaction in Primary Schools: The Relation to Work Environment" (student essay, Department of Education and Special Education, Göteborgs Universitet, 2017), https://gupea.ub.gu.se/bitstream/2077 /51390/1/gupea_2077_51390_1.pdf.

40. See http://www.konkurrensverket.se/globalassets/publikationer/uppdragsforsk ning/forsk_rap_2010–6_betygens_varde.pdf; and http://www.ifau.se/globalassets /pdf/se/2016/wp2016–09-impact-of-upper-secondary-voucher-school-atten dance-on-student-achievement.pdf.

41. Odd Eiken, "The Kunskapsskolan ('The Knowledge School'): A Personalised Approach to Education," *CELE Exchange, Centre for Effective Learning Environments* 1 (2011), http://www.oecd.org/education/innovation-education/centrefor effectivelearningenvironmentscele/47211890.pdf.

42. Yann Algan, Pierre Cahuc, and Andrei Shleifer: "Teaching Practices and Social Capital," *American Economic Journal: Applied Economics* 5, no. 3 (2013): 189–210.

43. Ibid.

44. Jean-Benoît Nadeau and Julie Barlow, *Sixty Million Frenchmen Can't be Wrong* (Naperville, IL: Sourcebooks, Inc., 2003), 183.

CHAPTER TEN: THE FUTURE OF PARENTING

1. Thomas Piketty, *Capital in the Twenty-First Century* (Cambridge, MA: Harvard University Press, 2014).

2. See also Roland Bénabou and Efe A. Ok, "Social Mobility and the Demand for Redistribution: The Poum Hypothesis," *Quarterly Journal of Economics* 116, no. 2 (2001): 447–87. These authors discuss the political consequences of social mobility.

3. Miles Corak, "Income Inequality, Equality of Opportunity, and Intergenerational Mobility," *Journal of Economic Perspectives* 27, no. 3 (2013): 79–102.

4. See, for example, Daron Acemoglu and David Autor, "Skills, Tasks and Technologies: Implications for Employment and Earnings," *Handbook of Labor Economics* 4 (2011): 1043–171; Daron Acemoglu and Pascual Restrepo, "The Race between Machine and Man: Implications of Technology for Growth, Factor Shares and Employment," (NBER Working Paper No. 22252, 2016); Guy Michaels, Ashwini Natraj, and John Van Reenen, "Has ICT Polarized Skill Demand? Evidence from Eleven Countries over Twenty-Five Years," *Review of Economics and Statistics* 96, no. 1 (2014): 60–77.

5. See Daron Acemoglu, Philippe Aghion, Claire Lelarge, John van Reenen, and Fabrizio Zilibotti: "Technology, Information and the Decentralization of the Firm," *Quarterly Journal of Economics* 122, no. 4 (2007): 1759–99.

6. Alex Williams, "Robot-Proofing Your Child's Future," *The New York Times* (Thursday Styles), December 14, 2017.

7. Robert D. Putnam, *Our Kids: The American Dream in Crisis* (New York: Simon & Schuster, 2015).

8. OECD: "Education at a Glance: Transition from School to Work." See https://data.oecd.org/youthinac/youth-not-in-employment-education-or-training-neet.htm.

9. John Maynard Keynes, "Economic Possibilities for our Grandchildren," in *Essays in Persuasion* (New York: Harcourt Brace, 1932), 358–73.

10. Ibid., 372.

11. For an extended analysis of these trends, see Fabrizio Zilibotti, "Economic Possibilities for Our Grandchildren 75 Years After: A Global Perspective," in *Revisiting Keynes: Economic Possibilities for our Grandchildren*, ed. Lorenzo Pecchi and Gustavo Piga (Cambridge, MA: MIT Press, 2008).

12. Edward Lazear and Sherwin Rosen, "Rank-Order Tournaments as Optimum Labor Contracts," *Journal of Political Economy* 89, no. 5 (1981): 841–64; Andrei Shleifer, "A Theory of Yardstick Competition," *Rand Journal of Economics* 16, no. 3 (1985): 319–27.

13. See James Heckman, "Four Big Benefits of Investing in Early Childhood Development," https://heckmanequation.org/assets/2017/01/F_Heckman_FourBenefits InvestingECDevelopment_022615.pdf

Index